Interference
Tapehead versus Television

Interference
Tapehead versus Television

Jim Shelley

Atlantic Books
London

First published in 2001 by Guardian Books,
an imprint of Grove Atlantic Ltd

Frontispiece: drawing courtesy of Kez Glozier

1 3 5 7 9 8 6 4 2

A CIP catalogue record for this book is available
from the British Library.

1 903809 25 8

Printed in Great Britain by Mackays of Chatham PLC, Chatham, Kent
Design by Helen Ewing

Grove Atlantic Ltd
29 Adam & Eve Mews
London W8 6UG

Contents

Foreword
Tapehead unplugged

Tapehead was the brother I never had. The one I never wanted. He was the popular one, the bad influence, the demon seed. If you've seen him in Primal Fear, you can picture Ed Norton playing him in the movie. The best thing about Tapehead was that he gave me the one thing any journalist would kill for: freedom without responsibility, power without price. It wasn't me, it was him.

Tapehead didn't care, he really didn't. He called Jamie Oliver an irritating little fuckwit and said that, with a hairdo like that, Mandy Jordache had it coming. (Trevor Jordache was only trying to knock some sense into her.) He lamented Donal MacIntyre's failure to suffer violent reprisals for his awful investigation series and said Jacques Cousteau couldn't swim. When he claimed John Lennon had shot himself to get away from Yoko's nagging, The Guardian's Corrections and Clarifications section was forced to issue a correction saying this was factually incorrect.

The next best thing about Tapehead was that he made it OK for me to watch so much television. 'I'm working,' I could tell anyone trying to get me to do something. Or, my mantra in life, 'I can't. I've got to watch this.' I've spent my whole LIFE watching television. The idea of hobbies was always a mystery to me. When I was young, apart from listening to records, watching television was the only hobby I ever had: from Land Of The Giants and Captain Scarlet to Revolver and The Rockford Files. Having failed (or tried) to find a better hobby, even now you can put me in front of a David Attenborough documentary, an episode of Taggart or any kind of horse race or football match, and I'm contented. It's probably the only thing that makes me really relax.

There is literally no limit to the number of documentaries about jelly-fish, prostitutes in north London or two-part episodes of The Bill I can watch. People complain that shows like Silent Witness, Holby City or Cardiac Arrest are well-made but mindless pap, valium for the eyes, but that's what I LIKE about them. To me, there is nothing better than really great television: The Sopranos, David Caruso-era NYPD Blue, David Wicks and Cindy in EastEnders. Even a really good film is not as good.

(You don't even have to go out.)

When I was growing up, my whole family, whilst not quite rivalling The Royle Family as critics, spent all our time watching television: in the kitchen while we were eating, hauling the portable upstairs so we could watch TV in the bath. (Not, I hasten to add, all together and not actually risking getting electrocuted.) There was some kind of tacit complicity to the way I was late back to school every afternoon because I was at home waiting for the verdict on Crown Court.

The day video recorders became affordable changed my life, introducing the revolutionary concept of going out on Saturday night without having to miss Hill Street Blues or Alex Higgins versus Jimmy White. I have been maniacally taping everything ever since. (While I was doing Tapehead, people were always remarking on how much TV he/we must watch. But I never really watch television. It's all on tape.)

I can remember the first piece that I wrote about television: an essay at college in which I had to compare the production values of BBC's Breakfast Time and TVAM. The lecturer didn't think that my view that Frank Bough had been chosen as a presenter due to his resemblance to a boiled egg was very funny so he failed me. (If we ever meet, I must tell Julie Burchill, given that it was her joke.)

When I was first asked to write Tapehead, in the summer of 1993, for the dummy of the Guide, I said 'No', repeatedly. God knows why. Somehow I ended up doing it every week for seven years. If you're going to watch so much television, you might as well get paid for it. In the early days, Tapehead was founded on the (deranged) idea of compiling the ultimate, 180-minute compilation tape of the next week's viewing: a brilliant idea but too much like hard work for Tapehead.

By the fourth week, he was doing Taz and watching live transmissions of the World Chess Championships all afternoon. Old episodes of Geraldo, programmes about Subbuteo, dominoes or the love life of the centipede were not very far behind. He commendably used his column as a platform to declare his love for the likes of Tina from Casualty, Fiona in Coronation Street and Alan Hansen. He wished George Best a happy birthday and seized the once-in-a-lifetime opportunity to tell Kate Moss to stop calling him.

At the start, Tapehead was positively evangelical, unlike even the most successful TV critics who, to this day, seem to write as if writing about television is a drag and something that stops them enjoying the fresh air or writing books. Tapehead couldn't watch enough of it. Tapehead campaigned for people to watch Oz, Gazzetta Football Italia, Brass Eye and Homicide: Life On The Street as if his life depended on it, which in a sense it did. He devoured documentaries (Cutting Edge, Modern Times, True Stories, Short Stories, First Tuesday, Arena, Horizon, Straight From The Heart) and dedicated himself to crime (The Vice, Harry, The Cops, Murder One, Touching Evil, Out of the Blue, Millennium...)

Somewhere along the line though, there was suddenly hardly anything good on. The turning point could have been the departure of Barry Grant from Brookside and the arrival of Bel and Ollie Simpson. Or it could have just been TFI Friday. But something snapped. Channel 4's decision to scrap the fifth series of Homicide and stick Oz on in the middle of the night got Tapehead down. Suddenly, Zoe Ball and Nick Hancock's grinning faces were everywhere. Baddiel and Skinner could just make things up on the spot. Jo Whiley was taking herself seriously, though no one else was. Tapehead started running feuds with the old bags from the Italian Kitchen, with Prince Edward and with Richard E. Grant. When Reg left a message on Mrs Tapehead's ansaphone, it made Tapehead happy for months.

'Hello cunt features,' Reg's voice smirked. 'I read your review last week and it was like being sprayed with hot shit. Absolutely astounding that somebody of your supposed intelligence and education should have been so personally vitriolic to the degree that you were. I'm just absolutely staggered. Shame on your head really. I hope you get some life-threatening disease very soon.'

By the time Tapehead tried to start a fight with Badger, one of us was going slowly mad.

Above all there was Brookside. As far back as 1996, Tapehead sent out a mayday: 'Earth calling Brookside. Earth calling Brookside. Please phone home. Get well soon.' But of course they never did. Phil Redmond, signing his letters 'Professor', complained directly to Alan Rusbridger and several times Brookside threatened to sue me for libelling Lindsey Corkhill, admirably unhindered by the fact that Lindsey Corkhill does not (I hope) exist. When they heard that I was going to be writing for the Mirror, Brookside's lawyers fired off a warning letter before I'd even started, asking that 'Mr Shelley is restrained from making these false statements'. Their letter catalogued all the insults that Tapehead had directed at Lindsey – '"On September 4th 1999," he wrote of her, "the benefits of being built like a rugby league prop forward paid dividends"' – with the net result that their letter was far funnier than any of the columns.

A kind of Tapehead mania started. One thing I could never understand was when press officers would ring up, offering to send me tapes and virtually begging for the programme they were working on to be in. Emmerdale lobbied to be mentioned with the other soaps. 'I can get Undressed for you every week,' promised one of Channel 4's tape service, memorably.

I learnt the sorry lesson that there's only so much telly you can take. I had become the sort of person who pressed pause on the video during Coronation Street when he goes out of the room to make a coffee. Unrequested tapes of 999 Emergency and Vets In Practice piled up around the room. I was staying up, watching two or three programmes simultaneously, hurling mini bottles of Absolut at the screen, like a modern-day Jerome Newton. Every Friday was taken up with a constant stream of dispatch riders trudging up the stairs of my seemingly desirable flat opining, 'Cor, this place is a fucking dump' or 'Fuckin' 'ell, I hate it round here'. Every Saturday morning, when I went to collect my mountain of packages, the blokes from the sorting office would lay into me. 'Here Jim, when are you gonna get a proper job, yer cunt ?'

Tapehead had gradually taken over. Friends of friends, I used to hear, loved Tapehead. Every time someone asked me, 'Are you Tapehead?', I was never really sure. Pretty soon, nobody remembered my probing in-depth profiles of Christopher Walken, Anthony Burgess or John Malkovich, or the myriad of travel pieces from Arizona to Timbuktu.

One of us had to go and sadly it was him. In August 2000, Tapehead was unplugged. But I know he's watching.

Jim Shelley, July 2001
tapehead@tapehead.co.uk

Introduction
by Julie Burchill

couple of years ago, when American television first started
thirsting for English game shows, I had a brilliant idea. Lemming
Rehab: combining animals, death and fierce competition, how
could it fail?

Three teams of three people – Blue, Green and Red – are taken to a
place where lemmings are due to take the big leap and, using nets and fire-
men's equipment, each saves five lemmings apiece. The fifteen lemmings
are painlessly tagged with their team's colour on a back leg and then for
two weeks they are shown that there is more to life than death as their min-
ders take them away and, with the clever use of various foods, music,
amusements and sex toys, attempt to re-awaken that all-important life
instinct. At an appropriate time, the fifteen lemmings are taken back to the
scene of their attempted mass suicide; the team to put the biggest number
off the idea of an easeful death wins. Intro music: 'Heaven Knows I'm
Miserable Now' by The Smiths, outro music: 'Happiness' by Pizzaman;
presented by Daniella Westbrook from an original idea by ME.

But whenever I mentioned Lemming Rehab to anyone, they laughed
awkwardly and then changed the subject. After a while I began to mutter
mutinously to myself, 'Tapehead would understand... Tapehead would
love it...' Until one day, one person – obviously not as nice as the others –
said rather meaningfully, 'Well, exactly!' And funnily enough, I never mentioned it again.

For Tapehead is a strange lad – king of a kinky castle, fiddler of a lonely furrow. Bedazzled by too much televised invasive surgery, mad penguins
and Emily Shadwick, he reels around the cathode-ray tubes of post-ironic
England, blinded by the light of the white dot. If we are indeed a global
village and TV has made us that way, then we must be in need of a global-
village idiot savant to explain us – and excuse us – to ourselves. For that
strange and lonesome task, performed par excellence, Tapehead's your
man.

I've always believed that nine-tenths of love was not about liking the
same things but about hating the same things and here Tapehead and I find

the perfect union. Whether decimating John Lennon ('Weak, nasal singing voice, dull haircut, awful granny glasses, zero sex appeal. Even Ringo had more talent'), Jimmy McGovern ('A trembling, vindictive voyeur'), John Peel ('So busy doing commercials for multinational oil companies and building societies it's a wonder he has time to bolster his flagging credibility by listening to any music') or Jo Whiley ('Her interview technique is certainly innovative – namely asking her guest a question, then interrupting with an anecdote about herself… The sheer volume of close-ups of her scary Terrahawk features is presumably a contractual requirement she just has to put up with'), Tapehead is both wise and fair and, better still, he knows exactly where to squeeze.

Evading both the effete sneering of the other broadsheet critics and the lumpish leering of the majority of tabloid TV writers, he is forever the little boy hanging from the lamppost, pointing out that the emperor has no clothes, and the two old blokes in the theatre box in The Muppet Show, pointing out that the show's crap. This, his first book, is the only legal reason I can think of for turning off the TV RIGHT NOW.

Hail, Tapehead!

Brighton, 2001

Welcome to the
Church of Tapehead

1993–94

TV heaven

n the last ever episode of Thirtysomething, a sensitive young child asked her extra-sensitive young mother, 'What's heaven like?' A *real* existentialist, she then added, 'Is there TV?' We should obviously plan ahead, just in case.

The clock shows 00 minutes, 02 seconds and counting...

When we get to TV heaven, Frank Burnside will surely be there, if not as one of its patron saints, then as one of the bouncers. The best television hardman since John Thaw's Jack Regan, in this week's episode of **The Bill**, Burnside departs, crosses over to the other side, the first essential TV exit since Elsie Tanner's or Mick Belker's and well worth preserving on video. With no friends and no private life, Burnside, looking like a cross between a Millwall hooligan and a silverback gorilla in a CID suit, has been roaming South London for years now.

He, and he alone, has made The Bill what it is today: a modern-day, half-hour version of A Clockwork Orange. Its quota of 'ponces' and 'toms', 'snouts' and 'grasses', 'Juvis' and, best of all, 'giving it loads of verbals' is, thanks to him, unrivalled. No one, besides maybe Harvey Keitel, could give lines like 'Five per cent of the population is slag' such stylish menace. Whether The Bill can survive his departure, coming, as it does, right after that of WPC Viv 'awright guv' Martella, is doubtful. We shall miss him.

The clock shows 29 minutes, 58 seconds and counting...

Possibly only a woman like Oprah Winfrey, one of television's angels, could handle a man like Burnside. This week's **Oprah Gold: Men In Love With Female Criminals** is, like every other Oprah Gold, unmissable material. It's like research. This is America, heaven or hell. Even Oprah can't handle studio guest Dr Larry Weinberg, a Man In Love With Female Criminal Sonia (15 years for selling marijuana, theft). 'Help me,' cries Oprah, genuinely a-mazed and defeated. Like some product of the disturbed minds of Hunter S. Thompson and Woody Allen, Dr Larry walks away with Tapehead's Wacko of the Week Award. Curiously, Oprah's main talent (like Tapehead's) is that she really loves the stuff and somehow has a happy knack of looking worried in all the right places (also like Tapehead). 'Coming next,' Oprah says, 'a man who says Falling In Love

With A Convicted Murderess Was The Biggest Mistake Of His Life.' Tapehead knows how he feels.

The way **Grange Hill** was driven out of its traditional Tuesday and Friday afternoon slot after Newsround was a crime as heinous and, make no mistake, as political as the dismantling of the NHS and an appalling waste of what is the best long-running, soap-style series on TV. Sharp writing, effortless acting, The Yoof Of Today explained. Essential research.

Madman or genius? Someone at Channel 4 is responsible for the sporting event of the year (and another genuine television event), the return of **Pro-Celebrity Golf**. Five hours a week (*five hours?*) could, perhaps, be overkill and will almost certainly drive any man insane (even Tapehead). Five minutes every day, however, should be a low enough dosage and a perfect fix to prepare us for next week's solid high, the full 60. The excellently-named Hale Irwin and Sam Torrance are the pros. Guest celebs are: Friday, Tim Brooke-Taylor and Gavin Hastings; Thursday, Christopher Lee and John Parrott; Wednesday, Bobby Charlton and Bruce Forsyth (divine); Tuesday, Val Doonican and Colonel Gadhaffi; Monday, Terry Wogan and the excellently-named Rachel Heyhoe-Flint. OK, it's not true about Rachel Heyhoe-Flint.

Wednesday's **Hawaii 5-0** features an appearance by the exceptional, exceptionally-named, veteran character actor, Clu Gulager. When we get to TV heaven we can be sure that whoever wrote this episode, called 'Fools Die Twice', will be waiting.

The clock shows 179 minutes, 47 seconds and counting...

September 4–10 1993

Cool as a cucumber

Cookery makes for perfect TV – not to watch but to video. No more trying to keep up, dashing in from the kitchen up to your neck in lightly flambéed duck's liver every 10 seconds to see how Delia is buttering her toast. Don't bake it. Tape it. As a great vegetarian, Tapehead is, understandably, furiously taping **Great Vegetarian Dishes** every day this week. Aussie presenter Kurma's first appearance on screen in the opening credits is characteristically disconcerting, furtively milling around the markets fondling fruit, rubbing an aubergine, sniffing a kiwi

3

and nodding at the camera in a decidedly suspect fashion.

There's something faintly suggestive (not to say erotic) about everything Kurma says or does as he makes the dinner; a knack he has of letting little intimate details slip, with a deliberate hint of frisson: 'I like to stir my rice while it's still hot and fluffy,' he demurs absentmindedly. 'I like to use a wooden spoon.' The biggest of these revelations comes on Tuesday ('Sweet and Sour Walnuts'). 'I like to use a wok for practically everything it's so versatile.' (Dah-ling!!) But the way Kurma cryptically mentions, 'There are certainly so many nice things you can get from the cow,' is faintly sinister. Of course, if Tapehead could really peel potatoes and carve them into one-inch cubes or sculpt cauliflower into 'little florettes' ('Cauliflower and Potato Supreme'), he would be a contestant on The Krypton Factor. Besides, aren't florettes what you suck for a sore throat? 'I like to put a tape on and relax when I'm making my sweet rice,' says Kurma. 'Consciousness is a very important item when you're cooking.' I suppose he means being conscious.

If Tapehead could invite someone to share a candlelit great vegetarian dish, it would surely be Alan Hansen, **Match Of The Day** analyst, the Bryan Ferry of football and a man whose resemblance to Captain Scarlet has caused many a striker to miss an open goal. Dressed as a high-class model or an assassin, Hansen deconstructs the day's best moves with the seriousness, sexiness and stylishness of Derrida by way of a ruthless TV confidence. Like the rest of us, Des Lynam adores him.

After Elvis And Me ('Germany, a strange, foreign place') and The Jacksons: An American Dream, Tapehead is here to advise you which moments of the four-and-a-half-hour mini-series **Sinatra** to get on tape. The bit where Frank (who actually looks like Tom Hanks) reveals 'there's a baby on the way' by telling Bogart (who looks like Leonid Brezhnev wearing a couple of those Richard Nixon masks) is obviously essential, as is the scratchy miming – by Hanks and a 60-piece orchestra (also miming). Lines include: 'I just wanna be somebody, Pa'; 'Frank, as your friend, you're killing yourself'; 'Honey, I just don't know you anymore'; and 'I just want you to think about this self-destructive path you're on'. A path that is about to self-destruct? See if you can spot Frank Sinatra Jr's 'additional vocal performance'.

It seems to Tapehead that there's a thin (fishing) line between going fishing and standing in the cold doing nothing, so presenting your own telly series, **Go Fishing**, is nice work if you can get it. Every time he catch-es something, the presenter moans, groans, laughs and says 'Would you believe it?' as if he's just spotted a fleet of spaceships flying overhead. Carl Hiaasen, it ain't. The last in the series, this is real interactive television: Go Fishing. No, you go fishing.

Worms abound in **Charming Worms**. Tom Shufflebotham's world record (511 worms from a three-square-metre piece of turf in half an hour) is under threat at Willaston's World Worm Charming Championship. Channel 4 regards this as sport rather than documentary. An art, surely.

More art from **Mr Magoo**, a man who taught Tapehead everything he knows about style. Showing after Oprah Changed My Life, Mr Magoo makes Sinatra and Hansen look, frankly, shoddy. Keep taping.

November 8–14 1993

Clean

Besides the perils of RSI (Remote-control Seizure Injury), Tapehead's lifestyle does, of course, have its penalties. The outside world is a mystery, human contact is kept to a minimum. Tapehead's only friends are strung across the country, scattered forlornly across the wilds of Yorkshire, Merseyside and Coronation Street. Continuity and stability are essential ingredients in Tapehead's meagre existence, so every week he likes to fill at least one tape with soap. So this is real life. You're telling *me*.

Traditionally, of course, the storylines on **Take The High Road** would revolve around exciting incidents such as someone called Dougall or Morag buying a Dundee cake or losing their front door key. But, like The Archers, Take The High Road's latter-day forays into the modern world have exposed grannies and Tapeheads across the highlands to things like AIDS and heroin which, if nothing else, gives new meaning to the concept of just which high road we should all be taking. Maybe this will become street slang. You know, like chasing the dragon. 'It's not a habit. I just like taking the high road now and again.' Take The High Road is fine as an occasional fix but, hey kids, never forget you're only one episode away from an OD.

Bizarrely, **Emmerdale Farm** has also betrayed the traditions that made it great (grate). True, Seth Armstrong still boasts the finest 'tache on tele-

5

vision but Emmerdale has committed the cardinal soap sin: not content with changing its name, some idiot has changed the music. The once wonderful, legendary strains of Emmerdale's theme tune have been subjected to some sort of hideous raving remix. That's not to say that the characters still don't walk in to Ma Sugden's kitchen, wipe their feet and greet everyone with the immortal words, 'Eee bah gum, it's parky.'

Mercifully the great cocker-knee traditions endure in **EastEnders** this week: Fat Pat Cabs squeezes the word 'Janine' out of her pursed and lipsticked lips; rusk-heads Phil and Grant mess up Tricky Dicky's hair gel; Mike Reid shouts, 'You're getting right up my bugle my old son' before tipping his hat and exiting doing his Follow The Bear impersonation.

When it comes to soaps, Tapehead is fanatically conservative: nothing must change, no one must leave, unless it's due to dramatic and unexpected death.

Brookside has always favoured the occasional bout of culling and after Trevor Jordache, the killing of Frank Rodgers was a family-feuding, cocaine-fuelled classic worthy of The Long Good Friday. This week's omnibus is quintessential Brookside: Tony is on a life-support machine having had a Nintendo controller surgically removed from both hands. After several months in the series, Tony's big mistake was: he spoke. He is now in danger of becoming a vegetable. How will they tell?

Major barnies reign this week. Bev and DD argue about who gets rid of Ron first, causing his painted-on hairdo to get a bit ruffled. Chrissy Rodgers returns to slag it out with the widow Lynn for the house. 'Our Katie' gets to be even more miserable than usual. Alarmingly, Mark Hughes-lookalike, Barry Grant, persists in his hopes for a kid. Expect Anna to reply in the only way she knows how: 'Haf you got the forty quid?' A motto Tapehead has adopted with fervour. We await the return of Beth, the horniest creature on TV, with anticipation – not to mention her imminent sexual awakening, the thought of which keeps Tapehead awake at night.

Like Brookie and Emmie (but tragically not EastEnders), **Coronation Street** is suddenly packed with more babes than a Baywatch beach barbecue: lovely, lusty women of different shapes and ages. Vicky, Maureen, Tanya, Denise, Liz, Mavis – though they are, of course, all ravaged by pathos. Denise the hairdresser may be particularly worth forming a relationship with – an Elsie Tanner in the making, no less. Besides the legendary Reg Holdsworth and Jack Duckworth, the best comic character on telly is currently Raquel (played by the estimable Sarah Lancashire), the sister Tapehead never had. Raquel has stopped doing French lessons (just the way she nervously uttered 'Bonjour' was a delight) but still drifts around in a soft, anxious world of her own. This Wednesday, Raquel gets her first modelling job and the Beer Mat Poetry Competition is announced. Postmodern music hall for all ages and a great taping tradition.

November 13–19 1993

Penguin suits

David Attenborough, of course, is the ultimate loner; a man, like Tapehead, less alone in the animal kingdom. Not many people know what it's like to stand alone, a blue anorak in the Antarctic, surrounded by ten million penguins, but we do.

Life In The Freezer concentrates on one of the wonders of the world: David Attenborough in his natural habitat – on television. Attenborough's authority and passion, as ever, are impeccable. He could tell us we were watching tigers fly and we'd believe it. Life In The Freezer has things you need to tape in order to believe them: icebergs the size of cathedrals; baby penguins wrapped up in insulation blankets; the sight of an eight-foot tall, three-ton beach master seal scrambling over his harem of females in order to headbutt another bull seal (fiercely reminiscent of a scene from The Dog's Head on a Friday night). Rewind and learn by heart the courting rituals of the albatross.

This week, 'the most spectacular rush hour in Nature'. Thousands of penguins struggling to cross glacial torrents and climb near-vertical cliffs of volcanic ash to feed their chicks. Heroic. One of life's mottos: there is nothing funnier than a penguin in a hurry.

Penguin-esque, Harry Salter, the star of **Harry**, is a manic outsider: an adulterer, an alcoholic and, worst of all, a journalist. Good God, no wonder no one's watching it. No wonder also that Tapehead completely relates to Harry, and not only because last week he did a piece on two rave organisers whose only desire in life was to be in the *Weekend Guardian*. This week: the Video Diaries film, Snappy, a dockers' strike, 'the usual bollocks'. Just when it looks as if it's all getting very cosy, as usual Harry packs a fierce and gloomy punch. From the theme tune on, Harry has a haunted

7

quality: 'La. La-la-la, la-la-la.' If that's not enough, there's Alice, a Scottish Beatrice Dalle, who can file Tapehead's copy any day.

After Attenborough, the ultimate outsider is profiled by **Without Walls**: The Singing Nun – the patron saint of the one-hit wonder and the only pop star to be dropped by her record company for not being a nun. Classic archive footage of the convent-bound nun playing volleyball proves deceptive. 'What did you think of the names, The Smiling Nun and The Singing Nun?' asks an interviewer. 'I thought, whoever thought of that had obviously never met me.' Correct. Deeply enigmatic (The Nun's glasses, pallor and nun's habit give her a disturbing resemblance to Vic Reeves), she lived the classic pop dilemma. She took her music too seriously, fame went to her head, all the glamour was in the wimple. Her first song after leaving was the pivotal 'She is Dead'. Her ode to the Pill, 'La Pilule D'Or', lives in the memory, particularly for its resemblance to 'Knees Up Mother Brown'.

Tapehead understands The Nun like he understands all his loners: pursued by the Revenue, addicted to tranquillisers. Her last letter, like this column, was drenched in tears. Her suicide was Joy Division-esque. 'Her song, "Dominique", still haunts us,' says the narrator. When you hear it, you'll know why.

Another loner-cum-nun, Boy George, collides with the King (or Queen) of Loners, the estimable Quentin Crisp, on **Omnibus**. But better still, **Sister Wendy's Odyssey** sees the good sister gliding along like one of Attenborough's mad penguins, looking closely at rude artwork and explaining, 'If your lover is a swan, you can't have very much communication.' Something Wendy, Tapehead and Attenborough all know to their cost. Also to tape forever, Sister Helen Mirren in bed on **The Big Breakfast**. Lovely.

The divine Kim Basinger is a loner even in her own town, Braselton, as **Made In The USA** reveals. Local Public Access TV clips from Atlanta include: Deacon Lunch Box, a big Southern trucker in a beard and bra, shouting and banging a hammer on a metal drum; The Weather Channel (slogan: weather you can always turn to); and the Name of the Week, Mr Terry Ron Kitchens.

Finally, **Women Talking**. Janet Street-Porter and two women quizzing Mr Andrew Neil. Motto: 'If you can't make love to it or plug it into the mains I'm not interested.' A man after Tapehead's own heart.

November 27–December 3 1993

Prehistoric monsters

his week, a freeze-frame of humanity as it stands today. Tape and watch it only when you've got the stomach for it. **Readers' Wives** follows four women and their spouses (who take the snaps), pursuing the grand prize in *Fiesta* magazine's Readers' Wife of the Year. It is as thoroughly demoralising a study of modern men and women as you're likely to find. The programme-makers fail to explain why people do this, though occasionally they reveal why they think they do.

Lydia ('I've got a good figure but I've got no looks') talks about being raped more or less as she sends her pictures off. You can't argue with a rape victim whose explanation for being a Reader's Wife in *Fiesta* is that she's *helping* prevent other women from being raped. With such miserable women and their miserable men, Readers' Wives is more Mike Leigh than Mike Leigh ('Cor, she looks a bit ancient,' says a girl at *Fiesta*, judging the entrants) – and more depressing. 'Magic,' says the winner's husband, Gordon, when he hears that his snap of his well-proportioned wife, Gaynor, has won a prize. He proudly reveals that he has loads of pics of the missus – 2,500 of them – in a drawer: 'The bottom fell out there were so many.'

According to 'Firebugs', the first episode of Channel 4's decidedly dodgy series, **Walk On The Wild Side**, teenage arsonists were responsible for starting most of last year's 27,500 fires. Sadly, the interviews with these wasters and idiots are smothered in horribly dated Network 7 graphics and black and white footage of car parks and remand centres. The arsonists themselves add nothing to our understanding: 'I like... the flames,' fumbles one.

The arsonists look like angels compared to the subspecies exposed in the **Undercover Britain** programme on badger-baiting, 'The Killing Set'. Luckily, the scumbags stitch themselves up with their own stupidity. The undercover reporter simply rings up a dog-breeder to make tentative enquiries about illegal hunts, only for his wife to tell him her husband is out – hunting. In Ireland, where they provide badger-digging holidays, they ask him to video the kill. He high-tails it to the ferry with the footage after telling them he's nipping out to buy some fags. Nerve-wracking and sickening, the climax of this 'sport' is several huge blokes from Burnley, armed with shotguns, clocking the badger across the head with a spade

9

then lobbing it to the pack of dogs.

Horizon's 'The Last Mammoth' has more bad news: mammoths have been wiped out! Horizon examines the differing theories (too cold, too hot, dying vegetation) but the result is so incomprehensible that you'll need to rewind every two minutes. Experts around the world keep finding mammoth tusks, fossils and, most astonishing of all, a baby mammoth preserved in the permafrost, 40,000 years dead. An autopsy of its innards tells us what it had for breakfast. A cave in Arizona contains piles of mammoth dung that is (the experts say) 11,000 years old. Pooh!

You have the same reaction to **The Unpleasant World Of Penn And Teller** with guest Dawn French, who copes very well, considering. Excellent use of an industrial shredder. 'Come on,' shrugs Penn, 'it was just a rabbit.' Worth taping to learn the trick where you cut your own thumb off.

Finally, some human beings to love. The nurses at the Glasgow Teaching Hospital (**Cutting Edge**) have accents that make toodle-ooh the most wonderful word in the English (or Scottish) language and cry when their patients check out, alive or dead. 'Cheerfulness,' says the commentary soberly, 'is a nurse's main role. It's especially important when the patient is known to be terminal.'

Cutting Edge offers a valuable pick-me-up in a week when most people on TV make you despair. The closing postscripts providing the patients' updates are classic and, of course, grim. But just watching the nurses deal with it all makes you want to check in and be looked after. Toodle-ooh.

January 15–21 1994

Sons and (golf) lovers

After recent fly-on-the-wall exposés by Beam and Da Silva and Network First, the glamorous, partially-clad world of the supermodel receives another voyeuristic, gratuitous going-over this week. In Friday's **Captain Scarlet**, Angel Interceptor-pilots Destiny and Symphony go undercover in the episode 'Model Spy'. Posing as waif-like anorexics, Destiny ('it'll be great to get out of uniform') and her partner (the rather ropey Symphony) infiltrate the cocktail and cabin-cruiser set of Monte Carlo to protect the head of a French fashion house from the grip of the fashion-unconscious Mysterons. 'How do I look?' pants Destiny, as she emerges draped in Valentino. 'Wow!' gasps Captain Blue, hiding his feelings. 'Mmmh!' smiles the once politically-correct Lieutenant Green. Showing his customary dedication, Captain Scarlet provides deep, deep cover by posing as a hard-working, networking, PR man: 'Darling! How are you? We must do lunch sometime.' But can the cool Cap cope with the Mysterons' own undercover supermodels, one of whom looks exactly like Linda Evangelista – only more realistic?

More bitchiness and bad fashion in **Sabotage**, Channel 4's new, post-Big Breakfast, but not post-feminist, all-female quiz show where contestants such as the manageress of the Hacienda answer questions about Supermodels, Getting Married and Chocolate. Hosted by Maria McErlaine, it's a girly, giggly, gushy quiz show. At least one contestant proves that not all models are dumb. Some of them are *really* stupid.

This week's **Cutting Edge**, 'The Club', tells of the sort of deeply conservative golf club where *Daily Express* readers are actually regarded as somewhat left-wing and lady golfers are accepted only on the understanding that they are forbidden from playing on Saturday or Sunday mornings. But then, as one chap points out, the ladies will still be washing up after breakfast.

Conflicts develop as other new members ('artisans... working-class types') begin to infiltrate. Standards fall, and in a club where even the pall is expected to behave decently at the AGM, the club chairman admonishes one toff (a Greens Committee Member) by telling him, 'You've been highly offensive.' The star of the show is an eccentric long-haired buffer called Preston Lockwood ('God I'm a diabolical player'). Preston's golf swing is a sight to behold, a deranged, scything action that teeters unsteadily between elegance and collapse. As one member explains, even the loss of one's wife is regarded as a minor inconvenience as long as one is a member of The Club.

Conflict of a specifically Freudian nature erupts in this week's **Living With The Enemy** as psychologist John Heron forces a group of parents to confront their feelings about their children and their own parents. 'Imagine this chair is your dad,' Heron tells a fifty-year-old professional Punch and Judy man. He encourages him to tell the chair the things he'd wanted to say to his father when he was a teenager: 'Say, "Dad I need and want your love".' Heron then turns to the Punch and Judy man's son. 'Do you have any friends?' Heron demands of the boy, who is by now blubbing away like his father. That's the way to do it.

In front of an audience of equally traumatised parents, Heron forces both father and son to acknowledge the resentment they both feel towards the way their parents humiliated them. This, he concludes brightly, shows they *do* share common ground. Presumably he thinks humiliating them together on television provides just enough *extra* common ground to cure them.

Screened after the watershed (at 10.20pm), this is the kind of viewing that is actually too disturbing and hard-hitting for children or parents of any age.

February 5–11 1994

Speed freaks

There's nothing Tapehead likes better than putting on his leathers, making an exhibition of himself astride the back of a throbbing motorbike, giving himself a thrill at full speed. Luckily, he also loves speedway.

Champions: Speedway Stars follows Dave, Kelvin, Dean and Gary, the macho lads of the English World Speedway team, as they roam the country at league meetings in the build-up to the World Championships in Coventry. 'Gary comes second', 'Martin beats Gary', 'Martin comes last' say the subtitles, poignantly. How macho are they? Well, how about strutting round in front of the cameraman with your willy out after a blinding race – that's how macho. The lads (fag in hand, dripping in mud) all have the requisite ponytails and blonde girlfriends, who proudly wash the boys' leathers each night. In return, reveals Dean, the lads devote any free time to the girls – 'Watch the soaps with them, you know.' Explaining their win bonus-only fanaticism, the England team manager sagely sums it up: 'There's more to speedway than just having your girlfriend in the stand... At the end of the day, you've got a living to earn. If you don't score points, you don't earn. If you don't earn, I suppose you don't eat and if you don't eat, I suppose you die.' You don't get much more macho than that.

One contender could be the poor mites shown under the dentist's knife on **Dispatches** which looks at the legal action taken by the families of 100 children against several manufacturers of baby drinks. Watch as young

Carl, who has lost seven milk teeth out of twenty, is gassed and has his teeth yanked out with pliers. Or Jack, who, at the age of two, was drinking so much sugar in his herbal tea baby-feeder, he was having convulsions, mood-swings and tantrums and lost his four front teeth. 'His teeth were that soft,' says his distraught mother, 'the dentist pressed a hole right through with a hook [cue huge close-up of scary hook]. I didn't expect them to bleed as much as they did.' No wonder kids start smoking.

The Lowdown looks at how macho youngsters are stocking up, not on sugar drinks, but nicotine sticks. They all say the first one makes them sick but then have several more – to perfect their taste. We see several kids going around buying them for the cameras. One pregnant 15-year-old tells her disapproving friend she does it ''cos it keeps me occupied'. 15-year-old Lee demonstrates his macho smokers' cough.

But nothing, nothing, compares to the macho cane toads in **Encounters** which (hilariously) profiles the love–hate relationship Australians have towards the creature that, since its introduction in 1935, has conquered Queensland and is now taking over New South Wales. Fearlessly sitting in the middle of the road, copulating crossly and copiously ('one female can lay 40,000 eggs in one summer – that's a large number of eggs'), the toxic toads' diet is a truly macho mix of grubs, flies, mice and dog-food, even the occasional cigarette (presumably after a meal). Not content with that, the cheeky chappies poison any dogs, snakes or protected birds foolish enough to try and eat them. Some residents love them: 'I couldn't do without them. They're friends!' Others loathe them: 'I really go out of the way to run them over,' says one driver, swerving all over the road. Nymphomaniacs, necrophiliacs, haemophiliacs, the toads, say residents, are 'a bit of a rough bunch... walking disaster areas'. 'The Cane Toads are coming,' says the soundtrack. One of them is even riding a motorbike.

April 16–22 1994

Sex on legs

This week: sex, football and television – the finest three words in the English language. **Goal TV** has many highlights – a whole night of highlights: John Burridge, David Icke and Albert Camus goal-keeping; David Coleman introducing the 1962 Chile v Italy match as 'the most stupid, appalling, disgusting and disgraceful exhibition possibly in the history of the game'; Kenneth Wolstenholme describing Bobby Charlton's goal against Spurs as 'a goal good enough to win the league, the Cup, the World Cup and even the Grand National'.

But the star of the BBC's night of football mania is Tapehead's first love, the subject of the best programme of the night, a classic Hugh McIllvanney documentary profiling the sexiest player ever to grace a British football pitch. Welcome to **The World Of Georgie Best**, circa 1970, when Best, his dazzling blue eyes smouldering amidst a shock of black hair, still looked like a cross between Warren Beatty and Prince. Best is shown at home (with Mrs Fullaway, his landlady), at one of his boutiques (with a chick smoking what looks like a white opium pipe) and at a genuine discotheque (the night before a game) wearing an outrageous pink tie-dye T-shirt that no mere mortal could get away with. 'A person who doesn't like him,' says the barman, 'just doesn't know him.' 'There's a self-confident coolness about him,' McIllvanney purrs with awe, 'that unnerves some men and fascinates most women.' Best himself recalls years of defenders trying to break his legs: 'The only way to get back at them is to make them feel so inferior that they never want to play another game of football again in their lives.' George Best did this at will.

The best moment in **The Ball Is Round** is also (unsurprisingly) from Best. Just after The Fall's Mark E. Smith has described the way Best used to do nothing for 85 minutes then suddenly amaze, comes a clip, a black and white clip, of absolute genius. Best taunts the opposition with the ball like a matador and then, when they rush him, shimmies past them and elegantly tries to chip the keeper from 40 yards – just for the hell of it.

The Ball Is Round is about the pain, passion and exhilaration of being a football fan and includes the love of Tapehead's life, Billie Whitelaw, and a groovy sociologist who summarises football as 'a game for poets'. A bewildered Everton fan explains how (unwittingly) he now knows where all the league's referees come from. 'Like, when people say P. Don to me, I just say Anworth Park.' Another mad fan's passion for football grounds is so great he's started ticking off non-league grounds too. 'He has a peccadillo for photographing corner flags,' explains his mate. Sadder still is the Middlesbrough fan who asked his mate: 'Do you play Subbuteo against yourself? Well, do you find that the team you want to win often loses?'

Not many sights on a football pitch get sexier than Best or the sight of

Mrs Tapehead singing Chelsea's Celery song but soccer supremo Mike Alway and Douglas Hart's film **Brazil 1970: The Sexiest Kick-off** captures one of them. Not only were Brazil's 1970s goals better than anyone else's (Brazil's fourth goal against Italy, by Carlos Alberto, is about as total as total football gets), their names (Rivelino, Jairzinho) were cooler into the bargain. Better yet, Brazil '70 has a clip where Brigitte Bardot strides out to the centre-circle in fur coat, boots and hot pants and kicks off.

Pure sex. Pure football. Pure television.

May 28–June 3 1994

Food and drink

To start, salad of pig's cheek with leeks and lentils. Then a main course of either pigeon breast stuffed with smoked aubergine and pickled walnuts covered in game and garlic sauce, served with mashed turnips and shallots, or salmi of pheasant served with redcurrants and chestnuts and braised celery. Then, for dessert, roasted figs or caramelised raspberries and lemon posset.

Just another night in *chez* Tapehead and, by coincidence, the very same dishes knocked up on this week's **Masterchef**. For this week's semi-final, Loyd Grossman is joined by lunching legend Alan Yentob and Sally Clarke of Clarke's in Kensington, the first high-quality restaurant to offer set menus only. 'I actually decided long ago,' says Clarke, 'that I wanted a restaurant that would offer no choice to the customer.' Charming. 'Would you normally associate lemon grass alongside a dish like pheasant?' asks a suspicious Grossman. 'I would not,' exclaims Clarke, sounding uncomfortably like Lady Bracknell. She disdainfully summarises Contestant Number Two's menu as 'rather ambitious' and mercilessly taunts Yentob for admitting that, at home, he still uses sun-dried tomatoes (peasant).

By the end, Yentob condescends to offer the judgement that he 'would happily be cooked for by all of them again'. Big deal. Masterchef is one of those supremely enjoyable and relaxing programmes with shots of people sprinkling, whisking and stirring that are unrivalled on British television. The Masterchef quiz is so marvellous that they have '2,000 lines open till midnight'. When Grossman talks about things like 'that combination of the rosemary and the crushed coriander we were worried about earlier',

Tapehead simply nods his head in agreement: he was worried about it too. The highlight of this week's episode is Grossman's extraordinary pronunciation of risotto. Elsewhere, a cornucopia of wild mushrooms is outdone only by much talk of seasonality and rosticity – look at the *rosticity* on that. Masterchef is tastebudtastic, mate.

After all that lemon posset and roasted figs what could slip down better than a quick dram and **Wooldridge On Whisky**? So far this series has offered an abundance of remarkable (not to say, encouraging) anecdotes and traditional tales from people fond of a tipple or two, including the recipe for Queen Victoria's favourite nightcap (half a glass of claret topped up with malt whisky). Tapehead is ingratiated to the doctor who reveals that 5 to 10 per cent of liver transplant patients with cirrhosis simply start again, putting their new, revitalised liver to good use.

In this, the last of the series, up pops Tapehead's old drinking mucker, the Duke of Argyll, who shares the story of his first proper drink (aged four), after which, needless to say, he didn't touch another drop for 'a viry, viry long time'. His parents were having their 'usual daily cocktail party' (in Biarritz). A shaker of dry Martini later, he was out cold on the floor and whisked off to hospital to have his stomach pumped – all before his strict Presbyterian nanny found out and resigned. The usual story in other words. Inspired by this series, Tapehead is pondering a move up to the Scottish islands, to the sort of village where they pour whisky over their dead so everyone can pay their respects without too much of a pong. They'll sell their best milking cow to pay for the funeral too and rightly regard it as bad luck not to drink every last drop of the whisky provided.

This week, no doubt, they'll be toasting Taggart, whose sad demise has blighted Tapehead's TV week. Mark McManus's face will live long in the memory, as will his acid humour and iron courage. So, drink to Taggart.

June 11–17 1994

Orgasm addicts

Sex addiction is all the rage these days, and no wonder. Where better to meet dozens of horny men or women than a sex addicts' therapy session? **Fine Cut: I Am A Sex Addict** illustrates how sex addiction can lead to devastating debilities, for example S&M, pornography and violence, and the sort of massive self-loathing that causes one addict to describe herself as 'a hopeless romantic in a vibrator life'. 'What sex addicts have in common,' Fine Cut states, 'is their compulsion and the fact that they are people, just like you and me.' It looks as if you and me have a lot of problems then.

One addict, a scary exhibitionist, wistfully remembers his first erection and recalls the time a couple from Gravesend tied wax and gauze around his dick. With blushing sentimentality, a couple of hippy-swingers/addicts display their 'cum towel', a six-year souvenir of their outdoor encounters which she has kept, 'in case we might want to frame it or put it on the wall'.

A hardcore S&M addict helpfully explains the variations in his collection of whips and handcuffs and reminisces about putting fluorescent cayenne pepper in a girl's welts so they would glow in the dark. Happy times, happy times. Quirky voyeurism is all very well of course (Tapehead likes nothing better), but Fine Cut veers uncomfortably towards crass exploitation for Lori, an obese nymphomaniac and porn star, renowned for being generously well-disposed toward gang-bangs (as many as 33 times in one go). 'No one's interested in Lori,' she claims, so her alter ego Layla (the lay of LA) stars in flicks like Hard And Lard in which, she says, she is renowned for her jiggle-osity. Lori/Layla's lewd version of 'Rescue Me' is probably the most disturbing, pathetic sight of the week as she belts out, 'Gang-bang me/Take me in your arms/Gang-bang me/I want your throbbing charms...' etc. Seriously demoralising.

Sex addict and freak-lover Pedro Almodovar would feel for her. **The Indiscreet Charm Of Pedro Almodovar**, a Late Show special, looks at his fantastic passion, brilliant women and outrageous humour and includes the surprising sight of John Waters being superbly upstaged by Almodovar's mother. Well worth taping, if only to count Almodovar's costume changes – some of them seemingly in mid-sentence. The most extraordinary moment is Pedro stepping out of a limo with what can only be described as a hairdo even Kevin Keegan would baulk at. 'I felt like ET in the village I grew up in,' he remembers, and no wonder with that hair. The Indiscreet Charm Of Pedro Almodovar also features undoubtedly the best clip of a transvestite and a knitting teacher enjoying a golden shower that you'll see on TV this week.

More sex and madness in Jeremy Isaacs's **Face To Face** interview with Jeanette Winterson who concedes (er, reluctantly) that her books are a play on form, challenging a genre, like Virginia Woolf, even a rod, a staff for her readers, a guiding light. Isaacs praises the novel, experimental diversity of Winterson's language and asks gravely where she finds these words. 'In the dictionary,' Winterson elucidates. Contrary to recent opinion, it is not true that Winterson is incapable of modesty. She admits parts of *Oranges* are badly written – 'in the same way as, say, a book like *Wuthering Heights*'. 'My childhood was happy. I was a happy child,' she says at one point, bringing to mind a similar master of the language, revered for his plays on form. 'It is a fiction. I am a fiction writer,' she explains, an obvious allusion to that great writer/philosopher Chris Eubank and his (profound) statement: 'I box because I am a boxer. I am a boxer because it is boxing.'

A true insight into one of literature's most important influences.

June 25–July 1 1994

Hand jobs

The original Naked Ape-man, Desmond Morris, returns this week with **The Human Animal** which begins (promisingly) with the inspiring sight of a naked man and woman gliding in slow motion through a crowded shopping centre, a pleasurable part of the weekly shop Tapehead knows only too well. Morris starts with 'The Language of the Body', looking at gestures of approval, disagreement, greeting and abuse and goes human-watching around the world to find examples – from the traffic police in Rome, the stock exchange in Bombay and the ranters of Speakers' Corner to dog-track tick-tack men, American Football coaches and synchronised swimmers.

Watch out too for a distinct lack of smiling from the winner of the World Poker Championships as he receives his £1 million cash – poker-faced all the way to the bank. Well worth practising is the body language in Bulgaria, where a subliminal affirmative (yes, to you or me) is indicated both by a nod up and down and a sideways wobble of the head. 'This,' says Morris, 'creates total confusion. Why on earth they should do all this remains a mystery – even to them.'

Thoroughly instructional television: learn how to lie without body language (special note to Mrs Desmond Morris to tape this episode).

Insult-wise, footage of Harvey Smith's two-fingered salute is all very well but Tapehead is particularly taken with the Greek hand gesture that, according to Morris, means 'excrement being pushed into the victim's face'. Elsewhere this week, Tapehead's main body language remains the involuntary click of the thumb that indicates the remote is being pressed.

The principal hand gesture during **Short Stories: The Pitcher** – 'the greatest market trader that ever lived' who knocks out rubbish down at Birmingham's Bull Ring – is probably the gimme-gimme-gimme open palm of the hordes of punters clamouring for The Pitcher's give-away goods. 'Don't charge him eight. Don't charge him seven. Don't charge him six...' The Pitcher buys things that cost £8 and sells them for £1. 'How do I make a profit? Buy 'em for less than they sell. Which I think is the theory of business.' Let's hope Kenneth Clarke is taping.

The body language in **Paramedics**, where this week the ambulance-men (sorry, ambulance technicians) are on duty for New Year's Eve, mainly consists of people holding their head as the Great British Public celebrate New Year by puking up, trying to commit suicide and stabbing each other (and all because of Andy Stewart).

Mercifully **Medics**, where even the surgeons are sick, is getting gorier, meatier and juicier in every sense and, in terms of people spewing blood, rapidly heading into Casualty territory. 'Let's take out the spleen and then get her straight down for a brain scan.' So far in the new series, the gloriously camp Tom Baker's hairdo has battled it out with Sue Johnston's, who has been getting it on with the evil administrator who gets his kicks by rigging drugs trials. Apart from a kid who pours bleach all over his birthmark, the current storyline is a rather tasty hepatitis patient. 'She's been incubated and ventilated, her abdomen's distended,' says the doc, rapping like a mutha from South Central. Watch out for Baker, leering into the camera like Igor, asking the parents if he can transplant a diseased patient's organs. Virtually licking his lips, his impression of Jeffrey Dahmer speaks for itself. Requires no body language at all. Moving and sensational, Medics gets Tapehead's thumbs up.

July 23–29 1994

Not drowning but waving

Another sinister TV week to tape: a sick and successful serial killer; a sad and sorry sex change; and, most worrying of all, a squad of grinning synchronised swimmers.

A meticulously slick TV movie with a rare sense of the tense and the truly terrible events that took place, **To Catch A Killer** is a three-hour, two-part reconstruction of the case against John Wayne Gacy (recently fried for the murder and torture of more than 30 teenagers), centred on a chillingly steely performance from Brian Dennehy. 'Are you liberal-minded about sex, Billy?' he asks one kid, casually. Yes, playing pool with John Gacy was no easy matter. Dennehy controls the transformation from respectable businessman to murderous deviant with masterly restraint, giving Gacy a stare and smile that are genuinely menacing. His performance as Pogo the Clown will give you nightmares.

At the end of last week's **A Change Of Sex**, we left George/Julia plodding away from a sex-change operation, in slippers and overcoat, looking for all the world like Tommy Cooper in drag. Tapehead is happy to report the transformation from someone resembling Eddie Yeats or ex-Arsenal centre-forward Alan Sunderland into Penelope Keith (*circa* The Good Life), vintage Barbara Dickson and, finally, the singer from A Flock Of Seagulls is now complete. At the end of three weeks of agony and anguish, the result is that Julia now looks like Mandy Jordache, Gloria Hunniford or Fat Pat Cabs from EastEnders: yes, like a man in a dress.

She has spent the intervening 15 years staggering blindly from Amsterdam to Chesterfield, from poppers to alcohol, suffering various degrees of personal crisis. She has made up what she has lost in height (several inches) in weight (several stone). All in all, it's fair to say that Julia's life makes even Tapehead's look alarmingly uneventful. Now, 15 years of chaos after her op, she has turned, as any man would, to pottery ('I never saw myself as being artistic'). The series ends with Julia discussing sex changes with transvestites gathering at Transformation, a shop stocking magazines like *TV Tarts* and *Punished in Panties* advertising 'full gender reassignment' and selling items like 'corsetry for that hour-glass figure'.

Whether Julia is ready for synchronised swimming though must, sadly, remain debatable. This week's **Short Stories** ('Sync or Swim') looks at the inside world of synchronised swimming: stories of ruthless plans to knob-ble opponents, rumours of drug abuse and steroids, not to mention nose-clips. The great debate raging through the sport, dividing it in two, is (inevitably) sequins: 'We're trying it out for a year – to go without sequins. Try and make it more sporting athletically.' Disaster. Anyone like Tapehead who has spent years of his life contemplating the mysteries of the sport (aka drowning to music) will want to tape Short Stories in order to appre-ciate fully its subtleties. As one coach, Muriel Coombs, explains: 'A lot of strength and flexibility are involved. Also, you've got to hold your breath under water.'

It's not really swimming and, sadly, half the time it's not really all that synchronised either: by the time they hear the music they're already out of sync. Bristol's finest 12-year-olds demonstrate manoeuvres like The Submarine Ballet Leg or Dolphin Bent Knee and very similar they look too. Mind you, The Eiffel Tower should certainly come in useful in later life, proving particularly popular with members of the opposite sex. So perhaps the great mystery is solved. Maybe that's what they're smiling about.

August 13–19 1994

Fatal fame

'Knock, knock.'
'Who's there?'
'O. J.'
'O. J. who?'
'Right, you're on the jury.'

You'd have thought the world and his wife would have known everything there was to know about the O. J. Simpson case by now. Undaunted, **The Late Show** returns this week with 'O. J. Mania: The Media Trial Of O. J. Simpson'. Sadly, it begins by comparing the impact of O. J.'s plight on ordinary Americans to Late Show viewers imagining what it would be like if Paul Gascoigne was charged with a bru-tal double murder. Not very surprising at all really. The show purports to examine the media's role in the trial but can't resist doing so without dip-ping its toe in a few sensational samples, most of which you'll probably know already. An anguished Rolanda broadcasts her chat-show debate on 'Can O. J. Simpson Get A Fair Trial' live from outside the court-house. Sales of Bronco jeeps – as used by O. J. – increased by 30 per cent as citizens prepare to race police cars to the Mexican border. It's another tale of ordinary American folk.

The 911 tape of Simpson's estranged wife, Nicole, calling the cops during an earlier attack is worth another listen: 'What does he look like?' asks the concerned 911 operator. 'He's O. J. Simpson,' she says, describing him to a tee. The only Grand Jury witness to place O. J. at the scene (swiftly signed up by Hard Copy) reveals that when she saw O. J. he looked 'crazy... like a madman gone mad' (very mad then). Naturally, she was never called to give evidence. Worth taping if nothing else for an extraordinary appearance by *Hustler* publisher Larry Flint, whose lifetime of heavy breathing seems, finally, to have taken almost terminal hold.

Amidst all the O. J. mania, who remembers Tonya Harding and Nancy Kerrigan? How fickle we are. Like The Late Show, the telemovie **Tonya And Nancy: The Inside Story** attempts to disseminate the morality of the media in the world of celebrity. Tonya And Nancy begins promisingly with a shot of (guess what) an ice-rink, beautifully shot like an arty MTV video. But you know things are going wrong when the guy playing the scriptwriter for a TV movie on Tonya and Nancy looks at the camera and says, 'How do I write this?' From then on, T & N is never happy just being a dumb TV movie, although the line, 'I wonder what Tolstoy would think of Tonya's life: much war and little peace', is a classic.

After the attack (a whack across the knee with a ruler), the narrator/scriptwriter explains, 'The networks went crazy.' Cue postmodern scenes of network executives having meetings about how to make a decent Tonya and Nancy TV movie. 'The deal was made,' one of the characters complains, 'but when ABC and Disney went partners, how could we compete with theme parks and a mouse with more money than God?'

After 'The Day Today', the ultimate (minor) celebrity Alan Partridge's first episode of his own series **Knowing Me, Knowing You** (ahhha) is such an accurate, straight parody, any actual jokes have virtually been left out altogether. Wonderful guest introductions though. 'Fame. I'm gonna live forever. Fame. I'm going to learn how to fly. Of course I'm not. But in a sense my next guest did...' 'If music be the food of love, play on. That's what William Shakespeare said. I'm not William Shakespeare, of course. I say, if music be the food of love, let's eat it.'

Let's hope Alan Partridge does not go the way of JFK and Tyson or O. J. and Tonya and find himself sucked from celebrity into terminal scandal and disgrace. What a tragedy that would be.

September 10–16 1994

Am I Black(pool) enough for ya?

'Yo, whassup, G? Where da f**k you at, man? Yeah we're getting busy y'all, just hanging, knowwadarmsayin*? So whassup wit chew man? Chill. Word to ma niggaz. Mad Bone and L'il Monster. Damn. Word up G... Peace.'

Yes, this week we're in Blackpool. B-l-a-c-k-pool and yes, OK, we're in Los (as in Lost) Angeles. Da Bank Holiday starts here. Best of all, we're in the TV Dreamland that was ATV-land, so a big shout to Tapehead's OG, fly nigga, MC Roger Moore: 'He is larger than life, never eats butter, he's Just Mr Television.' Yeah, 'nuff respect to Lew Grade, aka Louis Winogradsky, World Charleston Champion, Man Who Could Sell Fridges To The Eskimos and creator of this week's Bank Holiday viewing, ATV's finest: The Persuaders, Randall And Hopkirk, Man In A Suitcase, Jason King and Crossroads.

Check out **The Persuader: The TV Times Of Lord Lew Grade** for Sir Lew's resemblance to (a) Goldfinger, (b) Alfred Hitchcock and (c) a large sea turtle. 'I love talent,' says Sir Lew. Who doesn't, Lew? Who doesn't?

Meanwhile, based on the theory that 'the only true expert on gangs is a gang member', this week's **Witness: Eight Tray Gangster – The Making Of A Crip** follows the life and crimes of gang-banger Kershaun Scott, his brother Kody and his poor, magnificent momma, 'Birdy Mae Canada'. Kershaun describes his initiation into the Eight-Tray set when his mum moved the family to South Central; his participation in the '92 riots down on Florence and Normandie; in Eight-Tray territory; and his work trying to maintain the truce. The Crips have been going in LA since 1969 and the

23

film explains, at least in part, why the feuds are still running. 'Twice I thought I was gon' die,' says Kody. 'You would think you wuz gon' die too, you had blood pouring out both sides of yo' face.'

Another time, Kody was shot point blank in the stomach, in the back and three times in the leg. His buddy ran over to him sayin', 'What happened?' 'I said, "Damn fool, I'm shot, that's what happened."' Revenge, Kershaun explains, had to be swift. When he was shown the pictures of what he'd done, he says, 'I couldn't believe a shotgun could actually do a person like that. Made me respect the shotgun even more.' Not exactly remorse, but still. 'That person had no stomach anymore. It didn't look like a human being.' With a family of his own, but still a wanted man, now when he goes out Kershaun takes a bodyguard and stays out of the middle lane in traffic jams. But then, who doesn't?

Dreamtime: A Brief Anatomy Of Blackpool begins with Jayne Mansfield cooing 'that's the most fantastic sight I've ever seen in my life', taking the words right out of Tapehead's mouth. 'Blackpool's one of those places where you do things you would never do anywhere else,' says the head of tourism. David Thewlis remembers coming out of the sea aged eight covered from head to toe in maggots, which is certainly something you wouldn't want to do anywhere else. Needless to say, he has never been swimming again and now neither is Tapehead. Look out for the ultimate Blackpool holiday hat. Forget the love / Forget the passion / Whack it up her doggy fashion. Who said they couldn't rap in Blackpool?

August 27–September 2 1994

Career opportunities (the ones that never knock)

This week, Tapehead is thinking of changing jobs. The Guide have (thoughtfully) provided a selection of the week's prospects to hasten his decision. Sad to say, Tapehead has missed his true vocation, a job on **One Man And His Dog**, which starts this week with a new presenter and a new commentator. Yes, after 17 years and 132 episodes, Phil Drabble has stepped down to spend more time with his family (his family of collies).

The new series comes with a new course, 'with new hazards'. These turn out to be land-mines under the fetch gates and a small patch of quicksand in the middle of the run-in. Tapehead's theory that the dogs do everything on their own and the blokes whistling in the flat caps have no control over anything is borne out by the farmer who does nothing except say, 'Lie down. Come out. Lie down. Come out.' 'She doesn't do much on the farm, the wife,' he says, obviously rating her usefulness way below a collie.

Before the sheep are unleashed we get some quick analysis of the course, some team tactics and a pre-match potted history of the contestants. 'I never thought she'd walk again,' says one farmer about his accident-prone pup. In the post-match interviews, the farmers talk about their sheepdogs like managers eulogising about centre-forwards: 'Good temperament, fast feet, I knew Nan wouldn't let me down.' Nan agrees: 'Yeah, well, the gaffer sent me out to do a job and I think I done it.'

More dogs, sheep and animals in Tapehead's next job as a holiday rep (**Inside Story**) where 'Louise from Blackburn' is a besieged rep in Crete. There are 67 bars and six nightclubs on the doorstep of one of the hotels Louise looks after, although she insists that 'not everybody comes here to get steamboated out of their skulls for a fortnight'. Louise spends most of the programme vainly negotiating between gangs of mad English lads and their mad Crete hotel-owners. 'You cray-zee Ingleesh. Much drinky. Very cray-zee.'

Louise goes for the Vinny Jones school of diplomacy: 'Right you, Foghorn-on-legs.' 'Some of them you just feel like headbuttin'.' Like the beerboy who gets his heel clipped by a passing car: 'Did you go to hospital?' 'Naah. I sellotaped a couple of cold Heineken bottles to it.' Watch out for an excellent streetfight between drunken, sun-crazed young ladies, which you don't see very often (not nearly often enough as far as Tapehead is concerned).

This leaves **Come Dancing** as Tapehead's last chance, judging by the standards of the International Final (from Bournemouth), also known, bizarrely, as The International Proton Cars Trophy. The noisiest, most dazzlingest show on TV (like dancing on fast forward), some of the sights in this, the last in the series, are, as ever, extraordinary, especially the Cha Cha Cha. The costumes (notably the lime-green off-the-shoulder number that looks like a pair of sarin-soaked curtains with a set of pink poodles tied to the hem) are an inspiration. And some of the girls' outfits aren't bad either. The winners put even Tapehead's samba technique to shame. Mind you,

Real men

We all need heroes, Tapehead more than most. **NYPD Blue**'s Detective John Kelly is a natural: wise beyond his years, street-wise beyond belief, likes his girlfriend to be dressed in police uniform – in short, he's Tapehead's kind of guy.

The first of the new series, as poetic and elegiac as television can get, should, by rights, have been titled 'John Kelly: The Burden Of Sorrows'. Janice, Kelly's wild, pouting girlfriend is on trial. Kelly, of course, is the star witness. Intense and vulnerable, strong and skinny, head permanently crouched as if ducking away from the world's blows, David Caruso some-how has the face (or soul) of a little boy *and* an old man. This allows him to scatter wisdom like confetti, like someone who has seen too many episodes of Kung Fu, as if he's counselling not only the other characters but the whole audience, his public. Try practising his way, in the midst of a wildly heated, fraughtly complex situation, of gently saying, 'Am I right?' when he knows he is. Heroic.

Ultimately, of course, Tapehead accepts that one day (one day soon) Kelly/Caruso will make his exit and Tapehead's life will be devastated, des-olate, in much the same way it was when Sheila Grant left Brookside or when LWT killed off Dial Midnight. Never mind River Phoenix or Kurt Cobain, last year was all about Julian leaving Casualty.

This week, though, he's back, in **Dangerfield**, starring as a dashing, debonair GP who fills up all those irksome idle hours fiddling around as a Police Surgeon. Dangerfield is so slow, there's nothing for it but to start estimating how long it will be before we see Julian sitting suavely in his Range Rover again (sometimes it can be as long as, ooh, eight or nine sec-onds) or calculating how many thousands of pounds his mobile phone bill runs to: no wonder the NHS hasn't got any money.

Dangerfield is slower than Heartbeat, with more countryside than All Creatures Great And Small and dialogue like, 'Ooh, Dad! Don't forget your dictaphone.' To which Julian shouts back (as he dashes off debonairly into his Range Rover for a mobile phone fix), 'Don't worry, darling, I'll use my finger like everyone else.' All in all, Tapehead reckons Julian should get his gold lamé jacket out and go back to singing 'That's the look, that's the look, the look of love'.

Meanwhile, Julian's replacement, Mike, has a typically trying week in **Casualty** (but deals with it – heroically). 'Learning Curve' by Tony McHale has all the staple Casualty ingredients – teenage joyriders, teenage pregnancy, stroppy Scouse scallies and dangerous dogs – but all with good, juicy twists. Look out for a fainting Jehovah's Babe and, most startling of all, a strangely unpublicised guest appearance by Tapehead's old hero, Arnold from Diff'rent Strokes, making his comeback as an eight-year-old who breaks into a rich bitch's kitchen. A classic.

Last week in **Revelations** the truth came out about Thomas and Gabriel having a snog – 'I was wishing him well!' Gabriel protested (to his wife). This week, Charlie (Thomas's girlfriend, Gabriel's sister) goes on a bender (as it were) and gets nasty. All the while, Tapehead is no nearer to comprehending how one family, eight people, can contain so many enigmas. Why, for example, did Gabriel's mother (soap icon Judy Loe) confront her son's ex-lover and sneer, 'You're not a man, Thomas. You're nothing like one and you never will be,' when to Tapehead's eyes he is indisputably quite a lot like one (he's got a beard; he's doing both her son and her daughter)?

At least Tapehead's fascination with Thomas and Gabriel (the Tony Hadley and John Taylor of soaps), which has over recent weeks reached obsessive proportions, is no mystery.

Gabriel is extraordinary-looking, and not only because, in his dandy's blouse and Duran Duran waistcoat, he's a deadringer for Oscar Wilde's Bosie. With pouting lips, foppish fringe, sucked-in cheeks and gorgeously tousled locks, Gabriel is not only impossibly handsome, his resemblance to Tapehead is frightening.

January 21–27 1995

The beast of Brookside

The opening – a suffocating, blue nightmare – looks like one of those shadowy demon-ridden scenes from The Silence Of The Lambs or Elm Street. Murky, claustrophobic menace smothers the screen as the victim tries to thrash the fear away. Fists. Fists banging, smashing through the glass. On the stairs. Running. We know who it's going to be behind her. His face flashes through our minds. Then we hear

29

the voice, 'Mandy, Mandy. All right love, I know you'll need time.' *Trevor's back*. One day **Brookside** will be on every day. For now, though, it is Brookside week, a daily episode: Tapehead heaven.

Monday night and the patio slabs are coming up. Fred West gets a mention; a fellow demon. Then we see Trevor reaching up from the dirt, like a zombie, to drag his victims down. *He's back*. And he's badder than ever. There are people who thought Trevor was just too scary and, frankly, who could blame them. There are also those who thought you could have a story about wife-beating or child abuse *without* any wife-beating or child abuse. The sight of Trevor in bed next to his daughter Rachel, bare-chested in her bed, was just too much for them. For others, it was Trevor laying into Mandy behind the couch, fists flying. Pummelling her.

For Tapehead, though, gritty drama is what Brookside is good at. What upsets him more is Brookside's slapstick side – OAPs getting frisky, having a roll in the hay. Has Channel 4 no shame? What really gives him nightmares is not Trevor, but Mandy. Mandy's hairdo specifically. Back from the dead? The Night Of The Living Dead. A real horror show. Ever since she arrived on The Close bearing a distinct (disturbing) resemblance to Kevin Keegan, Mandy's barnet has gone through the creative wringer, until this week she looks like something much more surreal or supernatural, like that Sherri Lewis puppet, Lamb Chop, or Ermintrude from The Magic Roundabout. Something truly stupid. There's even a moment this week when poor Beth, forlornly, tries to persuade her mother to do something about it. 'Your face!' she complains. 'You look terrible.'

Tapehead can understand those feminists who objected to Trevor trying to beat some sense into her, but the sad fact is that Mandy Jordache is one of the most stupid women ever to grace the nation's TV screens. Since the murder, she has become more and more bovine, until her behaviour with loan-shark Kenny MacGuire was simply an insult to women. (This week, she's at it again, trying to coerce Sinbad into sleeping with her – having rebuffed him for months – just because she thinks it will avert suspicion.) It doesn't take long for Mandy to dominate Brookside week, swiftly occupying one other favourite place (the moral high ground) when Beth tells her she wants to reveal their gory secret to her new bit-on-the-side, Viv. Mandy moans that she can't entrust such a grave confession to a stranger. 'I didn't just pick her up, she's a friend,' protests Beth. 'She's more than that!' Mandy protests, indignantly. 'She's a lesbian.' (Nothing gets past Mandy). 'It's unnatural,' she complains, conveniently forgetting, as someone who not only murdered her husband and buried him under the patio but slept with her loan shark for money, that she's not exactly morally sound herself. Later, she has a go at Sinbad for stealing someone's car.

Poor Mandy, so deluded (with hair like that, it's the only explanation). On Tuesday she gamely plays the part of the tragic heroine/victim. 'All I wanted was a normal family and what do I get?' The fact that it might be something to do with *her*, the missing link (or more probably her hair), has obviously never occurred to her.

January 28–February 3 1995

I'm Mandy, fry me

A human tragedy, a tale of utter despair... a hellish journey... a story of psychosis, sociopathic domestic violence and incestuous rape.

Yes, you've guessed it, it's **Brookside**. What else could it be?!! Break out the bunting – five days a week, it's Beth and Mandy Jordache in the dock (Mandy's hairdresser stands accused). No wonder we're all having street parties. Not that Brookside's special editions are always cause for celebration. The Jordache Patio farce and the recent plague was presumably someone's idea of a joke, with Mick, in particular, behaving as if he was in a Chuck Morris movie, frowning hard and moving his eyes from side to side like an Action Man as he mans the barricades.

Luckily (sensibly), apart from a couple of irritating cameos from Ron Dixon and Julia Corkhill, each episode is filmed like Crown Court. The bit-part jury actors seize their chance to cross their arms and twiddle their pencils in their most Robert de Niro-like way possible. Brenna (Trevor's sister) keeps appearing (threateningly) in doorways looking like the woman from Widows or one of Macbeth's witches ('you left the poor man's soul in torment'). Rachel has gone back to looking like one of The Cure. Mandy arrives on the scene with her usual uplifting outlook on life: 'God, look at this place!' she moans, looking round the court building as if she was Catherine Deneuve or someone, adding with her usual spectacular stupidity, 'You don't think they've started without us do you?'

Strangely enough, they haven't. Tapehead has to admit he had never looked at Mandy and seen 'a clinical assassin' driven by 'manipulative prowess', but by the time the prosecution had finished with her, he was screaming *string her up!!!* at regular intervals. The prosecution begins with the words, 'I'd like to call Mandy Jordache…' but he sadly fails to call her anything. Instead, he scathingly recalls how she 'inflicted a sham funeral on her own daughter' and 'left Trevor's body in the extension' (contravening their planning permission). 'I had no choice,' Mandy bumbles. (Episode Three is not a good day for Mandy).

Contradicting her defence of diminished responsibility, the prosecution looks at Mandy and sees 'traits of criminal genius'. (Yeah, right!) 'As for your plea of self-defence, I'd say it was Trevor who was in need of defending.' As readers of previous columns will know, these were Tapehead's thoughts exactly. Trevor was only trying to knock some sense into her.

While Mandy sits in the witness box showing off a new hairdo that can best be described as early Eddie Izzard, Beth sits there, like a baby Winona, furiously pouting at the male jurors.

With a temperament the envy of Eric Cantona, Beth gets the week off to a great start, attacking a witness in the canteen ('she deserved it') and complaining about everyone eyeballing her all the time ('it's so embarrassing'), conveniently forgetting she is not only a lesbian sex kitten but a murderess to boot.

In Episode Four, the prosecutor, auditioning for The Accused and ignoring Anna Friel's heartbreaking performance, bizarrely insists Trevor's attacks were merely a product of her 'fertile imagination'. He follows this up by portraying Sinbad as a hapless pawn drawn to Mandy's Mata Hari-like web, 'like a moth to the flame'. The defence respond in kind by bizarrely complaining that Mandy and Beth were 'tired' during police questioning, having spent the previous week on the run in Ireland. (Ahhhhhh.)

Mandy predictably has the last word, claiming, 'I did it for all the women who suffered what I did' – which is palpably untrue. Anna Friel and Tiffany Chapman, in particular, are outstanding, and together the whole thing is better than Dostoevsky, though they never do explain why they buried him in the garden instead of just calling the police.

Two endings have apparently been filmed, but Tapehead's verdict is this: Beth gets an American mini series, playing Heidi Fleiss; Mandy gets to have her hair done in the electric chair.

May 6–12 1995

Mouth to mouth

I n 1991's **Hospital Watch** Mike Smith, Sarah Greene and Maggie Philbin spent a week presenting live broadcasts from the wards, waiting rooms and operating tables of Hammersmith Hospital. It was one of the most gratuitous, most intrusive and voyeuristic programmes in the BBC's fine, distinguished history and, this week, Tapehead is delighted to say it's back.

Someone has (sensibly) decided that undergoing an eight-hour operation during which the entire nation examines the inner workings of your intestines in intimate detail and then being interviewed by Mike Smith, is more than the human spirit can stand. Smith and Greene have been replaced by Tony 'Baldrick' Robinson and Sue Lawley – thus maintaining the TV tradition that decrees programmes about illness are hosted by people who make you sick. As most of the last series seemed to consist of innumerable microscopic cameras being fitted onto a variety of tubes and then inserted up every orifice imaginable, Tapehead only hopes Sue Lawley realises what she's letting herself in for.

The purpose of such a close-up look at the running of an everyday working hospital (Addenbrooke's Hospital, Cambridge) and all the hideous illnesses that can strike us at any time seems to be to prepare us for the worst. Hospital Watch does this by showing us the worst: showing what it looks like in gratuitous, graphic detail. It is not for the faint-hearted. Highlights in the last series included watching a colostomy being 'stapled' to someone's rectum and a trip inside the enormous, twisting red tunnel that was one man's urethra that was more thrilling than most of the rides at Alton Towers.

This year, amidst all the kidney operations and diseased gall bladder ops, Tapehead's highlight is 'watching a child with glue ear being fitted with grommets'. (Ouch! Mind where you're putting those grommets). So, get your BUPA application forms and doctors' almanacs at the ready. Let's hope no one croaks on camera.

The same should not be said for **ER**, whose depressing lack of fatalities has proved highly disappointing. This week's episode, though, 'shocked America'. (Good.) Tapehead still finds ER's principal characters horribly banal and the so-called gritty realism and black humour, tame and corny.

(Example: a student nurse complaining, 'Everyone round here is so old and sick,' to which someone replies, 'Hey, it's a hospital.' Pretty gritty black humour, eh?) However, the actions of Dr Mark Greene – modern-day America's equivalent to John Boy Walton – in this week's episode (the title of which gives away the whole plot) mean ER has risen in TH's estimation. The episode was written by 'Lance A. Gentile'.

Cardiac Arrest has been like a combination of ER and Hospital Watch, occasionally parodying them both into the bargain. The balance between black humour and dark drama has been brilliant, but the biggest surprise has surely been how good the programme is at sentiment/sentimentality. In this series, evangelical white light backdrops have been given lower priority to strong storylines – a pretty radical idea where Cardiac Arrest is concerned. Recently, members of the cast have been dropping faster than players in last year's Man United double team: James was HIV-positive; Scissors was upside down in a car crash; the gorgeous Claire Maitland was suspended; and ear doctor Docherty was pensioned off altogether – 'grateful to leave this bizarre set-up' (presumably meaning the series itself). The last in the present series, this week's CA is less about medicine than deception and betrayal; making deals and sleeping with the enemy; get-outs and getting-off-withs. Tim Robbins-lookalike, Dr Kirkby, is being hung out to dry.

The last shot of this mad, funny, scary series says it all, with saint-cum-sinner Dr Maitland actually smiling: mad, hysterical excitement plastered all over her beautiful, funny face. Look after yourselves.

June 3–9 1995

Pulp television

One of the great things about American television is the way in which an established series like ER will give young, up-and-coming talents a chance to make a name for themselves. This week's ER is a particular case in point because not only is the director making his TV directorial debut but he is actually a bit-part actor whose career has been blighted by a string of disastrously irritating cameos in no-hope, low-budget films like Destiny Turns On The Radio and Somebody To Love. The guy is such a loser his part in Reservoir Dogs was cut to shreds, finishing as a blink-and-you-miss-him role. Then, to make things worse, the sad schmuck overacted his way furiously through a scene in Pulp Fiction, hogging the camera from maestros Samuel Jackson and Harvey Keitel. Luckily, he makes a reasonable fist of directing ER, with signs that, all in all, he might be a name worth looking out for, though how far he's going to get with a name like Quentin Tarantino is a matter of opinion.

Yes, Tarantino directs ER. Frantic, shaky, handheld camerawork; dialogue you can't catch; too many characters: so what else is new? Just about the only clues that it's really him are: the freeze-frame shot of a bone-saw as a weapon; some chat about burgers; a good sun-lounger shot and a chick OD-ing on a speedball. Oh, and we get a girl-gang fight in which (guess what?) one girl gets her ear cut off. Ho-fucking-ho, Quentin... so funny. The best thing is the script and Tarantino had nothing to do with that. The real star is a bit-part actor/actress called (I kid you not) C. C. H. Pounder.

Whatever he does when he grows up, Quentin Tarantino will never be the director that Tom Clegg was, as Clegg's classic episode of **The Sweeney**, 'I Want That Man', demonstrates. As far as High Stylishness is concerned, The Sweeney puts Pulp Fiction to shame. From the graphics and opening credits to the two theme tunes, in terms of cool, The Sweeney had the threads, the birds, the hairdos and the car chases that Tarantino would happily have given his left ear for.

'I Want That Man' even has a jewel raid and a torture scene thrown in, not to mention a grass called Popeye, a snout called Jimmy Dancers and, best of all, Roy Kinnear as Frankie Little, tea-leaf and wheels man. John Thaw is at his best, revelling in the chance to run around shouting, 'See you back down the factory' and 'She might be the bird on that sparklers blag in Hatton Garden.' Forget Inspector Morse, where his accent was all over the place, when Regan walks out of the dugout at Stamford Bridge – his sheepskin coat and sideburns making him the perfect mentor for football managers across the world and Barry Fry in particular – Thaw is in his prime. 'Popeye likes football, don't he?' Regan asks his snout. 'Yeah!' agrees the snout. 'He likes the violence!'

There's a distinctly Tarantino-esque influence to the final of **Masterchef** as nerves fray and tempers fly. 'Just fuck off and leave me alone,' snaps Contestant Number One when Loyd Grossman and the indecipherable French chef, Raymond Blanc, come over and talk to her at the very moment that her ice-cream machine has gone on the blink and started turning her Iced Chocolate Pudding into liquid goo. Grossman then excels himself by describing the warm, smoked eel mousse as 'nice and warblay' (wobbly) and asking one contestant, 'Exactly what goes into a potato bake?' (Potato, Loyd, potato.) When Raymond Blanc starts rearranging the American contestant's handmade ravioli parcels into triangles, she asks nervously, 'Er, does it take longer to cook that way?' obviously thinking, 'Don't fucking touch that.' Finally, the third contestant's patience snaps when Grossman compares her delicately prepared Colcannon to 'leftovers'.

The last frame is a brilliant shot of all three contestants covered in flour, aiming their whisks at Loyd Grossman's head, frozen in a Mexican stand-off.

July 8–14 1995

Blasts from the past

Rock Family Tree sensibly passes over the fact that, apart from Blondie and The Ramones, none of New York Punk's contributions amounted to very much. (Anyone who mentions David Byrne will be taken out and made to listen to The Catherine Wheel.) Once again, though, we have to suffer the pathetic spectacle of Richard Hell claiming the credit for inventing the whole scene, even though not a single British band ever cited him as an influence eighteen years on. Hell is actually more famous for doing what he does here – whingeing about having to play support to The Clash, touring in (oh God!) a transit van and complaining that when he was in The Neon Boys the fans used to call out for his songs more than Tom Verlaine's. (Songs like 'Blank Generation' and, erm, 'Blank Generation'.) Tina Weymouth obligingly reveals that when they needed her to learn the bass, Talking Heads loaned her some Suzi Quatro records (oh, very intellectual). Not exactly the spirit of the Zeitgeist.

Vintage videos of Ms Harry bopping and smirking away to Denis certainly put today's meagre pop talents to shame, but New York's only true pioneers in those days were The New York Dolls, as everyone from Morrissey to Malcolm McLaren realised. True to form, Dolls' singer David Johansen (Tommy Lee Jones in nun's shoes and a dress) is the classiest contributor here. 'We would look like a bunch of Puerto Rican sluts at this point,' he growls, still looking brilliantly boxed.

The Ramones, inevitably, get the best lines: 'I guess we were just influenced by a lot of things around us,' recalls Johnny Ramone. 'Like mental illness. We couldn't really sing songs about cars and girls 'cos we had no girlfriends and no cars.' Five points for spotting how much Richard Hell now looks like Kevin Costner or American quarterback, Joe Montana. Ten points for noticing the resemblance between naff Rocky Horror Show pub-rocker Jayne County and either Teresa Gorman or Ivy Tilsley.

More double takes on **Match Of The Seventies**. Brian Kidd *is* one of The Verve. Paul Madeley *is* the actor Francis Matthews. Charlie George *is* the singer from the Red Hot Chili Peppers. As for Alan 'Sniffer' Clarke, has anyone ever seen him and Mark E. Smith of The Fall-ah in the same-ah room-ah? 'Turn-stile Psyche Goal-hanger Conspiracy,' as Mr Smith would say-ah.

Tragically presented by Dennis Waterman, rather than Stan Bowles or David Coleman, Episode One of this nostalgia-fed footie-fest vaguely traces the monthly ups and downs of the 1970–71 season as Arsenal and Leeds fought it out for the league title. 'And why did they invite you?' a journalist asks Arsenal boss and former physio, Bertie Mee. 'Presumably they liked the shape of my nose,' smiles Mee, enigmatically. Strange days. Despite an appalling script (understandably uncredited), there is still plenty of opportunity to *revel* at Alan Whittle's hair, Paul Reaney's sideburns and Norman Hunter's purple shirts. And *ponder*: who let Huddersfield and Burnley into Division One? How did a team with Gary Sprake ever get anywhere? And why don't they still play with those Subbuteo-style red balls in winter?

Worth watching principally to enjoy the sight of Emlyn Hughes 'writhing in agony' and for the moment when Leeds boss Don Revie (the man who took 'dirty northern bastards' as a compliment) sits down in the dugout at Anfield in a huge sheepskin coat, lights a fag and brusquely tosses the match onto the pitch. Now *those* were the bloody days. Eagle-eyed viewers will also spot a rare shot of a league table featuring Man City in second place.

Meanwhile, according to Channel 4, in this Wednesday's **Brookside**, 'the Jordache appeal suffers a serious setback'. Well, that's one way of putting it. As the closing credits roll, Mandy Jordache *is* Gloria Gaynor with her crushing rendition of 'It Should Have Been Me'.

July 22–28 1995

Master race

What *is* the point of **Mastermind**? The specialist subjects are invariably irrelevant or impenetrable and, as if to compensate, in this series, the general knowledge has been almost laughably easy. For example: which part of the body does alopecia affect? Too difficult? Try, 'Which mop-topped foursome from Liverpool had a hit with a song called "Love Me Do"?' Worst of all was the one asking, 'Which bridge – built in 1926, designed by Edgar Browingsdale – adjoins San Francisco?' (Rhymes with 'olden plate'.) This week's contender for Is Magnus Magnesium Taking The Piss is, 'Which flower is associated with Remembrance Day?'

The winner is invariably the contestant whose specialist subject is some obscure Cornish poet no one has ever heard of (1936–7) while the poor mug who takes on 'The History of Spanish Art... All of It' struggles to get into double figures. It's hardly surprising that the Wild West expert knows what Butch Cassidy's real name was (Tapehead would rather know what it was that made him so butch). Tapehead likes the way that the contestants nod knowingly whenever they get one wrong, as if they knew all along, and the way the last contestant – struggling to think of the answer – closes her eyes, frowns really hard and grits her teeth.

As usual, **Masterchef** is a study in viscious understatement. When Loyd Grossman says something like, 'I'm not totally convinced by the cream sauce on the red mullet', what he's really saying is, what a *peasant*. When he sees Contestant Number One's dish and knowingly describes it as 'the best thing someone's done with a black pudding for ages', he obviously hasn't seen some of the things Tapehead can do with a black pudding. While Italian cooking writer Anna del Conte natters away knowledgeably, special guest Mick Hucknall from Simply Red says, 'Cor, that tastes nice!' a lot and stuffs his face. Perhaps if he'd used his knife and fork a bit more rather than eating with his fingers...

As for the pepper tulle baskets, parsnip streamers, wild mushroom consommé and quenelles of sweet potato, that's the sort of thing Tapehead rustles up for his breakfast. The only thing that really has him puzzled is when Anna del Conte considers the preparation of the plate of venison and muses, 'It looks quite well hung.' Quite how she knows the deer concerned, Tapehead will never know.

Millionaires is a good idea for a piece of popular nonsense, but you know a new series is in trouble when it starts with the statement, 'When the Queen makes a state visit as important as the one to South Africa, how she *looks* matters as much as what she says or what she does.' So if the Queen said, 'Have you ever noticed that South Africans smell of custard?' or stood on the balcony smoking crack, the fact that she was wearing a turquoise two-piece with white shoes and handbag would be just as important.

This week's millionaire is the Queen's highly stylish, debonair dressmaker Hardy Amies 'or HA as he is known'. Future delights in store include Raymond Blanc and (say it ain't so)... Bruno Brookes. According to the press release, they will be 'revealing how they made their money and how they intend to keep it'. (Charming.)

The only interesting anecdote about Amies is that, when he was at school, his dad got him a job interview with the editor of the *Daily Express*, who told him they didn't think journalists should go to university and packed him off to go and live with a family of French farmers instead – exactly what the editor of the Guide did to Tapehead. Of course, this Carlton-made series is little more than a puff-piece, mere patronising PR, with Amies declaring, 'If it can be said that I am successful...' a lot, when he is evidently a multimillionaire. In fact, the tone of self-congratulation accelerates with alarming glee, until a moment near the end when Amies gets his wad out and starts screaming, 'Loads of money' into the camera. Absolutely shocking.

May 27– June 1 1995

Another close call

They just never learn, do they – the good people of **Brookside**. In fact, the more extraordinary the things that happen to them, the more stupid they are when it comes to anything elementary. Take Mick, part-time pizza man/part-time detective in Homicide. After months of being stalked by Mad Jenny the teacher, Mick has sorted out the problem superbly: he's let her move in. Sometimes, he even lets her take the kids to the park. Good work, Mick, you really should have been a therapist. Then there's Mandy Jordache. Her and Brenna are really close these days because, according to Brenna, 'we've been through so much together' (i.e. 'you buried my brother under your patio' – a genuine bonding experience).

The week starts with Brenna standing at the breakfast bar, brewing up some skin of toad and wart of dog, as is her wont these days. Mandy knocks it all back, in between being sick, telling everyone she's got a bug and wondering out loud whether 'the plague's come back again'. Anything except see a doctor. Such a good judge of character, Sinbad is still having difficulty in believing that Mandy didn't want to marry him – 'after all I've done for you' (i.e. bury your husband under the patio). By Friday, though, it looks as if Mandy and Sinbad will actually get married. The producers, it seems, felt a plague was one thing, but no one would believe that anyone could be dumped by Mandy Jordache.

It's a real bumper week (or bump-off week). Rachel gets her exam results (the result being: like mother, like daughter); Max and Patricia Farnham try to get Bing to invest in their business (never look a Gift Box in the mouth); the Farnhams decorate their flat to look like the one in Shallow Grave (Keeping Up With The Jordaches, presumably). As the wedding approaches, Mandy is looking more and more dreadful (and the poison's not helping either). For some reason, she is still walking around in a grey prison apron. Mad Jenny and Mad Brenna are both madly making puns, 'Ooh, you look dressed to kill,' etc. When Mad Jenny goes to visit her dead parents, Mick gives Bev's mate, Janice, an extra portion of the Pizza Parlour Special.

Janice, a vision of sophistication, reveals her idea of a perfect lie-in: 'A dirty great big cooked breakfast in bed, then watch Richard and Judy,' she winks saucily – obviously a girl after Tapehead's own heart. Janice gets ready in a hurry (short skirt, silver T-shirt, no lippy) and leaves dishevelled. 'Do I look dead rough?' she asks Mick. 'Do bears shit in the woods?' smiles Mick.

Next, on the grounds that it is Totally Improbable (i.e. a Brookside prerequisite), the scriptwriters get Ron Dicko to bond with Mandy. You know, 'Our Tony, Your Beth,' etc.

'I'd still be in prison if you had your way,' points out Mandy, with uncharacteristic sharpness.

'We'll have to agree to disagree on that one,' says Ron, as if they were talking about whether Ian Rush had scored more goals for Liverpool than

Kenny Dalglish. 'Oh, all right,' says Mandy, returning to type. Undaunted, the scriptwriters then get Ron to volunteer to babysit Mick's kids. Luckily, Mick is so thick he makes Mandy look like a member of Mensa and manages to forget Ron's racist hate campaign. Brenna and Jenny get to cackle and say, 'So this is goodbye.' Jenny gives Mick her farewell present: a book. Not the most obvious choice for Mick, but still. It's at this moment we realise Mick is in Really Big Trouble: Jenny's an Ian McEwan fan! 'First Love, Last Rites,' Mick reads slowly, predictably missing the possibility of any significance. 'It's my favourite!' explains Jenny meaningfully, practically twiddling her villain's moustache.

Brenna flies around the close on her broomstick; Jenny comes over all Reservoir Dogs. Outside the registry office, with characteristic sharpness, Sinbad has noticed something is wrong: the Best Man and the bride-to-be are not there! 'I'm sure there's a perfectly simple explanation,' says Jean – with characteristic sharpness. Mandy and Mick are certainly simple. The plot has been indubitably lost, so there is, as always with Brookside, no rational explanation. But no one could deny that this week's Brookside is absolutely perfect.

August 26–September 1 1995

The correct use of soap

In your hearts, you know it's the last thing you should do but, despite all your friends' entreaties, you cannot resist the temptation. A few free samples and you're hooked. Never mind the dangers of crack, when will the government act against the growing number of people succumbing to weekly doses of **Emmerdale**?

This week's episodes are Emmerdale 2006 and 2007, like sci-fi. Conclusive proof that Emmerdale is another planet (it's Yorkshire). After a spate of murders, sex scandals and more people playing away than Leeds United, Emmerdale has become so obsessed with notoriety that even the sheep are on drugs (watch that deranged one in the opening credits). A sex-with-animals storyline can only be weeks away. This week, Zoe the lesbian vet (there's a joke there somewhere) is recovering from an attempted rape. Sexy Kim Tait (who could be Sexy Cindy's mum if those roots are anything to go by) is having a rest and seeing what it's like to stay vertical.

41

Comedy capers are provided courtesy of the extraordinary Dingle family, who have the best one-liners this side of Preston Front: 'Shut up, slug-brain', 'Ooh you big jam tart', etc. Nellie, the Dingle mum, is the best comic creation in soap since Hilda Ogden, like Julie Walters doing Hylda Baker. 'If you've gone to that boozer,' she shouts at one of her dumb sons, 'I'll geld yer.' Nellie can also do things with a cocktail cherry not even Sherilyn Fenn would attempt. Watch out for an unexpected guest appearance by R. Kelly.

This week in **EastEnders**, David Wicks has a new dog (and I don't mean Tiffany). Robbie is torn between Well'Ard and Samantha. Even Jules and Blossom are doing the Wild Thing, butterfly-style. Bianca is losing everyone to Samantha: her best mate, Tiff, is now Sam's best mate. Her boyfriend, Ricky (or Greystoke as Tapehead calls him), is still Sam's husband, and her Dad (David) is Sam's boyfriend. 'Don't worry,' her mum consoles her. 'Everyone goes through this kind of thing when they're young.' (You speak for yourself, Carol Jackson.)

Elsewhere, Kath has been feeling 'a bit dodgy' ('It's me 'ormones playin' up. You know, The Change'); Nigel and Fat Pat Cabs are wearing the same blouses (D. H. Evans?); and Todd Carty's acting technique goes from Frowning to Frowning Really Hard, as if he's turning into an American Werewolf In London (in Walford). No wonder his wife Ruth is so miserable. Alternating between starring in EastEnders and singing for Portishead is about as depressing as you can get, and that indecipherable Glaswegian accent doesn't help.

More soap mania on **Dyke TV** ('Three Kisses And A Funeral') which includes interviews with Della from EastEnders and Anna Friel – the lovely Beth from Brookside – being her usual bolshie, mouthy self. Worth watching principally for re-runs of Beth's snogs with (i) Margaret, (ii) The Teacher and (iii) The One With Pigtails, the programme soon deteriorates into obscure lesbians giving their bizarre interpretations of The Significance Of Beth. Rachel Wilson declares, 'It's typical! A survivor cannot be seen to survive in the end.' (Eh?)

Their confusion between Friel and Beth grows more and more alarming until they start giving the young actress a hard time for posing in the press with her boyfriend and for 'stressing she's not gay'. One girl considers pictures of Friel wearing a fashionable baby-doll dress 'really quite disturbing bearing in mind she's a survivor of child abuse'. (Huh?) The truth is, Beth's popularity stemmed almost entirely from the child abuse storyline, as did Friel's most powerful performances. The lesbian storyline was tacked on to the character out of desperation for controversy.

Neither Beth nor Margaret were ever plausible lesbians. In fact, a scene on the beach (shown here) reminds us that the most convincing aspect about the notion that Beth was a lesbian was her mother. Now Mandy Jordache really does look like a lesbian.

September 2–8 1995

Suds-u-like

G iven that Phil Redmond, Channel 4's self-styled 'soap supremo', has written the first two episodes of **Hollyoaks** himself, it's tempting to see them as a sort of scriptwriting masterclass; an example of the master's art.

So here's how it starts: a car-customised chase; a recording studio in a bedroom; an 'invite-only' party flyer; a bare-chested hunk; a blonde babe; the police motorbike chase; the customised car exploding. It could be Beverley Hills 90210 but that would have, like, more dialogue. Any dialogue.

It's quickly obvious what Phil's formula is: short skirts, big tits, cheesy grins, lots of music, one black character, no Scouse accents, no obvious signs of intelligence. The young LA styling makes Hollyoaks look like a clueless version of Clueless. Like Baywatch but not as smart, or Grange Hill but not as scruffy, the strangest aspect of Hollyoaks is that it feels like something you used to watch in the seventies, during the summer holidays. (It's cornier than Double Deckers. It's even got Alvin Stardust in it.)

The party scenes have no groovy references to anything cool and contemporary: when he's in his bedroom, the hero does rock guitar solos instead of Ecstasy. As for razor-sharp repartee, we get lines like, 'Dawn... I knew she was called something to do with the new day.' (Oh stop it, Phil, you're killing me.) Phil's biggest problem is that his Travolta and Newton John – Natasha (Shebah Ronay) and Kurt (Jeremy Edwards) – are hopeless. Kurt says, 'Look, it's cool, OK?' at every opportunity and seems to be a kind of clean-cut Fonz (i.e. a total dickhead). As the village rebel, Kurt, in particular, gives Hollyoaks an uncomfortable resemblance to Follyfoot.

Meanwhile, the omnibus episode of Phil's series about Care In The

Community, **Brookside**, moves to Sunday to accommodate live basketball (Huh?!?). Our Carl has blown it with Your Sarah. Our Katie (Little Miss Miserable) is, er, miserable. Jacqui Corkhill's hair salon has got more staff than Tesco (although you have to wonder who would go to a hairdresser who had a hairdo like Jacqui's). Luckily for us, Susannah has come back to torment Max (and Patricia). As the press release puts it, 'Max is finding it hard to control his libido, but he's determined to be faithful to Patricia... But how long will it last?' Ask a stupid question... Who would go for a PR girl called Patsy wearing what looks like a pinafore over her T-shirt (erotic?) when he could go for a pouting (panting), big-chested blonde called Susannah? Yes, The Battle Of The Blondes With The Big Backsides is on and poor Maxie is trapped, torn, like a kid offered two flavours of ice cream and forced to choose only one.

Tapehead has a soft spot for Max and his footballers' haircut (it's Tim Sherwood's old one) and, judging by the way she interferes with him in the restaurant, so does Susannah. Feathers ruffled, Patricia circles round him like a brooding pigeon. Sadly, this Bouquet Of Barbed Wire sub-plot is sidetracked in favour of our first glimpse of Mandy's new-born. We are confronted with the reality that Mandy has given birth to Mick McManus. Now that she's had her baby and got off for killing Trevor, Mandy obviously had to come up with New Ways Of Being Stupid.

This week's involves going round to rescue a battered wife who wrote to her in prison. At first it seems Mandy is trying to kidnap her. But then, as we wait to see whether the woman's husband is about to burst through the door, it looks as if she's just trying to create a situation where she can bump him off too ('Have you got a patio?'). Sadly, Brookside once again ends up looking nothing like as realistic as that other soap about life in The Street: Sesame Street.

October 21–27 1995

The lying game

To lie. To falsify. Prevaricate. Deceive. Mislead. Misguide. Misinform. Exaggerate. Distort. Dupe... Would Tapehead lie to you? Hell, yeah.

Little lies, big lies, white lies, they're all in **Horizon**, which manages to devote plenty of great, true lie material to a wholly rhetorical question: has science caught up with the lie? Lying is (obviously) too enjoyable, too useful and amusing for us ever to give up, so Horizon's suggestion that we are about to enter a world where advances in science will require us to tell the truth the whole time, thus ensuring society collapses around our feet, is both bogus and disingenuous. 'Everyone lies,' says a former judge and, let's face it, he should know.

To prove the point, Horizon even shows chimpanzees lying – deceiving their fellow chimps into thinking something frightening is going on so that they have time to eat all the apples. (And you thought Nixon was bad.) Nixon pops up, of course, along with Ollie North, Maxwell, Profumo and Philby: fine liars all, Tapehead's mentors ('the dog ate my Tapehead' being a virtual mantra round these parts). As we soon see, only very young children cannot lie – not even to stop Snow White getting snuffed out by the wicked witch. However, the CIA's scary new brain-fingerprinting machine can measure lies by 'uncovering guilty memories'. (Tapehead is full of these; full to bursting in fact.) The dodgy old polygraph merely measures physical giveaways. What Horizon is really missing here are any expert liars capable of beating a polygraph, rather than simply showing innocent people being exonerated. American spy Alrich Ames, for instance, beat the polygraph twice by 'lying calmly'. Forget yoga or meditation. Lying calmly, 15 minutes a day, will stand you in good stead for later life.

Modern Times features a special police unit in West Yorkshire which has mugshots of 144 liars on its walls. They are bogus callers, scum. Described by the unit as 'totally ruthless', these characters can make fortunes ripping off OAPs by posing as health workers or council workers. Some are children, trained by their parents. They scour the streets looking for hand rails, lace curtains, overgrown gardens: typical giveaways of OAPs living alone.

These are useless witnesses, perfect victims: people so old, ill or confused they can't remember who they owe money to or for what; people who trust others because they are so honest themselves. Many of them fail to recognise the man who ripped them off the day before. Addresses of soft targets are passed around so the number of visits increases. One old boy has 12 people currently ripping him off. 'How many?!?' splutters the outraged interviewer. 'He's definitely getting worse with the senile dementia,' says the neighbour of one old man who seems to spend the whole programme handing out money. At one point he pays out £30 for delivery of some knives and forks he doesn't even take. Thomas Alcock, sentenced to three and a half years for 892 such offences, admits, 'I have no morals.' A policeman from the unit describes him as 'the worst in West Yorkshire... absolutely excellent. Thinks on his feet, ruthless, often violent.' He denies the unit's job is depressing on the grounds that 'it's beyond depressing'. He's right. A thoroughly demoralising, relentlessly appalling study of cruelty and lying at its most ruthless, this is a show whose moral is not 'Be careful who you trust', as its makers might think, but 'Never grow old'.

The eight students on **University Challenge** (obviously) all lie about how clever they are, relying instead on a series of lucky guesses. Contestants at modern Middlesex poly claim to be reading marketing and herbal medicine. Students at Exeter are reading politics and law. (Guess who wins?!) The girls at Exeter get very excited when the bonus questions are about trade unions (that's students for you). Tapehead's gift to you (finger on the buzzer) is that the answer to the first question is... Eric Cantona. No lie.

October 28–November 3 1995

Pop tarts

'**H**ave you had it yet?' asked the Channel 4 press officer with concern. 'Have you had sex with Paula?' It obviously needed explaining. Just because Tapehead is (a) male, (b) a media star and (c) hung like a llama, it doesn't necessarily mean he's had sex with Paula Yates. Even if it is Christmas.

What he meant, of course, was 'Sex With Paula'. (In Paula's love life, a pair of inverted commas can go a long way.) Back in 1986 (apparently) Paula was commissioned by Channel 4 to make a series that 'explored the connections between love, sex, morality and pop music'. Instead, she made **Sex With Paula** which explores none of these things or indeed any other things instead. The series was never shown because in the pre-post-politically correct climate of AIDS anxiety, Paula was just 'too frank', 'too flirtatious' and 'cunning' (which is not something you can say very often).

The highlights are as follows: George Michael says 'wanking'; Elton John offers us the benefit of his years of experience ('lubricate your knob'); Lemmy says he'd pay good money to see a man fuck a pig. It's a Channel

4 Xmas Special in other words. The main thing to remember is that this show was made back in the days when Paula was just silly and attention-seeking, rather than plain stupid and sad – sucking her thumb or twirling her pigtails as she swoons, 'You're in a group and everything' in a gooey voice, about as sexy as Shirley Temple (or less). 'Do you think young girls feel a certain amount of pressure to go out and lose her virginities?' she asks Patsy Kensit, which makes you wonder just how many chances she thinks a girl gets.

Poor sap. Her idea of what's sexy or controversial is so tame, so spoilt and suburban. And what terrible taste she had in pop stars too. Gary and Martin Kemp, the bloke from Cameo, Ben Poseur-Unpronounceable from Curiosity. Maybe they should all form a supergroup and do a charity record (for themselves). Needless to say, all the stars on offer say they regard sex with strangers or groupies as empty and unrewarding – which is easy for them to say, considering they've had so much of it. (Bastards!) Only innocent young Patsy admits (all too eagerly) that people do fantasise about her. 'I'd like to meet them,' she giggles. Not as much as they'd like to meet you, sweet pea. Elton John prattles on patronisingly about how hard it is for a pop star's partner to cope with them being so successful (the idea that any of them could get a successful job of their own obviously never occurred to him – or them). But you watch it for Paula, of course – poor, desperate Paula embarrassing all these handsome young pop stars, clawing at them like some thin-lipped, musty auntie demanding a kiss at Christmas. Channel 4 really shouldn't encourage her. All the time she was groping them, forcing herself upon them, she was married and bringing up two kids.

For real musical talent, tune in to **The Eagles: Unplugged** (scarily subtitled 'Hell Freezes Over') which begins, of course, with Hotel California – 'Such a lovely place/Such a lovely face'. With energetic overacting and eye-closing guitar solos as they make love to their (acoustic) axes, not to mention Don Henley over-emphasising every note and nuance of the recorded version (the way buskers do), Tapehead's lighter was held aloft until the lampshade caught fire. 'You can check out any time you like/But you can never leave' – I think we all know what he's saying.

Compared to The Eagles, **Pulp (No Sleep Till Sheffield)** just haven't got the songs (they don't even have room for 'Lyin' Eyes'). Essentially one-hit wonders dragging out their 15 minutes, in years to come Pulp will look horribly ordinary – especially when people look back at this. On tour, Jarvis comes over as a sort of postmodern Charles Hawtrey, clutching his earner bag wherever he goes, moaning miserably about the travails of his sad, lonely life on the road. Guaranteed to make you wish you'd never bought his records and made him a star in the first place.

December 16–22 1995

Ho fucking ho

Apart from **EastEnders** and Arthur undergoing a rude awakening in prison, reliving some of the more unappealing moments from Scum (in the greenhouse – appropriately enough for the man behind the Flowering Wilderness campaign), Christmas TV is a veritable avalanche of so-called Christmas 'specials'. For Tapehead's money, the pick of them is clear.

'Whatever Christmas means to you, there's no doubt it's a magical time. And we'd like to share some of that magic with you tonight. Nine guests to share with us not only their singing but their thoughts and feelings as to what Christmas means to them.' Yes, as Matthew Kelly confirms, 'It's a time of gifts and mince pies/It's a time for the **Christmas Stars In Their Eyes**.'

First up is a woman who wants to be, and is probably meant to be, Ronnie Spector, but actually looks more like the spectre of RuPaul. Then some loony does Alice Cooper as Ebenezer Scrooge – an ingenious way of disguising the fact that he sounds, and looks, nothing like Alice Cooper (or Scrooge). A couple of desperate theatre actors perform a duet as kd lang and Andy Bell of Erasure, which suggests, if nothing else, that Stars In Their Eyes is developing a sick sense of humour. (Enough is Enough is about right.) Sadly, 'kd' is so much bigger than the real kd that they could have been Yazoo impersonators from a previous episode.

The bloke who looks like Michael Bolton certainly has the same haircut but even he can't quite muster the necessary level of atrocity. He more than makes up for this with his unmissable (unlistenable) rendition of 'White Christmas' – or 'Wer-Height Cra-her-ser-mas', as he calls it. 'Where treetops ger-liss-hay-en/And children ler-hiss-hay-en.' Spend a little time on Christmas Day thanking the Almighty that you don't look like Michael Bolton.

Knowing Me, Knowing Yule is, of course, the Alan Partridge Christmas Special ('Ah-ho-ho-ho') and reputedly the great man's last appearance. As such, it includes AP begging the new Chief Commissioning Editor at the BBC for a second series ('Knowing You, Tony Hayers – Jew; Knowing Me, Alan Partridge – Jew-liker'), giving Christmas presents to sick children and touring the local shops. 'It's at times like these, browsing amongst electrical goods at Tandy's, that I know who I am. I'm Alan Partridge.' The guest that proves to be his downfall is a wheel-chair-bound golfer. 'Your story is a fairy story,' Partridge grins. 'So Gordon Hansel and Liz Gretel, allow me, if you will, to be Hans Christian Alanpartridgeson.'

The set, he is at pains to point out, is an exact replica of Alan's real home – 'But don't bother taking that as an invitation to go out and burgle my *actual* home, as happened six times last series,' he warns, explaining that he has a bloke from Securicor and two Alsatians waiting. 'In fact, *do* bother. You'll be picking up yer teeth with a broken arm. You people are scum. Let's meet... the bell-ringers of Norwich Cathedral.' Tapehead trusts that, like Mike Read in EastEnders, at the very least, Alan will turn up every Christmas.

The **Eurotrash Christmas Special** makes a rather token contribution towards the festive spirit with an item covering the World Santa Games (a sort of Superstars for Santas that includes events such as Chimney Descending and Beard Quality). Things deteriorate somewhat with methane-farted Christmas carols. And, for anyone needing any last minute mail-order presents, Channel 4 thoughtfully take a look at an Italian shopping channel hosted by a transsexual and specialising in porno (ho-ho-ho).

The season of goodwill to all men goes further on Channel 4, extending as far as a mass orgy organised by Sergio and Engie, two porn stars-cum-aerobics teachers. Eurotrash confirms the end of the dominance of the *Pirelli* or *Playboy* calendar, announcing the advent of a great new calendar featuring animals' arses. Good to see that Channel 4 are starting off the new year as they mean to go on.

December 23–29 1995

Lip up fatty

Week one of the new year is dedicated, appropriately enough, to being fat. **Ricki Lake** – 'My Man Won't Be Seen With Me Because I'm So F***ing Fat' – is about men who claim they love their partners but are embarrassed by their size. 'When we go out together,' Gabriel moans, 'she's so fat. She's fat. And I tell her she's fat. "You're so fat."' (Not the most articulate individual, Gabriel has been married to Laura for seven years.)

Then there's Tim, an over-opinionated Neanderthal, who calls Jennifer names to try and shame her into dieting. 'What are some of those names, Tim?' asks Ricki. 'Oh. "Fat Pig". "Linebacker". "Heavy Duty". "Wide Load".' That should do the trick. Tim has a peculiarly pragmatic approach to being overweight. 'What's the weight for?' he shouts. 'It's not serving any *purpose*. If you want the weight, make it useful. Like I told her recently, grow a beard and join the circus.' Yee-hah. That really gets the audience going. Even Ricki loses control and lunges for his throat. When Tim's partner, Jennifer, walks out (or rather, waddles out), she kicks him on the shin. 'I'm fed up,' she complains, which is surely the whole point. If only she could just *stop* feeding up...

The whole episode is, of course, Ricki's idea of heaven. She defends the girls to the hilt, but you can see her eyeing them up, thinking, 'Fuck me, she's fat. I was never *that* fat.' By the end, Ricki's sassying around the studio with an extra slink in her walk (the minx). Last word goes to Antoinette, telling her boyfriend, 'I don' need ever'body tellin' me to "lose weight, lose weight, lose weight". I'll lose weight when I get rid of *you*, fool.'

A new series of **Roseanne** heralds the return of the original Becky, prompting a string of 'Where the hell have you been?' gags, a cute closing credits sequence with the Two Beckys together and lots of unnaturally maternal loviness from America's favourite Fat One/Pregnant One. Roseanne and Jackie go shopping at Mothercare and Becky and Darlene throw something called 'a baby shower' to raise some cash to be able to buy anything there. 'What's with the fruit?' Roseanne asks Becky. 'I'm making a fruit punch.' 'Well, I've always found the best way to make fruit punch is to open a carton of Fruit Punch and then open another carton of Fruit Punch.' As Darlene mutters, 'When she hugged me, I knew true fear.'

Arena: The Burger And The King chronicles the life and times of Elvis through the food he ate, from his roots in Tupelo, Mississippi, during the depression, to the Lauderdale Courts Projects in Memphis, Hollywood and, finally, Vegas. 'Elvis probably ate squirrel as a boy,' declares a Mississippi old boy, as he takes another pot-shot at dinner. 'You develop a taste for 'em.' (True.) The cast of characters is pretty great: Mary, Elvis's cook for 26 years ('First day, I called him Mr Elvis and that's all I ever called him'); his brother-in-law, Billy Stanley; his doctor; and lots of people obediently saying, 'This is what Elvis ate.' So we get recipes for pigs' feet, turnip greens and cornbread; barbecued pork pizza and cheeseburgers; peanut butter and banana sandwiches fried in butter.

Elvis: The Army Years are represented by 'SOS' (Shit On A Shingle): milk, fat, and beef stock. Yum-yum. The best story is about the time he flew from Hollywood to Denver and had a diner there deliver 22 enormous 'Fool's Gold' sandwiches to the runway. The King's order consisted of 22 large French loaves, 22 jars of peanut butter, 16 jars of jam, 22 pounds of bacon: 42,000 calories per sandwich. (Something even Jennifer would have difficulty putting away.) By the time he died, Elvis was on so many drugs, he couldn't feel the pain of his stomach exploding internally with all that food. The last character we meet is Elvis's undertaker. The closing credits feature people insisting that 'Elvis Lives'. But watching this, you could be forgiven for thinking Elvis didn't live even when he was living.

December 30 1995–January 5 1996

Disco divas

t's not often you feel any sort of sympathy for anyone whose job is 'something in the music business'. But when 'multimillionaire' Nick Stolberg and Paul Hawkins re-enter The Biz to assemble 'the new Take That' (not the most original or noble of missions), **Inside Story** manages it.

Auditions are so painful you can't help but feel (momentarily) sorry for the two masterminds, even if they do declare with a pout that what they are looking for are boys who are 'fresh, eager to be moulded'. The audition number ('Love Me For A Reason') is an inspired choice, full of wince-inducing high notes and great singing-in-the-shower opportunities. Watch out for the Lee Sharpe-lookalike who announces his arrival with an energetic Flashdance routine, then massacres every note known to man. The real stars are the parents who have the temerity to scupper the Svengalis' plans by consulting a music business solicitor and wonder aloud what Jean Paul Gaultier's got that Marks & Spencer hasn't.

Having perfected the group's image, Nick and Paul realise that they have overlooked just one thing: the songs. (Rather irritatingly, Take That have ruined the conventional Boy Band stereotype by writing their own material.) So they visit a music publisher and listen to potential 'hits' with fingers pressed to their temples, eyes tightly closed, while the publisher energetically rocks out and grooves on down, as if she's trying to convince them this is the natural reaction anyone would have if they heard it. 'I think it sounds like a smash,' they chirp when they find the right song. And, indeed, it is a hit. (It's 'Careless Whisper'.)

After a year's work and quarter of a million dollars of Nick's money, the song, the video and the band are all pretty good, only for the two big shots to screw the whole thing up by calling the band Upside Down. Tragic.

More behind-the-scenes musical insight in **The House**, which looks at the snobbery and vendettas, the chaos and ineptitude that is The Royal Opera House. In the first of an obviously addictive series of six, the stars are divine diva Denyce Graves ('I swear apples make you sing better, I really believe that') and Director of Public Affairs Keith Cooper, who is set upon purging The House of his inferiors. 'Andrew is still a problem,' he informs one meeting, 'that will need to be resolved in some way... Andrew has neither the seniority, nor I think does he have the intelligence, to cope.' Keith has been receiving hate mail, though he claims to be unable to quote any of it. Ms Graves, meanwhile, having lost her voice and collapsed at the end of the opening *Carmen*, visits a Harley Street specialist who begins his examination of her vocal cords by announcing, 'First, I'm going to look in your nose.'

The week's star expert, though, is Andrew Wiles, a shy Cambridge bod who from the age of 10 has been obsessed with solving the world's greatest puzzle: Fermat's Last Theorem, which has baffled mathematicians for over 300 years and will now do the same to viewers of **Horizon** (for half an hour on Monday). The solution to the theorem (something to do with Pythagoras, the Horizontal Iurasawa Theory and doughnuts) was so elusive that no one else was even trying to solve it when Wiles 'gave up everything' (including sex and water?) to spend seven years in his study scribbling down equations.

This bizarre, utterly compelling suspense story is told superbly despite a variety of Andrew's egghead colleagues who say things like, 'All I had to do was add on some extra gamma-zero venstructure. As simple as it sounds, it had never occurred to me!' and guffaw merrily about how stupid they were. Wiles's secrecy and subterfuge became so great that, in order to consult another expert without arousing too much suspicion or interest, he gave a course of lectures, which only his colleague would be able to understand (and thus attend). Rather than 'Eureka!', he describes discovering the first solution as 'the most important moment of my life... so simple and elegant'. Amazingly, to present the world with his findings, he quietly, casually, gave another lecture without revealing the point or punchline. What a showman! Final proof mathematics is the new rock 'n' roll.

January 13–19 1996

Hit the north

It would, of course, be fatuous to say **Our Friends In The North** is not as good as When The Boat Comes In – just they're both set in the north east. But let's face it, that never stopped Tapehead before and it's certainly not going to stop him now.

In Episode One, for example, not a single character came in covered in coal saying, 'Why-aye, bonny lad. When the buurrt comes in, why-aye' – although Peter Vaughan did talk about the Jarrow March and, this week, insufferable pub rocker Tosker does say, 'There *is* no other woman, man' to his wife. But whereas When The Boat... was social history without even trying, Our Friends... is going puce trying to sum up the history not only of the north but of the whole of Great Britain (and, in Episode Six, parts of Uganda). We've got to 1966 (funny little period police cars are everywhere, trrring-trrring-ing their sirens like alarm clocks). Woar Nicky, played by Christopher Eccleston (who looks like a big bloke stuffed into schoolboy shorts; a third-rate Hal Hartley character; a marionette), is still getting overheated, trying to Save The Working Classes, a storyline so irritating and clichéd that even the producers decided to head south. (Hurrah!)

Here we catch up with the improbably named Geordie. Surely Geordies don't go around giving other Geordies nicknames like Geordie – they'd be saying, 'Hello Geordie', 'All right Geordie' all bloody day. Geordie ended up involved in the porn wars of Soho (double hurrah), where the scene is about to be stolen in the most spectacular way by Malcolm McDowell living it up as a cross between Andy Warhol, Miles Copeland and a villain from The Sweeney, delivering lines like 'I've got nothing to offer you but hubble, bubble, toil and trouble' as if they were second nature (which, of course, they are).

It's a splendid effort – one that distracted Tapehead only momentarily from his true duty, i.e. the study of Mary's fantastic eyebrows, dancing sensuously in myriad different directions. Come on down, Mary (down south). You know it makes sense.

Tapehead's only other friends in the north are, of course, all fictional, namely the good people of **Coronation Street**, where young Jamie actually does say 'Ay-oop-our-mam' and Jim MacDonald sleeps in his parka and still eats hot-pot every lunchtime and stew for dinner parties – 'Call it casserole,' says Betty Turnip and, let's face it, she should know.

Trisha is in prison; Gail and her extraordinary hairdo are about to meet their long-lost brother and Denise the hairdresser has, improbably, left Ken for someone more boring. 'Are you saying that she's *gone*?' cries Fiona, as bright as ever – not having noticed she wasn't there with her, in the shop. 'With *Brian*!!' 'I do think she's disturbed,' says Ken. 'Psychologically.' Bloody right. Brian (Denise's brother-in-law) even looks disturbed – lucky to have a wife, let alone a mistress. (He looks like a virgin. A disturbed virgin.) 'Nobody knows,' explains Ken wishy-washily. 'The whole thing took place in a vacuum' – which shows you what *he* knows. (The whole thing took place in the flat above the shop.)

The battle of the anoraks is on. Speaking of which... 'There's two things I don't like sharing, Willy,' says Jim MacDonald, like Clint Eastwood about to put his cigarette out and go and get his fists bloody. 'And one of them's a sandwich.' Meanwhile, as Maud and Phyllis propose to Percy (they propose a rather creaky threesome), the sexual allusions are flying. 'You wanted a word, I believe,' says Percy. 'Is it your guttering? 'Cos I know it's sagging a bit at the back.' Ooo-er. Watch out for the way Phyllis's blue hair clashes with Maud's purple hat, which merges into Maud's hair without ever threatening to show the join. Through it all, Maxine's beautiful narcissism remains intact.

As for **Brookside**, we all know The Close stopped being part of the north long ago and moved to some other planet altogether. This week, everyone changes partners, Shane tells it how it is about smack and Jackie's cat gets wasted in a drive-by. 'If the police can't control the streets, then it's up to us,' says Ron Dicko, the Brookside Terminator.

EARTH CALLING BROOKSIDE, EARTH CALLING BROOKSIDE. Please phone home. Get well soon.

January 20–26 1996

Heartburn

Two days before Christmas, walking past the churchyard, Robert Wilson heard a voice. 'Will you help me please? They poured petrol on me and set me alight.' (**Modern Times: Tracey And Joey**.) Robert still looks traumatised, wracked with the memory and guilt. 'She was brown all over. Which I took to be a bodysuit.' Somehow you knew all along that it wasn't. 'I've seen burns,' says a policeman, 'but I've never seen anything like that.' She survived 12 hours. Tracey Ann Mertons, 31, abducted and set alight in Congleton. Tracey had no reason to be there, or to be killed.

Somehow, Modern Times almost manages to spoil its own story. It is pointlessly pretentious (mention a train, we see an arty shot of a train) and ridiculously written, like a student's essay (C+). The programme-makers are fed up that they can't solve the case, but for whatever reason they stick to Tracey's boyfriend, Joey, just the same. Joey is a smack-head, a crack-head and a crack dealer, which is not a crime in itself (well, all right, it is – but it doesn't mean he knows what happened). And after all he was in rehab. (All right, he was in there selling drugs.) We witness domesticity – Joey-style home life with heroin. 'For Joey,' says a voice, 'friendship came with the needle or wrapped in silver foil.' (Ooh, nasty.) 'His left hand has an abscess from injecting,' the narrator whispers menacingly. 'The stigmata of addiction.' (Horrible, nasty man. Horrible, nasty drugs.) 'The pattern down the years: drugs. Debt. Deceit. Chaos. Flight.' But that's enough about Tapehead.

For some real writing, a real lesson for Modern Times, **Straight From The Heart**'s 'Fool For Love' is extraordinary. Here's Bo talking about her love: 'I had feelings I'd never even had before. Everything was new. I just wanted him to love me. 'Cos I loved him. I just wanted to be with him. But he began to not want me.' As good a definition of being tragically in love with the wrong person as you'll read this side of Jane Austen. The other two true-life stories are even worse. This is how it goes wrong: coldness, homosexuality and bad handwriting. More murder. A man who was not a gynaecologist but a fertiliser salesman; a woman who was not an exotic beauty but a lesbian call girl; the phrase 'It never occurred to me that she was having an affair with her uncle.' Those terrible words: 'And I've never seen him since.' 'That was the end of that,' says poor Bo. 'This horrible thing happened. I didn't say anything. I must have an expressive face,' she adds chirpily. 'He spat and spat and spat in my face.'

Jilly Cooper couldn't write a single sentence worthy of Bo, though **Bookmark** dedicates an hour of our time to her, enticing us by making it steamy. (Hear the sentence 'He kissed each chestnut nipple', then see a man doing it.) The extracts overrule her claims to 'research' and suggest they should have made the show about her magnificent old mum instead. As far as Tapehead can see she is the silliest woman this side of Paula Yates. 'I do think things are more likely to happen to glamorous people,' she simpers, gushing about something called 'a bonk'. 'A terrific bonk!' The worst four-letter word in the fucking English language.

March 16–22 1996

Be my wife

When it comes to jealousy, Tapehead makes Othello look like an indifferent wuss. As one of the victims in **Straight From The Heart** explains, jealousy is not actually anything to do with the person you're with or worried about. It's about you. 'It's born of fear. Fear of losing.' Take Sarah, for example. Sarah cut up Jed's best clothes so that he couldn't go out looking nice without her. She wouldn't let him go to the bar in case he got served by a barmaid or watch Baywatch in case he fancied Pamela Anderson more than her. Veronica would follow her man in the car to see where he was going, who he was seeing and end up tailing him up and down motorways ('we went for *miles*'). The result was even worse than she thought: he was going to the football.

Then there's Linda and her scarred, scary, Scouse boyfriend, Austin. At night, Austin would quiz her relentlessly – where she'd been, who she'd spoken to. Then he'd let her sleep for an hour before waking her and asking the same questions to see if there were any sleep-hazed discrepancies. To all of which, Tapehead can only say: what's wrong with that? When you find out you were right and the affair is happening, as Veronica says, you feel nothing so much as relief. 'It's as if you've come to the end of your search.' Amen.

It all starts in childhood (Sarah admits she tried to ruin her stepdad's relationship with her mum because she was jealous) and there are plenty more jealous minds in the final **Cutting Edge**. Stepmothers, stepwives and stepchildren get it all off their chest. The children, their little bitternesses, are the worst. If they've divorced, they want their mum and dad to get back together. If they're dead, they want them to live again. What they don't want is their stepmum. Aidan's impossibly cute stepdaughters tell it to him straight. 'He's a bit strict,' says one tot, sucking her thumb. 'And boring,' announces the other. 'Very boring. He's going back to the stepdaddy shop. You ring the man up, he comes round and takes him away with a sack on his head and brings you a new one.'

When her husband's ex-wife died, Shelley was competing with an angel. One of his kids left home straight away, telling her, 'I'm not listening to you. You're not my mother. You're not even a member of my family.' The eldest girl was sympathetic, and so frighteningly mature, at first it seems Shelley's sense and determination to be a good stepmother are working, even though (with his father's approval) young Adam keeps his feelings inside, to himself. On camera though, suddenly he is less cautious. 'When I first met Shelley,' he shrugs, 'I knew there were going to be problems.' These problems are going to get worse when Shelley sees the rest of the programme. 'I could fit in with a stepmum. I just don't fit in with Shelley. I don't like her. I'd like my Dad to divorce Shelley and marry someone all of us like.' Tapehead hopes Cutting Edge are proud of themselves.

A blaze of ghostly white light and some typically blunt dialogue tells us **Cardiac Arrest** is back: 'FBC, U and E, calcium, LFTs, glucose... Can you see about a CT?' The only person Tapehead could be jealous of at the moment is anyone knocking off Dr Claire Maitland, although judging by this episode, this could be several (hundred) people before the 13-part series is finished. The patient has suffered a brain haemorrhage while making love to his wife. 'He won't live,' says one doctor. 'Who does?' Claire pouts, the heartless minx. 'One minute he's shagging,' she sighs, 'the next he's shagged,' before deciding to go off and have one herself. What a woman!

March 30–April 5 1996

Perversion

A neurotic TV writer, famous for interfering in TV adaptations of his scripts, writes a part in his series, **Karaoke**, in which an actor plays a famous neurotic TV writer, always interfering in TV adaptations of his script Karaoke. How ingenious can you get? There's nothing more banal or obvious than a writer writing a script in which a writer reads from a script. Only Dennis Potter would be lauded for it. 'Isn't that what my script's about? Karaoke as a metaphor,' asks the writer (Albert Finney) – several times. Er, yes, Dennis, we got that point. We actually got it about 35 minutes ago. After the 44th hint.

By the end, poor Albert is staggering around, drunkenly bumbling, 'I've got to have her. I must write a happy ending.' Potter made a mistake here. 'I must think of something else to say. Got to have a new idea,' would have been more appropriate. The first episode (pointlessly repeated on Channel 4) is devoted to two ideas: a writer convincing himself people are saying his lines (as if) and, er, Roy Hudd speaking in unfunny spoonerisms ('What do you think I'm ducking fooing?' he says – several times).

As A. A. Gill recently said of Potter, you shouldn't speak ill of the dead. But on the other hand, what are they going to do about it? The really boring thing about Dennis Potter was, as a self-promoted pervert, his taste in women never developed.

For a decent bunch of real perverts, Channel 4 is repeating the Equinox special, **Beyond Love** – though perhaps Beyond Help might have been more appropriate. Channel 4 merrily exploits three latent paraphiliacs: a man who, at 17, used to strangle himself in the mirror before masturbating ('then it got worse'); a woman whose perfect man is the corpse of a 16–25-year-old; and a man so obsessed with mutilation that he eventually chopped his own leg off (satisfaction guaranteed). A programme about us all, in other words – much more so than any of Potter's ever were.

One of the psychologists ingeniously explains how paraphiliacs' fetishes (leather, stockings, the usual Dennis Potter stuff) symbolise female genitalia. 'They tend to be pink, red, black, furry, wet, shiny,' he says delicately, later elucidating his analogy by turning to a man whose interest was (can you guess?) plucked chickens. 'Actually, if you think about it,' he says breathlessly, 'this is very close to the innate releasing mechanism I described earlier: a pair of pink, fleshy hemispheres and a mysterious cleavage down the middle.'

Lots more spurious scientific evidence is lobbed up on the screen to suggest we actually start masturbating at 18 months old (a good trick if you can do it). There are actually people whose *job* it is to check ultrasound scans and see which bonny baby fetuses are having a wank.

An Inspector Calls concerns London Underground's Revenue Control Inspectors, who go around catching ticketless foreigners and what they call 'people of the older persuasion', implying the ticket-dodging coffin-dodgers are just forgetful when, in fact, as we all know, half the OAPs on the underground are trying it on. One inspector, a particularly irritating streak of piss, is like John Major doing Eric Idle. 'I'm sorry if I detained you,' he whines chirpily to one penniless fare-dodger. 'It maybe would have been better if you had waited to buy a ticket in the first place... Don't forget,' he shouts, 'you can appeal.' It's funny how people like this always have voices like his.

April 27–May 3 1996

Liver and bacon

OK, OK, so Tapehead was wrong about **Karaoke**. Compared to this week's episode, last week's opener was a fast, funny, postmodern indictment of the sick state of the human soul and the fine line between fantasy and reality. Certainly nothing in last week's was remotely as slow and pointless as the scene in which Liz Smith (overacting almost as badly as Richard E. Grant) slips an armpit hair in Roy 'Kazy Lunt' Hudd's egg sandwich. Laugh? Tapehead had to reach for the dictionary.

This week's episode sees Potter's self-parody dragged to a new nadir with a simpleton's allusions to the Garden of Eden and nauseating doses of sentimentality. 'I can remember when I could make a whole ward sing,' says the misty-eyed, bedridden writer (Finney/Potter), harping back to the good old days of his early, funny series like The Singing Detective. Thanks for reminding us, Dennis. 'What's it called then, your story?' asks his (evidently rather thick) heroine, to groans from viewers at home. All together now: 'It's called Karaoke. I called it Karaoke because the song, or the story, of our lives is sort of already made up for us.' And so on and so on, presumably for the next two weeks. Frankly, in terms of writing for TV, The Bill's in a different league.

Speaking of bright ideas, the BBC has got Carla Lane to revive **The Liver Birds** along with Nerys Hughes, Polly James and Michael Angeli – a veritable troupe of clapped-out talent, the creative equivalent of a Nolan Sisters Christmas Special or The Who re-forming. You know a new series is already in trouble when the exciting ingredient is provided by (oh God) Mollie Sugden – as Nerys Hughes's mum. Like putting a big sign up on the screen saying, 'RUN OUT OF IDEAS', except more expensive.

Somewhere between the fake intellectualism of Dennis Pervert and the sheer Scouse stupidity of Carla, we have **The Works**, which purportedly seeks to elucidate the link between Velazquez's portrait of Pope Innocent X and Francis Bacon's Screaming Popes series. Psychoanalyst Darian Leader hops from half-baked theory to thoroughly foolish theory, hoping that all piled together they'll mean something. Bacon's Popes paintings flick past us so quickly that we're not allowed to form our own opinions and we are left wrestling with the sort of scrambled, pedestrian script that makes Potter look concise and relevant. For instance, lines like

'Bacon's father ran the household like a platoon' are immediately followed by footage of a sergeant-major shouting – just in case you didn't know what a platoon was. Bacon's own father is said to have looked like Innocent (although so did Terry Thomas on this evidence) but Leader dismisses this theory as being far too obvious (and presumably brief), despite Bacon's much-documented antipathy towards him. Instead he tries to twist Bacon's asthma and his aversion to his father's beloved horses from being a symbol of the distance between them into some sort of 'sign of love'.

Although it's supposed to be about Velazquez, Eisenstein's Battleship Potemkin and Poussin's 'Massacre Of The Innocents' are thrown in for good measure. Bacon regarded the mother's scream in the latter as the most powerful in art, but Leader focuses on the doomed child instead, 'very graphically gasping for breath' (his mouth's open) – an obvious link with Bacon's asthma and the, er, Battleship? From here, the final link is Bacon's 'Arab Walking With Child' which is not even part of the Popes series, though Leader gushes that, 'The form can hardly fail to evoke that of The Popes.' Well, it can actually.

May 4–10 1996

Best behaviour

Their third interview, midway through the **George Best Night,** and Michael Parkinson can't help asking Best where did he get so much talent from? All that talent for pulling the ladies. Best laughs. 'Well, I was gonna say it was a bit like playing football – 'cos it came so naturally.'

Personally, Tapehead could never understand how anyone could not love Manchester United – because of George Best. The years of Tapehead's childhood were riddled with suffering because of George Best, and not just because George Best was the first man Tapehead ever loved. He was waiting for Man United to win something. Look at the gallery of black and white pictures that opens the Parkinson show: the most beautiful man who ever lived; the best footballer of all time; and a cool name to boot. George was so cool he could make a pink tie-dye T-shirt look groovy. Glory, glory Man United.

In the first Parkinson interview, in 1973, asked why he lost his fitness and retired, Best sums it up simply as 'drinking, night life... general things.' It's the general things that make you wonder.

They are all here: his dad (with a picture of George dribbling the ball aged one); the scout who discovered him (and has a voice worthy of the coolest gangster); a man whose life's highlight is still that he used to wash George's hair. We see the Cookstown sausages advert ('the best...') and a marvellous ad for Fore aftershave, with George as a Pied Piper of females ('Phwoaaar' would have been more appropriate.) A week after the ad he grew a beard.

And here he is now, 50 years old. Happy birthday, George. It's a tribute to Best as a man – his charm – that he can use the words 'genius' and 'superstar' about himself and still seem shy and naturally modest. His talent for storytelling is almost as good ('I'll never forget it...').

In the latest Parkinson, he's immediately on good form: telling the world that Leeds United watched him when he was 15. Stayed 20 minutes and left! The Man U scout sent Sir Matt Busby a telegram telling him he'd found a genius. George walked out/went home on virtually his second day but eventually made his debut at 17, the week The Beatles released their first single. He trained his weaker foot so hard it became the stronger. Let's hope Ryan Giggs is watching.

This is a night devoted to Mephistopheles as much as to George, as the picture of him being carted off to Pentonville suggests. Best was soon getting 10,000 letters a week (rather more than Stan Collymore) – the first football superstar. No one knew what the rules were. Best was a playboy, but never predictable. Although he took up gambling to replace the excitement of football he quit after a night in the seventies in which he won £26,000. Parky returns to the key question near the end: 'How many girls, though?' Best blushes. 'Well, how many times were you in love?' 'A couple of thousand, I suppose.' If all this wasn't enough, Parky gets him to tell the 'Where did it all go wrong?' story.

Tapehead trusts the boys in **This Life** are watching. (Well, it is real, isn't it?) Sadly, Egg has other things on his mind – impotence, unemployment, the fact that his dad is fucking Anna, things like that. There is also the fact Milly glows like a candle every time her boss acts manly. Egg turns, as any man would, to pornography; but Milly, tragically, is not interested. 'I'm just getting to the bit where they insert the wooden penises,' complains Egg. So it's left to Miles to demonstrate why This Life is Tapehead's favourite show and explain why English teams never win in

Europe. 'We've stopped passing the ball, you see,' he complains. 'I mean, you wouldn't have thought you could *play* football without passing the ball, but you can.' As the clips show, Miles, George Best did.

May 18–24 1996

A load of old bollocks

Don't you worry sometimes about the amount of gratuitous filth on our screens? About the effects on our children and what it says about us as a society? No, neither does Tapehead, but if he did he would surely be in uproar about the licence-paying public's money being wasted on programmes about punk like **Dancing In The Street** and the absurd notion that shit-eating pseuds like David Byrne and Richard Hell should get any of the credit.

Punk, as Paul Simenon once again so ably demonstrates, had nothing to do with being an intellectual – or even intelligent. The Ramones, whose every song began with the shout 'Wah-tun-free-fuh', understood this. 'Dee Dee would always do the counting – don't know why. It just came natural to him. He could count to four very well.' They deny they only played short, mindless thrashes, regarding them as 'long songs played quickly'. Compared to The Glorious Slits or The Mighty Buzzcocks, Richard Hell (the Kevin Costner of punk) was the sort of one-hit wonder who made Plastic Bertrand look prolific. Patti Smith was a rock singer. And as for Talking Heads, they had a *keyboard player*, for God's sake.

The Pistols, of course, were punk, as the programme eventually realises, with Jones and Lydon two English epitomes of how not to give a fuck. You can tell McLaren still loves them. Just watch his affection and admiration for the riot they inspire at Randy's Rodeo in Texas when the beer cans start flying and Jones just stands there 'nutting them back like a footballer'. The programme closes with Talking Head Tina Weymouth's attempt to sum punk up by quoting 'Never Mind the Bullocks'. Quite.

Ten years ago, if you'd told 'Mad' Frankie Fraser that when he got out Channel 4 would come and ask him to make a programme called **If I Were Prime Minister**, he'd have nutted you for taking the piss. Now 72, Fraser spent a total of 56 years inside, a result of his irritating habits of taking people's teeth out when there was nothing wrong with them and torturing their testicles with home-made electrocution devices. Now, thanks to Channel 4, he gets to go on TV pontificating about sex offenders ('people tampering with women and children'); pensioners ('they should be allowed everything for free – everything'); and immigration ('no more carte blonk – the time has come to say no').

'Thick' Frankie Fraser would be more appropriate. One Algerian political refugee gets into a furious slanging match with him. Presumably Channel 4 neglected to mention to him what Frankie was famous for – or how lucky he was not to have his goolies barbecued.

That the BBC, once a fine organisation, is now stooping so low as to compete with the already depraved Channel 4 saddens Tapehead. It was bad enough when Bing got all frisky in Brookside; now, in **Coming Of Age: Grey Sex**, our screens are sullied with dozens of perverted OAPs revelling in the sordid details of their disgusting grey sex lives. 'I only have to look at you and you have an erection,' giggles Pearl, 70, to Frank, 69. Ex-army officer Donald (74) boasts, 'By God, I can go on for ages,' and after 50 years of marriage, Ian and Joan are experimenting with vacuum pumps to sustain Ian's 'nice, healthy erection' – which in Tapehead's book is one step away from plastic bags and satsumas. They are all (obviously) completely deluded, virtually senile, but still... the BBC should not encourage them. Tapehead has, as you know, campaigned for as much sex on TV as possible, but you have to draw the line somewhere. Keep this (old) filth off our screens.

August 3–9 1996

Pump it up

Four stories of spectacularly low moral subterfuge, **Inside Story**'s 'Betrayal' starts with a quote about 'the naturalness of lying... the almost non-existence of an idea of right and wrong', and this is a bishop talking. Documentaries about betrayal always feature couples relating how their marriage went horribly wrong. But not many have stories where the adultery took place *during* the wedding.

Nigel and Marie's wedding was the happiest day of Marie's life. She felt loved 'loved and sick-ewer'. Husband Nigel was less certain but, even so, when he saw Marie at the altar, he felt 'a lump in me throat'. During the reception, Nigel got gravy on his sleeve and nipped home to clean it – taking the best man's wife, Debbie, with him. The best man, who was responsible for the wedding video, actually filmed them leaving together (the chump). By the time they came back, Debbie was practically doing handstands. The honeymoon, sighs poor, betrayed Marie, was 'brilliant'. 'We were together. It was just me and Nigel,' she says with awestruck amazement, as if (perhaps understandably) she couldn't quite believe it. Five weeks later, Nigel and Debbie were at it again.

The other three tales of betrayal are all, in their different ways, even worse. In fact, the whole programme is a masterpiece of understatement ('There was a bit of an atmosphere'). The editing is exemplary: 'She was fine about it'… 'I was destroyed'… 'Carol enjoyed it – up to a point'… 'I did nothing but cry'. The moral in the end is obvious. Neighbours, best friends, sons and sisters: never trust anyone.

There are horror stories of a different kind in **Dark Secret**, another video nasty from the BBC, which looks at three treatments for impotence available at the Royal Hallamshire in Sheffield. Three couples in their sixties are desperate for sex and Sister Patricia Allen is there to help them. Cyril and Nellie haven't had sex for eight years. 'You forget about it,' Nellie sighs. 'Keep yourself busy.' The battery-operated vacuum pump is the first remedy. 'So what you do,' Sister Allen gushes with enthusiasm, as if she's preparing a recipe on The Generation Game, 'you stand up, put your jelly on your penis, push well down and then switch on.' But the pump has its drawbacks: it lacks spontaneity, the penis can be a little cooler than normal, it can look 'a bit mottled'. Cyril inwardly shivers. He doesn't think the pump is right. 'Or there's the injection.' He watches the video of a man injecting a large needle into his penis when he wants to have sex. 'Er, I'll take the pump,' Cyril says, virtually snatching it from her. Tapehead could be wrong, but Nellie looks so frustrated she wants Cyril to try the pump and the injection together, if necessary. After a few weeks with the pump, she can hardly walk.

The next patient watches the injection video with his mouth agape, going grey with horror. He goes for the metal rod implant which, Sister Allen explains, gives you a permanent erection. 'You bend it up when you want to do it and bend it down when you don't want to do it. It's like a bendy toy.' After the operation, we see Rod, covered by a sheet, being wheeled away with an enormous ridge where his groin is, like a magician, and what looks like a smile on his face.

Philip goes for the injection which, the nurse assures him, is painless. We watch as the large needle goes slowly into his penis. (Up his penis.) 'Well, was it painless?' asks the nurse brightly. 'Well... ,' he gasps, with tears in his eyes.

His tears were nothing compared to Tapehead's, who was by this point openly sobbing, screaming, pleading for it to stop. Praying for it never to happen to him.

August 17–23 1996

No friends of mine

Having never watched **Friends** before, it didn't take Tapehead long to realise why it's called that. Joey, Phoebe, Rachel, Ross, Monica and Chandler are friends. They don't have any others and are clearly never going to. It's no wonder they cling to each other so tightly. There they are in every scene – joined at the hip, crammed into the shot like a family photo, looking like some sort of grinning six-headed monster. Just a bunch of everyday, middle-class, young Americans, in this Superbowl Special, the friends get to go on dates with Brooke Shields, Chris Isaak, Jean-Claude Van Damme, Julia Roberts. How cool is that? Not very, but then they thought going to a Hootie and the Blowfish gig was cool.

As for the acting and writing, this episode makes early morning pap like Hangin' With Mr Cooper look challenging. Most of the jokes are so obvious you can see them coming from so far away, you wonder if they were dreamt up by sky-writers. The scenes of Lisa Kudrow's funny kids' lyrics are just excruciating.

The one moment of quality comic acting is from Homer Simpson (Dan Castellaneta).

Jennifer Aniston and Courteney Cox are so generic as to be totally indifferent and David Schwimmer is a complete dodo. As for Matthew Perry and Matt LeBlanc, overacting furiously, Tapehead says: bring back Diff'rent Strokes.

War Cries looks at another group of people with no friends: Leeds United fans. (Nowadays, the combination of Howard Wilkinson, Lee Sharpe and various old-age pensioners means even Leeds fans don't like Leeds.) One of those almost home-made public access programmes about

English football fans abroad, War Cries makes you appreciate the fact that most TV is made by writers/directors who have received some training. Bona-fide fans describe how they were beaten up, banged up and, to the presenter's horror, not even allowed to go to the toilet. (This is nothing to the punishment Leeds inflict on their own fans every week.)

It's all been said before. So clubs like Chelsea and Man Utd care more about money than their own supporters? Never! The Dutch and Turkish police are *really horrible*? You don't say.

Thank God for **Cutting Edge**, which looks at sextuplets and the sponsorship deals and media attention that invariably accompany them. The first of these was the Waltons, who somehow resisted the temptation to name their six kids, John Boy, Jim Bob, Jason, Elizabeth, Mary Ellen and, er, Grandma. Sextuplets that followed became progressively less newsworthy. The Colemans got free baby clothes for a year but after that, nothing. (And why should they?) Proud father Arthur can't even remember them all: 'That's Gary, Hannah, Nicola, James, Stuart and, er, the last one.'

The tabloids seized on the Vince family after they discovered the mother's 'ex-father-in-law was a murderer'. (They did let her give her side of the story. They just never printed it.) Jane Underhill's six babies only weighed a total of nine pounds but, amazingly, survived an anxious first few weeks in intensive care. Hell, not happiness, was round the corner though. Today, Charlotte, the smallest, who weighed just one pound, four ounces, is a sweet-looking kid with poor sight and a terrible stammer who spends much of her time looking through photo albums recording the births and then, sadly, the deaths of her brothers and sisters. One by one, the others died – five funerals within nine months – until every morning her mother was frightened of going into Charlotte's room in case she had joined them.

This is one programme that presumably Mandy Allwood will be watching.

August 31–September 6 1996

How's your father

Anyone who thought the BBC's decision to cancel their documentary about the life and times of Terry Venables during Euro 96 hinted at any kind of controversy will be warned not to expect anything too exciting by the title they've given the programme: **Terry Venables: The Man Who Would Be King**. Hopes for Tel Boy: Right Dodgy Geezer will have to wait. Still, the programme proves its own point that the media has always loved Tel, if only because, Tapehead suspects, Terry has always loved it back. Not only does he own a nightclub, he even named it Scribes.

From his first TV interview as a child prodigy at the age of 16, we see Terry through the years, dazzling the press with his witty quips, salt-of-the-earth *bon viveur* charm and over-enthusiastic crooning. The programme-makers fall for it all over again (bewildering), figuring that anyone who knows the likes of Eric Hall, Adam Faith and Bill Wyman must be a diamond geezer. They whizz past little inconveniences like the dirt dug up by Panorama, glossing over the minefield of El Tel's dodgy dealings and legal battles in favour of rehashing the glorious failure that was Euro 96. They imply that managing England was the pinnacle of Tel's career when everyone knows the real highlight was writing Hazell.

Terry, for his part, appears grinning winningly throughout, filmed in a hideous England sweatshirt that makes his head look as if it's been super-imposed on top of it like a cardboard cut-out. Their summary is embarrassing: 'He bowed out, a hero in defeat... Villain or victim, one thing's for sure: we haven't heard the last of Terence Frederick Venables.' As if that's some sort of achievement. We haven't heard the last of Myra Hindley or Status Quo either.

Tommy Docherty steals the coaching honours with a half-time team talk from the sixties that displays all the tactical genius that made him great. 'It'll come good in the end,' he tells them. 'Keep playing that football!' **The System**, sadly, is not about Terry's love of wing-backs, but the traumas and turmoil that follow in the wake of the Child Support Agency.

Four out of five single mothers receive nothing from the fathers, leading to the obvious conclusion: all men are bastards (and let's face it, Tapehead should know). David, a millionaire with a £400,000 house and an £80,000 car, refuses to give the mother of his child a penny, insisting that he didn't want a baby and doesn't see why he should pay for her to have one. He even has the audacity to compare himself to Emmeline Pankhurst, although the fifty-pounds-a-week maintenance is nothing. 'I don't care whether it's a fiver. I don't want to pay it.'

Paul, on the other hand, is a hapless, penniless individual, whose life has been ruined – first by the fact that Helen chucked him out and second because, he says, she is now using the CSA to batter him the way she did when they were together. 'I didn't do anything wrong,' he whimpers. 'We met when we were very young,' she says charmlessly. 'I grew up and he didn't.' Paul knows he's losing his grip, mainly because every time he hears songs like Elton John's 'Sacrifice' he starts weeping. Tapehead hopes Elton John's proud of himself. Paul complains that the CSA should be targeting genuine absentee fathers. The problem with this, as Paul rightly points out, is simple. 'Nobody knows where they are.'

In the end, the CSA has no sympathy for anyone, no matter what sex they are. Neither does Tapehead, apart from the bloke who complains his maintenance payment isn't fair on the grounds that 'I could lose my television'. And hats off to the woman who told the CSA she didn't know who the absentee father was because when she got pregnant she was hanging out of a window being sick. So *that's* how you get pregnant.

September 21–27 1996

Worship

The thing about fame is that it does not replace loneliness; does not compensate for your lack of love. For several of the subjects in Channel 4's new series, The Fame Factor, the only effect the bright lights of fame ever had on their unhappiness was to highlight it.

An expert on stalkers emphasises their loneliness, lack of intimacy and the emptiness of their existence, but as the most pertinent and poignant moments of **The Vanishing Of Richey Manic** make clear, he could just as easily have been talking about the recipients of the stalkers' adoration. The facts of Richey's disappearance are needlessly interspersed with perspectives on fame from the likes of Boy George and Shaun Ryder (now fully mutated into something out of Rainbow), but they are mostly interested in talking about themselves more than Richey.

There is nothing of the Manics' music and not much of an insight into Richey's state of mind, save an MTV interview in which he reduces life to something that grows more depressing the older you become: 'Your energy dies. Your friends die. Your dog dies.' The boys and girls who worshipped him for his services to self-mutilation, anorexia and badly applied make-up techniques still wait for him, as does the taxi driver who dropped him off near the Severn Bridge services.

You can cling to the ambivalence of his disappearance, but the tone of this film will not leave you in much doubt about what happened to him. 'Fame,' ex-Coronation Street star Lynne Perrie assures us with authority, 'is like taking drugs: the more you get, the more you want.'

'The story of a woman who lost herself in the search for stardom', **The Ghost Of Ivy Tilsley** begins with Perrie musing on the 'years of adulation and wealth' and her lost identity while sitting under a hair-dryer seemingly infested with flies. When Lynne was 'not feeling quite right,' Perrie gushes, 'Ivy was always there to rely on and take over. But in the end, Ivy couldn't handle the troubles that Lynne had.'

Flicking through scrapbooks, watching old reruns of Gail's scary hairdos, Perrie is beset by regret. She could have been a film star. Men, apparently, slept with her because of who she was. 'I'm happier now, since I've left the Street,' she confides to strangers queuing up to meet her during celebrity appearances at bingo, where she is still billed as Ivy Tilsley. She says it over and over again, presumably in the hope that if she says it often enough it might be true.

Ivy has stalked Lynne Perrie far more effectively than anyone on **I'm Your Number One Fan**. Dr Klaus Wagner, Lady Di's notorious admirer, has clearly ruined his life far more than Diana's. He is convinced that Diana is being destroyed by Her Majesty the Beast (Elizardbeast), as predicted in the Book of Revelations – a theory that certainly convinced Tapehead.

DJ Mike Read's stalker (Blue Tulip Rose Read) has a history of mental problems and it's hard to see how her inclusion here is going to help him, or her. Like the heroine of Jane Campion's film, Sweetie, Blue Tulip needs someone to look after her and has convinced herself it is going to be Mike, as her T-shirt with the words 'My husband Mike Read' illustrates. 'I want to marry you, Mike,' she howls, sobbing desperately. 'If I've caused a bit of harm I've not meant it.' Read's assistant holds up a photo Blue Tulip sent in of her washing machine. On the back she's written, 'This picture proves I have a washing machine. I have called it Mike Read.'

Scenes of her in her room, wearing a feather boa, dancing and barking like a dog to classical music, or sitting naked at the typewriter, are truly disturbing/disturbed. It's hard not to conclude that Channel 4 have tormented and exploited her in a way worse than any stalker.

October 5–11 1996

72

Drag

Tapehead has lived in Soho, and God it was awful – full of drunken prats, clichéd clones, Norwegian tourists, arse-holes in advertising and, worst of all, people sitting on the pavement who weren't even homeless. It is astonishing how many people in Soho think that sitting outside a café sipping cappuccinos liberally laced with petrol fumes is cool.

Quite how writer/director Christopher Terrill has crafted a series as monumentally monotonous as **Soho Stories** is beyond anybody's guess. It starts ominously on Monday with the description of Soho as 'a film set full of characters learning to play their parts'. Sadly, through Tuesday's and Wednesday's episodes, we realise the film set in question is some tragic Broadway musical – an idea that anyone who saw Absolute Beginners will regard with horror. Judging from the second episode, Soho was also the scene of the most boring bomb scare in history.

Most of Terrill's characters – the 'director' at the Raymond Revue Bar, a dresser for 'Les Miz' and even a cheeky-chappie bespoke tailor – just aren't interesting enough, while an absurd drama teacher, 'Garbo' (a victim of a bizarre mascara splatter attack), proves Soho's 'characters' can be as severely irritating as anywhere else's. Mystifyingly, Terrill fails to bestow any kind of poignancy on his subjects, and in terms of bringing out any good stories, Soho Stories seems to be full of people who don't really *have* a story or if they do, they fail to articulate it.

The exception is Gwen, a bonny student making some money stripping at Raymond's, whose brief biography ('I was aiming to do astrophysics but I'm doing English – Shakespeare's my favourite') immediately eliminates her from further episodes on the grounds of not being superficial enough.

This is certainly not an accusation you could level at Danny. Danny dominates this week's Soho Stories in a way that you can only presume the director wishes he would dominate him. Either that or he has never really met a drag queen before and thinks that they're so weird that their fascination is endless. (If only!) Either way, this is the most boring love letter ever written. 'Do you prefer buying men's clothes or women's clothes?' he asks him. (Not exactly Cutting Edge.) Danny has obviously never thought about it. Poor Danny hasn't got the, erm, *equipment* to justify all the coverage Terrill gives him. He is left floundering. Danny waffles away about how incredible he finds it that something called 'straight society' can thrive in Bar Italia, a mere 20 yards away from gay Old Compton Street. Why is not clear. Given that he lives in Soho, you'd think he'd have got over it by now.

Click-clacking his way to his spot at the drag cabaret bar, he gets antsy as soon as he crosses the gay border, uncertain whether to demand to be treated the same as anyone else or to get slightly irked that no one's paying him any attention. Mostly, though, he is happy to let Terrill portray him as just another sad drag cliché – one who wants to give the whole thing up ('another two years and I'm stopping') in order to concentrate on his dreams of singing/dancing/acting – none of which, on this evidence, he appears to be very good at. We're spared his up-tempo version of 'Stormy Weather' ('I am such a fucking nancy'). Then he goes back to what he – or Terrill – likes best: shopping. 'Now *that's* a handbag,' Danny gasps, picking up (guess what?) a handbag.

Danny, the truth begins to dawn, is just the dullest drag queen in Soho. Terrill lays every one of his painfully unamusing asides before us until, in the end, all poor Danny can think of is to give us his fifteenth Bruce Forsyth impression so far. Judging by these, his acting prospects are even lower than those of his singing. Let's hope he's a fucking good dancer.

October 26–November 1 1996

Hopelessly devoted

Is there anything worse than well-meaning members of the aristocracy? **Cutting Edge**'s 'Great House Wives' looks at three women nobly struggling to manage their husbands' stately homes. When Lady Pamela Mansfield married her witless husband, she also married this 'enor-mous hee-ouse' to which she has devoted herself, while he potters around Europe pretending to be a politician. Said hee-ous is Scone Palace, which is appropriate considering she is a MacDougall ('of the self-raising sort'). Lady Peven becomes concerned when a commoner has a heart attack in the gr-eeounds. And not just because he spoils the view.

When Lady Montagu of Beaulieu wants to see her husband, she has to talk to his secretary and even then it seems to be in order to satisfy her obsession with preparing his lunch. (So there might be a lunch?) Her bedroom used to be part of the tourists' tour. Now at least she can watch Coronation Street in peace. The sight of 200 toffs singing 'Rule Britannia' round the piano almost makes you feel sorry for her.

Lady Cobbold's husband maintains, 'If you live in a stately home (Knebworth), everybody thinks you're very rich, you stay in bed until lunchtime and employ lots of servants. But it's bloody hard work.' As he works in London all week, the bloody hard work is left to the missus. She has even learnt caning (to upholster the chairs, she reckons). Every night she drives to London on the grounds that he doesn't want to commute and it's 'better all round' (going *against* the traffic). 'He needs looking after,' she blushes, obviously aware of her humiliation. Lady Cobbold, Tapehead needs looking after too.

Don't Leave Me This Way, a marvellous, hugely depressing film by James March, suggests Brian Connolly's version of an ancestral home-he-has-given-his-life-to is seventies glam rock band The Sweet. With the added pressures brought about by alcoholism and a broken marriage, the band took what seemed like its final toll on Connolly, who had 14 heart attacks in 24 hours. He was given the last rites and his ex-wife was told that if he lived, he would probably be brain-damaged. What happened instead is almost worse.

At the Bognor Regis Butlins club, Manhattan, he is helped to the microphone the way you help an old man to the toilet. His drink is pinned to the mike stand because he can't reach down for it. He sucks on it through a straw, like oxygen. His eyes are virtually lifeless, his face is withered with age and illness. He speaks with his hands shaking constantly, walks with difficulty, as if his jeans are full of rice pudding.

Connolly's sorry state is highlighted by the enduring health (and hair) of the rest of the band. Mick the drummer's is even longer than it was in the seventies, like Bonnie Tyler's run riot. Andy, The Sweet's ex-guitarist, sums Connolly up: 'It's like a fried egg – once it's been fried you can't unfry it.' Ex-bassist Steve Priest disagrees. He prefers 'scrambled'.

Speaking of scrambled, it's a tough week for Joe in **EastEnders** (aren't they all). After his Jeffrey Dahmer phase (an unhealthy interest in Auntie Nellie's dead pussy, a bout of pyromania), and mounting sexual frustration (storming into pubs and demanding that total strangers 'tell me about women'), Joe is still recovering from the video evil in Nigel's shop. ('They get into yer 'ead and you can't get 'em owt.') Every scene ends with Joe either frowning blankly or jogging out of the door and sprinting into the

Square. Where he goes, no one knows.

This week, as the residents of Albert Square enjoy Bonfire Night, Lorraine is worried about the effect it has on Joe. ('They get into yer 'ead and you can't get 'em owt.') Last week's bizarre cake-making episode came out of nowhere. Joe's pain was tangible as *Cakes and Cake Icing* joined the list: betrayed by a book about cakes.

November 2–9 1996

Randy old dogs

I t's hard to believe, but since the climax of the David and Cindy story-line, **EastEnders** has got better and better. From tomorrow's omnibus, this week just soars to another level.

Grant and Phil are still on Cindy's tail (as it were), although why is not really clear. At least it gives them plenty of excuse to do what they do best: run around the sidestreets of London like a couple of Weetabix skinheads from the Suedehead novels, 'having a larf watching Barry squirm'. As Phil babysits Baby Ben (at the bar), they start plotting military manoeuvres in Paris (Grant in Paris could be even better than when he went to Ibiza). Even Martin, one of those soap kids who grows a year older every episode so they involve him, finally gets his first storyline. This is a symbolism spectacular. Broken mirrors: broken lives. Bonfires: lives going up in flames. Robbie's phallic firework, with Claire looking on…

Then there's Joe, The Running Man. After Auntie Nellie's smelly pussy, writing 'EVIL' on his chest and weeks of cowering in kitchens chanting, 'Satan's here' (a phase which, let's face it, we've all been through), firework night is a pyromaniac's paradise/hell. The Prodigy have got a lot to answer for.

Then, on Thursday, when David ventures into Joe's room, he makes 'a shocking discovery'. David has become positively Shakespearean, practically tragic, a Lothario destined to self-destruct. He is EastEnders' Guy Fawkes. Randier than a hutch full of bunnies, David is almost as randy as Claire, the foxiest girl on the square, who is reading up on snogging lessons. He is now on course to alienate the few cast members whose lives he hasn't already tarnished. How they can even consider getting rid of him is a mystery.

Judging from the opening scene of a fantastic **Secret Lives**, Errol Flynn was almost as good a kisser as Claire or David Wicks. Born in Tasmania, a teenage delinquent expelled for truancy and seducing local girls. Flynn's life carries uncanny echoes of Tapehead's. He was a pearl diver, gold prospector and jewel thief, stood trial for murder and starred in a panto in Northampton (he was sacked for throwing the director's wife down a staircase). Secret Lives says Errol's appetite for living was strangely contradicted by an equally manic talent for self-destruction, but this seems inevitable. Despite – or perhaps because of – an estimated 12,000 sexual partners, in 1943 he was charged with having sexual relations with two under-age girls (one of whom breaks a fifty-year silence on this programme). During the trial, in true David Wicks style, he dated an 18-year-old from the courthouse.

Errol died aged 50, of a heart attack (and no wonder). He was found by his 17-year-old lover, Beverley. He died, the narrator says, sombrely, 'a victim of his debauchery', which, to Tapehead, seems as good a way to go as any.

The canine equivalent of Errol and David appears on Nick O'Dwyer's brilliant Modern Times' 'Dog Trouble', which follows the Dog Warden service round an estate in Sheffield. 'In all the years I've been in this business, I've never seen a day without dog trouble,' says the warden. Mother-of-two Maxine sits in the living room of the council house she shares with 13 enormous Akita dogs watching one shagging another in front of her. He's not called Randy for nothing. The downside is people like Mr Fox, a grisly Neanderthal who makes Harry Enfield's Slobs look like something out of *Tatler*. He has mistreated his dogs so badly that, back at the pound, one of them sits facing the wall, head miserably pressed into the corner, permanently cowering from any human contact. Sadly, it looks as if they put down the wrong one.

November 9–15 1996

Hang the DJ

Once in a while, you get a glimpse of what **Shooting Stars** could be like. This week's savage, surreal moment comes when What-Are-The-Scores-George-Dawes turns on special guest Dave Lee Travis and, in his best cockney barrow-boy accent, asks, "Ere, you seen

Pretty Woman?' 'Yes.' 'So what?' he says, suddenly menacing. 'It's been on telly four times. It's on video. What, you're a film buff now are ya?'

Vic and Bob, on the other hand, are too cosy with celebrity to antagonise or humiliate their guests. Which is a shame. There doesn't seem much point in having DLT on unless it's to savage him. Last week, when they winched up Ulrika, was the first time she's actually served any purpose. As pin-ups go, Ulrika is a dull icon – neither stupid or smart enough; just a weather girl. This is not to say that Tapehead doesn't always join in with Vic's crooning club-singer and admire Mark Lamarr's apathy and amusement. (Lamarr is one of the few radio personalities to have worked out that, on TV, you should say as little as possible.) But surely the impressions round should be more humiliating or personal.

Watching **TFI Friday** these days makes Tapehead long for **The Word** which, after two years off air, is (bizarrely) being revived as a series of three-minute Pepsi adverts in between Baywatch and Gladiators. Evidently, brief highlights include snippets of Terry Christian interviews, men eating dog-food pies in The Hopefuls, and sex-kitten Dani Behr – the girl with more footballers than Birmingham City.

It's easier to remember something funny from The Word than it is from TFI Friday. And if Chris Evans ever does a sketch or a joke that is actually funny, you can be sure he'll repeat it, continue it, or re-show it in slow motion until it isn't – a sign of a truly mediocre entertainer. The desk-drilling thing summed it up. Evans's comic instinct is so poor on TV, he can't even employ good gag-writers. This leaves him simply gabbling away to his own ego. He starts every show commenting on what people have been saying about him that week, like an Eastern European leader, and is continually referring to his production office/running order/crew (as if anyone is interested). 'Did that gag work, Danny?' must surely be one of TVs no-nos. Hiring Danny Baker (another DJ-with-delusions whose TV shows are now used as manuals entitled *How Not To Do TV Comedy*) is bad enough. But to keep mentioning it only reminds us of the mistake.

The sight of Evans showing off the Beatles posters he'd bought at auction for pathetically inflated prices, saying, 'I'm *trying*, OK? I'm *trying* to spend the money you pay me,' showed how complacent, indulgent and dull he has become – a man whose idea of cool is defined purely by his own success and has no connection with his audience at all. As DLT and Danny Baker eventually proved, once a DJ, always a DJ.

November 16–22 1996

Psychiatric help

'You know,' Dr Frasier Crane says to his brother Miles on this week's one-hour bonus of **Frasier**, 'I'd forgotten what a weird little person you are.' And, let's face it, there are a lot of them around, particularly on television. Nutters everywhere. Quite why, is, as Frasier says in the same episode, 'one of the questions that makes life so rich. And makes psychiatrists richer.'

Eddie Izzard may be 'two lesbians trapped inside a man's body', but that doesn't mean he can't be as boring as the rest of us. (His resemblance to Fee from Brookside's better-looking younger brother, or a benevolent mini-Honey Monster, is a different matter.) **TX – Je Suis A Stand Up** follows Eddie's tour from Bexhill and Iceland to Paris and New York. Yeah. Eddie is a soft and endearing type, not to mention hilarious on stage, but the rest of this programme merely confirms that comedians are best left on stage where they belong. We see Eddie going back to the tearoom where he worked as a youth, hot air ballooning in Sweden and having a 'mare on stage in France (in *French*). None of it, though, is very funny or interesting. The main problem is that we see far too much of 'the real Eddie' being real (i.e. dull). Maybe it's just a consequence of being interviewed by too many regional journalists.

Hours later, another cross-dressing champion, Tricky, shows Eddie how madness is done on **Later With Jools Holland**. While the other bands obligingly rock out the hideous blues-boogie intro theme tune, the camera pans round to find Tricky's band just sitting there glumly, admirably refusing to jam or grin at the camera like the rest of them. When they finally do vent, Tricky jogs manically up and down on the spot, eyes closed, hydroponic kicking in or coming down, a thick (mad) headband pulled down almost over his eyes, before promptly rocking out. Like a mutha.

For the second number, Tricky, a man whose idea of chilling out is to walk the streets of New York on mushrooms, doesn't even show up. 'Tricky, ladeeez and gentlemen,' Jools Holland gestures at the end of the show, indicating the stage, even though Tricky is still not there. What a trooper. (Watch out for Sting, too, a man whose idea of cool – vest and leather trousers – proves he is still truly delusional.)

Detectives On The Verge Of A Nervous Breakdown in **Homicide**. Bayliss is losing it and so is Pembleton – his cool, that is, which, given his role as the coolest detective on TV, is pretty grave. The war between them is now raging. 'I don't work for you, Frank, I work with you,' Bayliss complained last week. 'You never say please and thank you.' 'Please don't be an idiot,' responded Pembleton, regaining his ultra-cool. 'Thank you.'

This week's show starts with the one thing guaranteed to drive Tapehead nuts – more Homicide bullshit about giving up smoking. Luckily, from then on, this is a classic. Bayliss and his new goatee, already thinking of quitting, are haunted by the bloody body of a child, stabbed and molested and left in an alley. 'She looks just like her,' Bayliss moans gently. 'Just like Adina Watson.' The Adina Watson Case (four years ago now) was the best long-running storyline Homicide ever had. Homicide is so classy, they never really solved/resolved it. It's been haunting Bayliss ever since. (Rather like Tapehead and Beth Jordache.)

Finally, 'Are people who are not conventionally good-looking discriminated against?' asks the BBC. Let's hope so. 'Watch **Esther** to find out.' Let's face it, she should know.

December 7–13 1996

Faux pas

The vagaries of fashion continue to bewilder us all, and none more so than **Network First**. Making a film about the horror that is Harvey Nichols without being funny, frank or scathing must be fairly difficult, but for some reason, Network First contrived to try. From the first carping words of the commentary – 'Some people get very excited by fashion' – you sense the level of observation will indeed be truly mundane. (Loyd Grossman produces and Nick Lord directs but, fittingly, no one owns up to having written the script.) The voice-over (by Graham Norton) is appalling, sneering snidely about everything obvious: 'Everything has to make the mouth water.' What's wrong with that?

Fashion people may be funny (planning spring-wear in autumn), but what else can they do? When it comes to the individuals, Modern Times or Cutting Edge would have stuck the knife into someone like Mary Portas far more fabulously. Mary (Harvey Nichols's marketing services director) has taken the rather strange marketing decision to appear on national television looking as if she's dressed in clothes from C & A.

OUT THERE

Her most recent masterstroke was the Harvey Nichols Barbie Doll. 'Lots of what Barbie stands for, we believe our customers stand for as well,' she beams. How the customers will feel about this is anyone's guess. 'She's about glamour, sex... She's also extremely timeless.' (She's made of plastic.) In fact, customers like Amanda Wilson-Barrett are neither as charismatic or intelligent as Barbie. 'Yah, that's gr-eat,' she says, admiring one garment. 'You wouldn't look stupid in it, d'you know what I mean?' Actually, Amanda, I'm not sure I do. (And by the way, grey really isn't your colour. And cover those arms up.)

Mind you, even Amanda understands fashion better than Network First. She patiently explains to them why not all of us want to buy our T-shirts at Mr Byrite. Instead of simply sticking with sticking the knife into the customers, the programme aimlessly whizzes past menswear and goes (fleetingly) behind the scenes in the kitchens, while the launch of a branch in Leeds (a gift) is totally wasted. All in all, this is a programme with far less substance than its subject.

Nicola Roberts's tour round the photographs of Guy Bourdin in **Dreamgirls** at least acknowledges and understands why fashion can be exciting. There are only fragments of biography (mainly the influence on his work of his relationship with his mother) but Bourdin's fashion photographs are expertly used to illustrate the elegant decadence and strange eroticism of the seventies. The senior director of Sotheby's sees Bourdin as 'a kind of dark genius', but it was more noir than dark, with echoes of murder and a dazzlingly cinematic style. His photographs, someone says, were 'about the problems of desire, the problems of connecting'. Following his S&M contest with Helmut Newton's work in the pages of French *Vogue* every month would have been a hobby worth having.

Now that summer is over, at least Georgia from **Brookside** is no longer allowed to pursue her fashion *faux pas* any more (i.e. those denim shorts that make her legs look fat). Nice chunky winter jumpers are a much better look. Not exactly dressing to kill, but still... 'Why do you have to be so intolerant?' she pouted last week, accusing Max of forcing his morality on everyone else. Has anyone worked out if we are meant to sympathise with her and Nat?

This week: worries that Georgia might be up the duff and about to produce the first two-headed baby on the Close. Another Brookside breakthrough. At least it won't be as gormless as its father. Still, an incestuous pregnancy: how fashionable is *that*?

December 14–20 1996

81

Homosexuals can't swim

Memo to Tapehead: 'Following a searching editorial review at the highest level, of both **Brass Eye** and its making, C4 is now satisfied there is sufficient public interest in the programme to merit transmission within existing guidelines.'

Yes, those wild and crazy characters at Channel 4 are at it again! Last year's media fuss over Brass Eye now looks as over-inflated as the East 17 palaver, although hoaxing Home Office minister Tom Sackville into answering questions in the Commons about the dangers of a new drug ('Cake') sweeping the nation's youth is pretty funny. The good news is that Brass Eye is all Chris Morris and no Armadillo Iannucci. The sight of his Paxman character jacking up what the *Guardian* calls 'smack heroin' gives you an idea of the edge Morris gets, especially when he declares, 'The heroin I use is harmless. But what about other people, less stable, less educated, less *middle class* than myself? Builders or blacks, for example.' His piercing parody of the desperately pedestrian Pulp and an officer's objections to gays in the Navy will surely become legendary: 'Homosexuals... can't swim. They attract enemy radar. They get up late.' Some of it may be too warped, but anything that pisses off Noel Edmonds this much constitutes a public service.

More strange goings-on in **Fortean TV**, with items on freaks of nature like 'the day it rained straw in Norfolk' – an episode witnessed by a child, so it must be true. (Unless she'd been on the Cake.) David Heppel – 'the world's leading authority on mermaids' – says the best-documented sightings of mermaids come 'from the island of Yell', which is not a great start. Heppel has 'sworn affidavits' from fishermen who actually captured a mermaid but then *let it go*. Great going, lads.

We witness the first autopsy on a mermaid's remains – a fishlike skeleton with a demonic human head – destroying this rare specimen by removing its head to examine it. A fascinating exclusive marred only by the fact that it's actually two pieces of wood joined by Airfix glue. In one town alone, 'the vampire goat-sucker of Puerto Rico' El Chupacabras has slaughtered over 150 goats in six months. 'Panic has spread,' say locals, especially the goats. The killer creature is described as 'looking like a kangaroo, with the snout of a pig; huge, slit eyes and is, above all, strong and vast in a way that a kangaroo isn't.' Not very much like a kangaroo at all, then.

Travel insurance might be advisable in Kingston, too, if **Jamaica ER's** sensational look at the city's public hospitals is anything to go by. While sulphuric acid is the weapon of choice in what they quaintly call 'domestic disputes', machetes get the job done nicely on the streets. The doctors say things like 'This man have a big wound in him head', enthusiastically asking patients, 'Who chopped ya sir?' With dub-plates booming around the wards, whenever a doctor pronounces 'lac-er-ation', you expect him to follow it with 'inna Babylon nation, seen?'

One man with a broken neck has to be operated on in the ward under only local anaesthetic. A clamp has to be fitted (to his head) and then brandishing a nifty Black & Decker, the doctor prepares to drill some holes (*in his head!*) 'Hello!' he says cheerfully, leaning over a surprisingly peaceful patient. 'You should feel a little noise now. A lot of noise now,' revving up to a noise not unlike someone drilling into concrete or a small plane taking off.

All of which leaves Tapehead with only one thing to say: anyone got any Cake?

January 25–31 1997

Family affairs

Tapehead has been straight for months now, but this week he has once again succumbed to temptation, quit the Cake and gone back on the soap. A Coronation Street-style cull is overdue on **EastEnders.**

Get rid of Pauline, Ted Hills and George, Peggy's fake-gangster boyfriend. Get rid of the pirate-radio boys (whatever their names are), the whitest black jungle DJ and the Welshest Welshman on television. As for Martin, only days after his first speaking role, he's already on the rob. If we don't get rid of him soon, he'll be raping and pillaging. Send him off to Borstal for some Sleepers treatment.

As for Alistair the God Squad Snogger and Frankie The Man-Killing Lizard (who's not good-looking enough to tempt either heterosexuals, gays or clergymen), they can go too, preferably together. In tomorrow's omnibus, Alistair's followers give him a birthday cake covered with candles. 'Now blow!' Frankie tells him, with the sort of ease that only comes from experience.

Getting rid of Lorraine or, as we call her in Tapehead's household, That-Bitch-Lorraine, is more difficult. This week, Lorraine is not sure if she should worry about Joe reading the Bible ('It's good to see him having an interest,' she witters brightly), prompting Tapehead to give her some advice. Where Joe is concerned, if in doubt, worry. Taking after his dimwitted, bleating bitch of a mother, Joe is also worrying: 'How will I know if I do start getting ill again?' Well... motorways, window ledges, mirrors and TV screens covered in tin foil and gaffer tape, rocking back and forward next to the Zanussi... You'll know. OK?

This week, Tiff and Bianca are reunited. Tiff is ready to drop. Grant takes the plunge and Sanjay and Gita consider IVF treatment. (Is it any wonder Sanjay can't get it up when he's married to his grandmother?) Tony comes over all maternal – but still reckons he might not be gay after all. 'What are you doing?' Tony groans the morning after a heavy night out. 'Bad head?' jeers Simon. 'No, I quite enjoyed it actually...' The big question is: will Tiff's baby make it through her first episode? Have your hankies ready.

More tears and traumas in **Brookside** as the Corkhills finally get to bury Our Little Jimmy. Jackie drops the bombshell. There's no culling necessary in Brookside (although Jack Sullivan, Cassie and Our Elaine can go) as this month the whole cast go into therapy (and so do the audience). Even therapy doesn't stop Bel from moaning. 'It's like the whole family's on trial,' she clucks, looking as if she's speaking with a piece of rotten lemon in her mouth, as always. 'We're all in the dock,' she gasps, even though she's the one accusing Ollie and Ollie's dad of corrupting Nat and Georgia (as if such a thing were possible). Now we know why Ollie's got that train set in the garage.

The big question is: who will Ollie molest next? 'I've just been watching a horde of teenage boys building up a sweat,' he mocks, with rather more fervour than can be wise, really. He doth protest too much, Tapehead thinks, and so does she. They are both after Daniel. 'Don't tell me I'm not old enough to understand,' he whines to Ollie. 'I am old enough.' A dangerous declaration under the circumstances. 'Come here,' coos Bel, giving him a hug (a rather big hug) after Daniel asks if Ollie's moved out because he's having an affair (with Matthew? Or Emily?). Daniel is the one to watch from now on (the albino rabbit impersonation will stop). Already the most fucked-up member of the whole family, in years (or months?) to come, Daniel will make Nat and Georgia look like amateurs.

February 7–14 1997

Under pressure

S tress. Tapehead has heard of it and now, finally, he's experienced it – watching **Modern Times**' programme about it. (Previous knowledge was confined to occasions when the VCR taped Morning Worship instead of The Waltons.)

The film looks at four men who, like Travis Bickle, could not take it any more, going from thriving on stress to cracking up because of it, cases of men working seventeen-hour days, 'sitting in a room shaking his head and talking to himself' and 'roaming around at night, unable to sleep, *making milky drinks*'. Ray, who worked for the DSS for 23 years, once picked up a kitchen knife and asked his wife, 'How many fingers would I need to cut off to never have to go back to work again?' (Tapehead's guess, Ray, is eight.)

As his business was destroyed by Tesco, Martyn, the corner-shop owner, would start the day 'crying a bit, getting the shakes, throwing up'. When he finally went bankrupt, the man from the receivers asked for his cheque cards, took out a pair of scissors and cut them up in front of him. Happily, he made it through. 'If I owe anybody my future, I owe it to Cassie,' he says, 'not Jean.' Jean is his long-suffering, unswervingly loyal wife who appears on the show throughout. 'When I was really poorly,' he explains, 'I spoke to the dog. I could unload without being criticised or judged' – although this last detail is more than Tapehead or the RSPCA really need to know.

All in all, Modern Times is the most stressful experience Tapehead has had since the last series of **Homicide** ended with Pembleton's 'Jacob's Ladder' of a heart attack. Four months of suspense as to whether he made it end pretty swiftly thanks to cowardly Channel 4 who have decided that the first two episodes of the new series should be withdrawn on the grounds that the storyline (a school hostage scenario) has something to do with Dunblane – a reading of 8.7 on Tapehead's new stress metre.

Prison-riot storylines, apparently, are OK, so we get a kind of Greatest Hits of previous Homicide bad guys including the copycat sniper, the video park-bench killers and Claude Vetter, a lowlife who killed the woman he loved ('I guess I'm just a hopeless romantic'). All the minor irritations that accompany a new series of Homicide remain: Kellerman going on about quitting smoking, Bayliss's new haircut, the number of awful rock songs (three). The weaselly video guy, Brodie, seems to have had a makeover on Ricki Lake. On the plus side, there is a new post-Seven credits sequence and a conversation about which animal produces the largest sperm. Tapehead is happy to see Mick from Brookside still moonlighting from the Pizza Parlour, mumbling incomprehensibly as jazz hipster Meldrick Lewis.

A new series of **Murder One** would be cause for great celebration if Tapehead hadn't ruined it for himself by watching it already on Sky, where he also saw actor Anthony LaPaglia tell David Letterman the show had been axed (4.2 on the stress metre). The new storyline has James Wyler (LaPaglia) replacing Teddy 'Shinehead' Hoffman for a case in which the governor of California and his mistress have been shot by foxy blonde Sharon Rooney. As soon as Sharon tells Wyler she did it, we know she didn't – the sort of soft-option choice that made ABC kill it off, along with Teddy's staff of saps and smoothies, Justine, Arnold and Chris Docknovich. Too much LA Law, not enough Homicide. From his great opening scene onwards, LaPaglia is terrific, a fascinating blend of Jamie Redknapp and Shakin' Stevens, with some Billy Corkhill and Oliver Hardy thrown in. And he can say, 'We're done here, people' with the best of them.

Finally, in **Brookside** on Friday, Tapehead's own cull continues. Snuffing out two children in any soap is always good news and, even if Georgia has to go (for now), anything's worth it to be rid of Nat. Tapehead wishes him good luck in Hollyoaks.

April 5–11 1997

Low

Witness surveyed 250 men, 'to find out why men go to prostitutes for sex'. One man – get this – went, 'for no apparent reason at all other than that he enjoys it'. Can you believe that?! The rest are a sad and not-very-sorry bunch of inadequate misfits and scary-looking wackos (and that's just the women). At least the men come up with some good excuses.

Wayne's excuse is that he was, 'run over by a kid in a go-kart'! (He went for a massage and before he knew it, he was watching a porn video and being covered in baby oil.) Bill seems to blame his first wife, which is a nice touch. He considerately explained his use of prostitutes to his second wife as 'just something I need and enjoy doing', like DIY.

Monty's justification is that he is 'unlucky in love'. A 36-year-old DJ from Romford, an intense-looking, podgy Goth, Monty puzzles, 'It's a mystery to me why I struggle.' Of course, Monty mate, going on national television telling everyone you f*'*k prostitutes probably isn't going to help. Sometimes he leaves a prostitute's room, wondering, 'Am I a bit of a sad tosser for doing this?' – a rhetorical question if ever there was one. At least Charles, a quiet, deeply disturbed mannequin dressed in the truly scary combo of brown leather waistcoat and tie, goes for 'pure lust'. ('I was hooked on illicit sex.') The line of cuddly toys on his bed is genuinely alarming.

Too Much Too Young's 'Chickens' (on two teenage rent-boys operating in the parks and, appropriately, graveyards of Glasgow) similarly fails to rise above the mundane, merely confirming the clichés. Despite its level of access to the boys (as it were), the programme's tone is flat, trivial and almost chatty. Inane observations like 'I do believe I'm providing a service' actually have no value at all, likewise anodyne advice like 'You need a sense of humour throughout everything: life, work, whatever, or it's gonna be a boring old, depressing world.'

The boys' irritating endless chirpiness – with more naff singing than a Pet Shop Boys/Erasure head-to-head (as it were) – is not even endearing. Some subtitles would have come in handy too. Mumbling in heavy Scots accents, especially for anything risqué, results in a series of lines like 'I do believe I'm good at ma job because I'm known to be an och-aye-tha-noo-werrfiupfffstrurgff.' It is also surely time drag contests were banned, at least from TV documentaries.

The only thing lower than going on the game or paying to have sex with prostitutes, you might think, is being a traffic warden, and **An Inspector Calls** confirms you'd be right. 'If it wasn't for us, the city would come to a standstill,' says one pompous jobsworth, while another, an ex-army officer, declares, 'I'm still wearing the Queen's uniform to a certain extent.' Warden Karen Carr has developed 'such a thick skin' that 'insults no longer hurt'. A dumpy, plain, flabby-faced busybody, as far as Tapehead can tell, whose thick skin is her most attractive feature.

The city's longest-serving warden, David Raglan, is such an officious, petty-minded irritant that even when he got promoted, he insisted on going back on the streets to persecute honest citizens like your good selves. That red herring 'jovial good humour' surfaces again. (Raglan is so remorselessly, humourlessly 'chirpy' even a former policeman had no option but to throw him through a shop window.)

What none of them realise is that in the absence of any commission, their low wages (£186 a week) and good-bloke good humour actually makes them *worse*. 'It's not me personally that they can't stand,' smiles one, 'it's the uniform.' (No, really, it's you.) Raglan's Percy Sugden-esque rage at finding one of his parking tickets has been ripped up is priceless. 'That's the respect they've got for the law y'see. They'll have to pay in the end. They don't know I've got a copy.'

Look, you idiots, we know we'll have to pay in the end. We know you've got a copy. Seeing how much the ripped-up ticket hurts and outrages him is inspirational. So, rip up all your tickets, readers. Even if it only annoys one or two of them this much, it'll be worth it.

April 12–18 1997

You're the one (for me fatty)

When the BBC has 'a Panorama Special' it's invariably about education or the Lebanon. A 'World in Action Special' will focus on the NHS or the homeless. This week's **Cutting Edge Special**, being Cutting Edge, is about One-Night Stands – i.e. something much more important.

The film follows four one-night-stand specialists out on the pull, demonstrating the sort of inane perspectives that documentary-makers think make them great philosophers of our time. 'It's the nineties, innit?' laughs one of them. 'Liberation.' 'It does make me feel very independent to have sex with someone I don't know,' muses another, missing the point that you can't be much more 'independent' than single/chronically lonely. Bonnie, a 24-year-old Zoe Ball lookalike with a young baby daughter, says she has 'always been single. Even when I was living with Layla's dad, I was single.' Her baby, she says, is 'like a husband' to her: 'I clean for her. I cook for her. I wash her.' Which makes you wonder what sort of husband she's expecting.

The only relationship that Jean-Yves, a delicate, softly spoken 34-year-old man, is looking for is 'with myself'. 'I like to look at a pretty man, but also a handsome man, a masculine man... I like men who look like men, behave like men...' (Between you and me, Tapehead reckons Jean-Yves might be homosexual.) Every Saturday he goes out cruising, ending up 'totally screwed up, in a place like Bethnal Green'. (Good God.) Watching him rubbing nipples with several strangers in a club called Substation (as opposed to Substandard), the tension as to whether Jean-Yves will indeed have a one-night stand, er, mounts. In fact, the day Jean-Yves or anyone else ever manages to leave Substation without scoring will be such a freakish event as to be worthy of an entire series.

Cocky Scouser Mark's excuse for his aversion to serious relationships is that he did it once and 'was always being quizzed about it'. His chat-up line is: 'So, er, when did you last have sex, like?' In Liverpool this passes for suave.

Bonnie's one-night stand ends, fittingly, with Cutting Edge looking longingly up at the curtains so we can only imagine what she's up to and then goes sniffing around in the aftermath. The worst thing that can happen to these characters is that they cop off with someone they genuinely like. A pretty sorry state of affairs, really. Poor Jean-Yves can't even commit to a second date.

Ron Wankling, the star of **Mad About Machines**, met his wife 125 years ago at the pictures by screwing up a ball of paper from the programme and throwing it at her. Rather than a bordello or cunningly-equipped dungeon in Bayswater, 'House Of Tricks' turns out to be about an old bloke in Warwickshire who can make lawnmowers from a Hoover handle, a push-bike brake lever and the handle of a tea urn (whatever that is). He ruins perfectly good biscuit tins by turning them into light-fittings and has knocked up a kitchen-roll dispenser, a used-plastic-bag holder and an incredibly realistic cat. His wife/assistant ('Betty, press the button') explains his fanaticism by saying, 'He always has to be busy. He doesn't like time on his hands.' Which seems strange since he's invented so many time-saving devices.

Masterchef is still the only food programme Tapehead can sit through, despite the prevalence of the opinion that cooking is 'The New Rock 'n' Roll' (you might as well just say 'The New Leprosy'). Judging this week are

Anouska Hempel ('That's just me as a girl coming from my opinion') and boring tosser Rick Stein ('He's chosen exactly the right duck for that dish') who join Loyd to waffle on about 'the fashionability of fish'. (Fish are the lead singers of The New Rock 'n' Roll.) Contestants are Barry in the red kitchen ('crayfish interleaved with red mullet, aubergine crisps and a chestnut parcel'), Ann-Marie from Virgin Records at Heathrow airport ('mussel and butternut squash soup and salsa stacks') and Fred, a policeman in the (ho-ho) blue corner ('foaming crème anglaise, you have the right to remain silent…'). Fred's experience of grilling prisoners, battering suspects and cooking up evidence will no doubt prove invaluable.

Finally, on **Ricki Lake**, 'You're Too Fat To Be My Friend'. Quite right.

April 26–May 2 1997

Dark hearts

After **Millennium**, the quaint idea of TV thrillers and 'murder-mysteries' will never be the same again. Never again will the murder scene fail to be covered in semen or poems written in human blood. And never again will the investigating detective just be some sort of ordinary Joe. He will have to be at least as fucked-up as his suspects – if not more so. The writers of Miss Marple have a lot of work to do.

Millennium has totally moved the goalposts of how horrible you can make things, in much the same way that Seven has done with movies – mainly by copying it. Most impressive of all is the total absence of the token 'dark' humour that programmes like Cracker or Prime Suspect go for. Frank, Millennium's semi-psychic investigator, does not crack a lot of jokes. He has seen so much scary shit that when he turns up, it's amazing that the victim's relatives don't just call the cops and tell them, 'He's here. We got the guy that did it!'

The last episode of the first series on Sky (shortly to be repeated on ITV) will no doubt be some sort of sick, celebratory special. A couple of weeks ago a man graphically gouged his eyes out with his thumbs and ended up toppling, naked, out of his tormentor's fridge. Besides nubile young women, last week's serial killer had moved on to horses and, ultimately, a lorry-full of hogs, cutting their throats and leaving Frank looking for semen (the killer's – not the horses'). A close-up of a fly crawling around a young woman's eyeball suggested she wasn't doing too well. 'We're witnessing the birth of a psycho-sexual killer,' Frank mumbled. 'That's why he wrote HELP in human blood – meaning "help me".' To which you might say, 'No shit, Sherlock' (but not to his face). By the close last week, the killer had abducted a horse-loving vet and strung her up in a slaughterhouse next to several horse corpses, and looked on in a state of sexual excitement, licking one of them. You wonder if ITV know what they've let themselves in for.

Desperate to absolve himself from Robson And Jerome and Soldier, Soldier, Robson Green's new thriller, **Touching Evil**, copies from Cracker the way Millennium does from The Dead Zone or Jacob's Ladder. Beside Robson's flashbacks of his near-death experience (on Top Of The Pops?), it has its own mystic in the form of a fat psychic 'snout' called Cyril (stop sniggering), a Stan Ogden lookalike that Robson refers to as 'the Nostradamus of the underworld'. Last week's chilling child-abduction plot was (depending on how you look at it): (a) a high-quality Morse or Out Of The Blue; (b) a darker, quite nasty Touch Of Frost; or (c) a relatively cheery Millennium. The ultimate in outsider detective stereotypes, Robson plays his part as the strong, silent type, emotionally cold (except when he Cares Too Much) – and sensibly so, because when he needs to do anything more than this, he can't. (His voice rises into Paul Daniels' squealing territory.) His character is cocky but totally charmless, and so insipid he makes Tony Blair look like Abel Ferrara.

Just as, no matter how dark he thinks Touching Evil is, Robson Green will always be That Wanker From Robson And Jerome, we will always think of **Melissa** as Jennifer Ehle as Calypso from The Camomile Lawn, especially if she continues to play everyone the same way by demonstrating her fabulous talent for talking and giggling simultaneously. Melissa is Alan Bleasdale's version of Francis Durbridge's sixties tale of 'mystery, crime and passion' and a right old yawn it is too. Calypso's character, Melissa, is 'a femme fatale', 'a glamorous publicist', as if there was such a thing. Only someone as dull as her principal suitor, a foreign reporter played by Tim Dutton, could possibly find her 'enigmatic', so she understandably overlooks his nauseating middle-class smugness and self-indulgence (not to mention moon face).

The other characters are equally awful, caricatured and portrayed in a mundane way by a troupe of well-known Bleasdale actors who seem to think that just because some of it was filmed on a cruise liner, the whole production should be done as amateur dramatics. This underlines the impression that Melissa is about as thrilling as something that actually was made in the sixties, despite Bleasdale's embarrassing efforts to show us he's heard of Quentin Tarantino. The music is awful, the satire of publicists and PR pitifully thin and clichéd. Even the opening credits are rubbish. All in all, about as gripping as Alan Shearer's handshake. (Tapehead didn't like it much.)

May 10–16 1997

Banged up

'If I told the whole story of my private life, I'd probably make half a million pounds, but I'd have to spend the rest of my life in Tahiti and I don't really want to have to do that.'

So says the star of **Secret History** – Tory peer and PPS to Winston Churchill, Lord Boothby, during a (to say the least) candid interview on the Tonight programme back in the 1960s.

An MP at only 24, Boothby was a high-flyer whose rogue charms and snappy soundbites made him the first TV star of British politics. But, Ludovic Kennedy suggests, 'He did have one or two flaws.' Although we learn he was cavalier with both his money and his affections, a gambler, playboy, adulterer and an inveterate liar, we never learn what his flaws were. Besides being a gambler and liar, the narrator tells us, darkly, that Boothby 'was marred by a third flaw'. Known by the name The Palladium (on the grounds that he was twice-nightly), he was beset by 'an uncontrollable urge for sexual adventure'.

Openly bisexual, he was married twice and had a longstanding affair with Harold Macmillan's wife, which was surprising, Ludo remembers rather ungallantly, not because he still rose so high (as it were), but because 'she was rather horse-like. Huge hands, like hams.' What (finally) threatened to derail his career was a set of photos, taken in 1964, showing Boothby with Leslie Holt (East-End boxer, cat-burglar and Boothby's lover), Reggie Kray and another London gangster, Teddy Smith (*Mad* Teddy Smith to give him his full name), who was also what the programme calls 'an active homosexual' – as opposed to one who sits around all day watching the telly, doing nothing.

Kray, states another villain (perhaps rather unwisely considering his brother's imminent release) was also 'a raving poof', exchanging 'prospects' with Boothby, corrupting young boxers and 'importuning young men at dog tracks'. When the secret service leaked the photos, *Mirror* proprietor Cecil King thought he had another Profumo scandal on his hands to help him suck up to Labour leader Harold Wilson.

Tune in to find out how Boothby ended up not only winning a printed apology but a whopping sum of cash from the *Mirror* – thanks to the fourth man in the picture who was also 'a voracious homosexual' (like, a really hungry one?). Thanks partly to these pictures, the press, the politicians and even the police laid off the Krays, resulting not only in criminal carnage across London, but endless claptrap in the press about the golden-hearted Twins and, even worse, Gary Kemp's film career.

Harold Wilson pops up on **Breaking The News** in some behind-the-scenes footage of his barney with David Dimbleby. A rather rushed compilation of UK and US TV news in the sixties, it chucks in some from the Soviet Union for good (or bad) measure. Footage from the first televised presidential debate in 1960 shows Kennedy arriving looking 'tanned, handsome and well-tailored' while Nixon was suffering from what they ambiguously call 'an infection', 'looking green and sallow'. The debate takes place in what seems to be an enormous padded cell. Don't miss Cliff Michelmore outdoing Chris Morris opening the Tonight show by blasting a shotgun into the camera.

Alf, one of the prisoners on Banged Up's **Drugs, Dogs And D-Wing**, was sent down for life in the sixties, a time when, according to Alf, 'there was no drug problem in prisons'. It's the same today. Say the word 'drugs' and someone else will say 'no problem'. Prison officers at HM Prison Preston deploy random strip searches, mandatory drug tests ('Take this drug, you bastard!') and sniffer-dogs like Zak the German shepherd. The service relies on donations from the public – not of money, but actual dogs – 'dogs that are a bit difficult to control'. When he first arrived, John Stringer's dog would not go anywhere near humans. As he had pneumonia, fleas, sores, conjunctivitis and worms ('heavy worm infestation'), the feeling was probably mutual. The brilliant bit is that to train them to sniff out drugs, they reward the dogs by letting them play with their favourite toy – a cracker packed full of... *drugs* (to reinforce the smell). Tapehead would search for drugs himself to play with that cracker. See you in Tahiti.

June 21–27 1997

Mob deep

Television, increasingly, is just becoming a study of madness. This week, we have a veritable Blind Date of dementia with veteran contestants Rutger 'The Hitcher' Hauer, 'Mad' Frankie Fraser and 'Doolally' David Icke. These days, Frankie Fraser is on TV more often than the weathermen. (He was last seen on Brass Eye being branded 'as mad as a lorry'.)

Frankie, it seems, has turned into a right old tart: a media tart. He even turns up on yet another bout of gangster nostalgia. **Inside Story**'s examination of gangsters and their women, 'Molls'. (Next week it'll be gangsters and their pets.) Frankie's other half, Marilyn, is the daughter of one of the great train-robbers. Her mum remembers realising he was up to somefink when they bought a van and some frilly curtains (hopefully not together). 'I knew there wuz gunna be a rob'ry,' she remembers, sounding eerily like Waynetta, 'because 'e told me to keep the kids away from the toy cupboard.' The programme's central premise – 'behind every successful gangster there's a strong woman' – is, of course, nonsense. Usually behind every successful gangster is a woman who does what she's told, doesn't mind a smack now and again and, above all, doesn't know what her boyfriend's up to. (Serious villains never tell their women anyfink.)

They wheel out done-to-death old lags like Charlie Wilson and Tony Lambrianou and numerous old molls who have been involved with various armed blaggers, Kray twins' associates and blokes like Dave Courtney who organised Ronnie Kray's funeral and famously never goes anywhere without a knuckleduster. One typically astute moll, Jo-Jo Laine, the former girl-friend of one of the geezers what done the Knightsbridge safe-deposit job in '87, declares, 'I actually feel protected by dangerous men' – which is OK for her, but what about the rest of us? Later she reveals, ''E tried to bite my nose off.'

Like all the other nonsense the BBC's Oxbridge graduates come up with, 'Molls' conveniently brushes over the fact that these geezers run protection rackets, loan-sharking, drug-dealing and commit acts of fantastic, sometimes random violence, usually aimed at the general public. Marilyn Wisbey also contributed to the stream of racist rubbish

Fraser came up with when he was (absurdly) on If I Were Prime Minister. Tapehead says: stick 'em all back inside. It's the only language they understand.

Rutger Hauer's peculiarly amused form of madness has been on the wane somewhat of late. But his performance as a Soviet nuclear submarine captain in **Hostile Water** is salvaged (unlike his submarine) by his depiction of the captain as a cross between an East German centre-half from the seventies and Coronation Street's Jim MacDonald. The moderately pointless moustache, tired greasy quiff and failed air of resignation are all in place. All that's missing, Tapehead feels, is Jim's parka. It's even got Gail Tilsley's Canadian brother in it, as a suit from the White House. Other bitparts seem to be played by Ian Hislop, Tony Hancock and Chelsea's token Englishman, Dennis Wise. Martin 'Charlie's Dad' Sheen is resplendent in a Captain Bird's Eye beard of the highest order. The matte shots of the submarine are, to its credit, better than Scorsese's Blue Peter efforts in Cape Fear, but it all becomes a bit too much like an underwater Star Trek ('Captain, the power's gone.' 'Switch to batteries.')

Rutger saunters through it all with considerable aplomb, bestowing upon even his most staccato speeches a kind of suave grandeur, like Clark Gable in The Misfits. On the evidence of **The Chair**, like 'Mad' Frankie, poor David Icke should be locked up out of harm's way. We would have learned more about him if Oliver James, The Chair's resident (querulous) psychiatrist, could stop interrupting. (Just get Anthony Clare for the next series.)

Icke reveals that, as a toddler, he used to cross the road to avoid people (now it's vice versa) and that football was his saviour. When he recalls the time people would laugh at him wherever he went, the juvenile James sniggers. Even when Oliver clears him of being schizophrenic – on the (erroneous) grounds that he has none of the classic symptoms – Icke scents a conspiracy. 'But who decided what the classic symptoms are and who told them, you see?' His paranoia certainly seems clinical and terminal. James cops out of giving his conclusion but, in Tapehead's view, the medical term for it is: bananas.

July 26–August 1 1997

Armageddon out of here

L ife is over. **This Life** is over, with Thursday's aptly named 'finale': Apocalypse Wow. All the big questions are answered. Will Miles get married? Will Milly confess? Will Ferdy come out? Tapehead's pledge: you will never guess what happens, though it is true Ferdy finally comes out and admits, yes, my real nickname is Fatty.

Don't miss Egg's Marlon Brando impersonation or Milly and Rachel auditioning for Lady Macbeth – not to mention the brilliant final freeze-frame. Tapehead's only reservations about this series have been over the producer's fascination with Ferdy (at Egg's expense) and the famous five's penchant for pyjamas. Alan Shearer's wages could be used to persuade the big five to stay. If Milly comes back, let's hope they buy her a new coat (one that fits) and Jo and Kira must marry. Cult viewing doesn't come much better than This Life, but we still have King Of The Hill, Millennium and, of course, the cult of cults, **Brookside**, where the race is on to be The Close's first serial killer. Two rhetorical questions from Friday: 'How will Danny react to Eleanor staying the night?' (badly?) and 'Will Christian see the funny side of the joke?' (not fucking likely). Better start preparing the patio.

House Gang, Channel 4's new sitcom featuring three actors with learning difficulties, is guaranteed cult viewing. The opening 15 minutes are so stilted, so badly acted and so awkward, it makes Hollyoaks look like Homicide. The protagonists can't act, can't speak and, even worse, are Australian. Things pick up when their landlord and his daughter Chloe move in and Chloe starts raining insults on her three handicapped co-stars ('Give Me That You Bitch' etc.). All faintly fascinating.

Inside Story's cult viewing looks at the 39 members of the Michael Cimino Appreciation Society, Heaven's Gate, who committed suicide in San Diego earlier this year, departing the world, according to their leader, by a spaceship tied to the tail of the Hale-Bopp comet. Like members of the Church of Tapehead they were dressed in Nike trainers and grey uniforms, their heads covered by purple shrouds sponsored by Silk Cut. Some were asphyxiated with plastic bags containing alcohol and pheno-barbital. The Heaven's Gate leader, Marshall Applewhite (who founded the cult in the early seventies), seems to have renamed himself with the Simpsonsesque exclamation 'Doh!'. Creating 'a fusion of Christianity and New Age science-fiction', Doh!'s church promised disciples entry into the Kingdom of Heaven without the tedious minor detail of having to die first. 'I'm from the Kingdom Level Above Human,' he says on one of his eerie recruitment videos. His big ears and clown eyebrows, the shaved silver hair and playschool manner of addressing people back up our impression of him as a genuine simpleton.

We meet several ex-Heaven's Gate members, all of whom have Doh!'s scary tranquillity and alien shaved head, like extras from Third Rock From The Sun. One of them, Richard Ford, had been reborn as Rio D'Angelo, which is definitely an improvement. 'The Virgin Mary,' he tells us, 'was impregnated by being taken up on a spaceship.' 'It sounds, like, unbeliev-able?' he admits (sounding like a Bret Easton Ellis character who can't end a sentence without a question mark?) but points out this version's better than the virgin birth theory because, 'It's, like, technical?'

Parents of the members who died maintain that Doh! had brainwashed them and former members confirm that their behaviour was monitored so closely they could only shave using downward strokes of the razor (which is also, spookily enough, recommended in those *How To Shave* guides you get in *Arena* every month). Sex was considered 'too human' and enemas were used to 'cleanse the vehicle' – not your Renault 5, but the vehicle of our soul. Such 'special purges' used 'the master cleanser' – a mixture of lemonade, cayenne pepper and maple syrup. (Do not try this at home.) The Church of Tapehead is working on perfecting this recipe even as we speak.

August 2–8 1997

Les EstEndeurs

Grant looks down at the menu, raises his Nookie Bear eyebrows and tuts, 'This is all in French.' Yes, **EastEnders** is on its travels for a one-week special again. It's almost as good as when they went to Ibiza or thought they'd ended up in Calais for Ricky's stag-night but had in fact gone to Kent. They are staying at the Hotel Gustave Flaubert, which shows you just how good it is.

Phil is looking forward to it already. 'Anyone starts looking down their nose at *me* they're in for a good kicking.' Or, as they say in French, une bonne kickeeng. Grant is enjoying himself too. 'Brilliant or what?' squeals Tiffany with excitement. 'Act your age,' he mumbles back. That's not to say they're all getting on. 'S'abaht time you grew up!' shouts Grant. 'S'abaht time you shut up,' replies his bruvver.

Kaff and the Goddess Tiffany have abandoned their babies at the first opportunity and Rick-ay and Bianc-ah are staying with Ricky's sister Diane, who after several years out of the series has blossomed into a young Myra Hindley and a glowing ad for motherhood to boot. 'A 36-hour labour, I had an epidural, forceps, stirrups, the works,' she says enthusiastically. 'I ended up ripped to shreds. "Enough stitches to sew up the Bayeux tapestry" the nurse said…' – which is rather more detail than we needed. She has shocking news that Rick-ay is not as thick as we had thought he was. 'He just got this label put on him when he was young and he believed it,' she says, which suggests we were right in the first place. You can still see the label on his back from time to time.

Bianca is worried she might be up the duff ('going to have a bay-bay' as she puts it) and becoming as close to Nell Dunn's Poor Cow as you can get. 'It's not the end of the weld,' the Goddess Tiff consoles her. 'Have you been sick at all?' 'Well, I ain't puked, if that's what you mean.' Bianca also seems to be saving up for an arse, or an 'orse. (Actually it's an 'ouse.)

The main event is the lovely Lorna and Phil, who is cracking under the strain. He is dying to go on une bender and is acting so hard his face keeps fluctuating through the myriad shades of the rainbow (from puce to crimson). He's suffering so much guilt about what he's done to Kaff he could teach the Bad Lieutenant a thing or two. (The Bad Mechanic?) 'You don't know Lorna, do you?' he cries to his bruvver. 'No you don't. So shut yer marff.' In fact, Lorna has written Phil a letter and of course Kath wants to know what it says. 'It's full of the sort of stuff a drunk person says,' Phil explains helpfully. (Things like 'hic, burp, belch, Johnnie Walker's, puke'.) 'Lorna's a bit loopy,' he explains, coming over all romantic. 'She gets upset. I think she's fallen off the wagon. She could do anyfink.' Let's hope no one's bought baby Ben a pet rabbit.

More proof (if proof were needed) that All Men Are Snakes also turns up on **Ricki Lake**. Brigitte, Tanisha and Rigel (don't ask) all believe men are rats, will lie at any opportunity and are only interested in sex, so what the controversial debating point is is anyone's guess. 'Where you lookin fo' yo' men?!' demands one male defender as he's going to whomp them. Tanisha in particular makes Rosie Perez look shy and retiring. 'Every guy in the universe is a dawg,' she says with authority.

Hank Hill, of course, is an exception, as **King Of The Hill** confirms. His meeting with his hero, Willie Nelson, truly stirs the soul. 'Hey Hank,' Willie Nelson greets him, 'your son Bobby's been telling me all about you. I hear you like playing guitar and that you've got a narrow urethra.' Hank wonders why his son can't turn his energy into something more useful, 'like that boy with no legs that ran across Canada'. But he bonds with him like the good man that he is. 'Now I'm going to show you something you can do with a guitar that *doesn't* involve cheese.'

Back in EastEnders, by the end of the week Grant and the Goddess Tiffany are getting all romantic. Tiffany reveals that, as children, she and her brother Simon used to play kings and queens. 'I bet you did,' mutters Grant. 'I won't ask who was who.' Grant is 'Louis the Whatever' to Tiffany's Marie Antoinette. She just wants Grant to woo her, to offer anything she desires. 'All right then,' Grant concedes romantically. 'How about a beer?' Tiff, Tapehead will woo you any time you like.

August 23–29 1997

And another thing...

apehead, as you know, is not one to complain. Well, OK, there was Candle/Hamster In The Wind being played at Wembley. And episodes of Homicide being pulled because of Dunblane, Garth Crooks on Match Of The Day, the idiot who now presents The Clothes Show, people who play frisbee in the park, the weathermen (liars)... But nothing, nothing, compared to **Cutting Edge**'s 'The Complainers'.

David Walsh, Alan Birkin and Barry Ritchie are tormented by complaints: driven, disturbed. They are protest pros, argument addicts. Monty Python sketches come to life. They are only happy when they have something to complain about. By comparison with the other two, David Walsh is almost genial, trundling down to the supermarkets equipped with his magnifying glass and fruit knife to badger regional managers with his daily inspection of suspect labels and Tesco pears which he considers 'cold and hard as usual'. (Everyone knows that pears are ripe for about four minutes before they go off.)

Alan Birkin is pure Yosser Hughes. He's even got the same moustache and haircut. You can picture him lying in bed at night ranting on about Esso charging for air to fill his tyres up with. To himself. 'I'm trying to compromise here,' he argues with the blokes from the carpet shop who (understandably) won't give him his deposit back. 'I just want me money back.' Nothing makes him happier than the moment he realises he's being ripped off. You can see his eyes gleam. That's why he always goes to the same lousy fast-food place, even though he knows the number of French fries you get for 70p leaves him feeling maniacally short-changed. (Or short-chipped.)

The third complainer, Barry Ritchie, is just damaged. He's one of those self-made men forever infuriated by the inadequacies and apathy of others less deranged than them. He is a Rik Mayall character written by Steven Berkoff when he was brutal/good. 'Nothing's up to scratch is it?' he rages. By the time his final explosion erupts, you can't help but wonder if Cutting Edge's cameras haven't driven him to the verge of a heart attack.

The last two in particular are ultimately just savagely unhappy. As you can see when Yosser takes his Hoover back to the repair man, even when The Complainers get what they want and win the argument they are not happy. They are far from happy. In fact, they are pissed off that they won't be able to complain any more. Tapehead hopes Cutting Edge paid them properly. Imagine the complaints.

In **Animal People**'s 'There's A Penguin In The House', Bryan Campbell is livid. Having moved into an expensive, secluded beach-house, his nearest neighbours set up an animal sanctuary or, more specifically, a 'penguin hospital'. Pretty soon, loads of penguins were fighting, fucking and regurgitating their fish in his front garden. 'I'm the only one it affects,' he rages, reciting a speech that sounds well-practised from the times he's spent talking to himself. 'No one was giving the consideration to my family that the penguins are getting.' Narrator Peter Sallis suggests the dispute with neighbour Viv Hextall was 'quite amicable enough at first'. 'She's an unfortunate spinster with nothing else in her life,' Campbell says 'amicably'. 'I will not lay down and be walked over by her and by her penguins,' he says, obviously by now in the midst of some bizarre sexual fantasy. 'Penguins have a special character,' Viv explains, 'partly because they're native and partly because they are cute' – not exactly scientific analysis, but still.

The penguins (Little Blue penguins if you're interested – the smallest, noisiest, smelliest breed) are great little skittles whizzing across the lawn on fast-forward, tripping up with better comic timing than Buster Keaton. Eventually, an injured penguin is carried away in a bucket, like a mad handbag, and taken out for a ride in a canoe to see if he's strong enough to swim away, the way people go rowing in the park. When they bring him back in, you can see the penguin thinking, 'Well that was a nice afternoon. Nicely rested for making more havoc for Mr Campbell.'

The little bleeders regularly wander round town. 'Visitors have never seen a wild animal walk into a nightclub,' says a local. The bouncers ask if they are members, but they just walk right in and mingle. 'They don't even seem frightened.' The only way to stop them coming in is by playing Elton John songs.

September 20–26 1997

Greed is not good

Are the nation's programme-makers trying to tell us something? Their fascination with bisexuals/transsexuals seems to know no bounds. Still, if nothing else, the nature and quality of programmes like **Seven Sins** confirm: love (or lust) is blind.

Take Paul Farquarson, for example, a black bisexual included to demonstrate how bisexuals represent Greed (because they like men and women, even though they very sensibly refute any association with promiscuity). Now, Paul is charming, passionate and, er... cute. But, honey, you ain't no rocket scientist. Paul, like a lot of bisexuals on TV, feels the need to announce that he doesn't recognise 'conventional terms' (i.e. words) like 'gay', 'heterosexual', etc. 'I mean, how do we define being black?' he demands. 'By the fact you can dance or you've got a big cock? And if you can't dance or you haven't got a big cock, does that mean you're not black.' (No, Paul, it doesn't.)

If Seven Sins is suggesting Paul's excitable, schoolboy insights are representative of bisexuals/blacks/black bisexuals, then they can only have been included to indicate how ridiculous they are. And if not, then what's the point? Most of Seven Sins is taken over by Felicity – caterer, masseuse (which she rhymes with moose) and a 'greedy' bisexual who resembles a sort of plain Theresa Russell. Sadly, Felicity merely confirms how tiresome bisexuals on TV are: indulgent, narrow-minded, stereotyped and painfully inadequate and insecure (can't deal seriously with men or women, constantly needing to convince themselves they are sophisticated, scandalous, fascinating, etc.).

Bisexuals are so pretentious; the worst kind of show-offs. 'I love the sophistication of humanity,' Felicity announces dramatically, by way of explaining her dual sexuality. 'I love the fact that we can control who comes into our lives.' (We can't.) Explaining what attracts her to someone, she gushes, 'It's the way a person holds themselves. It's a pair of beautifully manicured hands... Beautifully painted lips, a well-designed bicep, a bulge in a pair of trousers.' So nothing superficial then. 'With women,' she says, 'you know how their bits work. You understand they're going to get shitty at certain times of the month' – which, as summaries of women go, certainly no male could say unchallenged. Felicity, of course, thinks she is fabulously, fascinatingly broad-minded despite announcing that when she starts a relationship, she always discusses the rules first. 'I have my own set of rules.'

Later, she predictably contends: 'Most people aren't intelligent enough for bisexuality. They prefer to play safe. They have dull, grey lives and petty-minded rules... I wanna touch. I wanna taste. I wanna feel. Take me to a buffet,' she shouts to the heavens, 'and I will taste everything on that buffet.' Judging by the difficulty she has squeezing into her more outlandish outfits, unfortunately, in this case, she's not speaking metaphorically.

'Cocktail Party' is Tapehead's first exposure to those roly-poly Wallace and Gromits of TV cuisine, the **Two Fat Ladies**, bossy-boots Jennifer Paterson and her unfortunate sidekick-in-a-sidecar, Clarissa Dickson Wright. The new series opens with a chortling, 'Oooh, I think I'm getting stiff – not enough red meat.' The level of humour and quality of insight are not much better than Viz. They are actually both rather frightful, dull snobs.

Correspondent is unmissable if only because of suggestions that it is secretly the work of Chris Morris. The reporters here – melodramatic, pompous bods – are funnier than Brass Eye's Peter O'Hanrahanrahan and Susannah Gekkaloys. One follows a London mother's 'desperate quest' to cure her heroin addiction by going to Thailand – which is like going to Las Vegas to quit gambling. She joins Buddhist monks at Wat Tham Krabok (The Temple of the Opium Pipe) where 'the path of enlightenment' lies in a tough regime combining toil, self-discipline and shit-loads of opium. OK, 'herbal purgatives'. To the strains of 'Born Slippy', and hilariously out-brass-eyeing Brass Eye, our correspondent announces, 'I've never been with someone coming off a Class A drug before,' as if the report was actually about him. If the detox fails, he declares, she will be 'condemned to the life of a hopeless junkie thief', branding her 'a junkie mum... a crackhead turned smackhead'.

In the next item, reporter Sue Lloyd Roberts becomes a vice girl – er, 'joins the Vice Unit in Hong Kong'. The give-away that the hand of Morris has been here is that the Vice Unit is called the 'Mon Kok Squad'. We miss you, Chris.

September 27–October 3 1997

Heaven knows they're miserable now

'For years I have wanted to live according to the morality of the majority and live like everyone else,' Albert Camus says in **Bookmark**. 'I said what was necessary to say in order to bond, even when I felt separate. The upshot of all this was catastrophic. Now I am wandering among the wreckage, resigned to my singularity and my disabilities.' Albert, me old mucker, Tapehead couldn't have put it better himself.

A large part of Booker Prize week has been given over to reiterating: there is nothing more guaranteed to make you miserable than being a writer. (Phillip Schofield and Jenny Turner never had such problems.) The Camus quote, by the way, comes in Part Three – 'Happiness'. Bookmark's approach is to be Deeply Serious, with sumptuous photography and pained piano music, though at 90 minutes you could read A Happy Death in less time.

Director James Kent predictably declares poor Camus 'in need of reassessment' but mercifully does nothing of the kind, instead dragging us through his life and loves, culminating with the fact that even when he won the Nobel Prize it only made him more miserable. The film is short on football, long on theatre and excellent on his many (mad, miserable) 'long-term lovers'. ('The windows of the clinic are always closed.' How true that is.) The line, 'He was a Don Juan and she was a Don Juana' is not exactly erudite, but pretty great nonetheless.

Sadly, gnomic French intellectualisms worthy of Brass Eye's Jacques Liverot abound – characters such as Roger Quilliot saying things like, 'From this moment, Meursault enters the world of judgement and the world of judgement is the discovery of man.' (Eh?) Still, at least Bookmark relies on its subject-matter to hold our attention rather than its presenter and has a decent (i.e. professional) narrator (Brian Cox).

The Works ('Kerouac', by Andrew O'Hagan) and **Omnibus** ('Oscar', by Michael Bracewell) confirm that while actors narrate and TV presenters present, journalists should journo. O'Hagan starts off with the 65 days Kerouac spent as the solitary fire-watcher on Desolation Peak near the Canadian border (next to Damnation Park and Mount Terror, right opposite Mount Despair), predictably (pointlessly) going up there himself and narrating as if he were speaking English for the first time. The remotest fire station in the fire service (a case of Off The Road) having cultivated his Catholic upbringing into an interest in Buddhism ('Boo-dism' as the Americans call it), Kerouac declared that, with no drugs or drink for company, 'If I don't get a vision up on Desolation Peak, my name ain't, er, William... Blake.' Already intense and miserable enough, Kerouac didn't get any religious visions but 'a feeling of desolation' (what, on Desolation Peak?! Who would have thought it, eh?), writing loads of tosh about 'abysmal nothingness' and being 'face to face with my old hateful self instead.' 'I learn that I hate myself – because by myself, I am only my self.' 'Everything is nothing,' he wrote. Indeed.

The most intriguing part of Omnibus is director Hugh Thomson's insatiable appetite for filming journo-presenter Michael Bracewell's back, watching him trudging gloomily down endless corridors and stairways, like a miserable version of the White Rabbit. We see more of Michael than Oscar. Of course, there's an obvious case for Oscar Wilde as 'the century's first pop star', as Bracewell puts it, but surely he deserves more than to be reduced to the status of some sort of Boy George/Ziggy Stardust self-invention. Occasional allusions to Wilde by the likes of the Rolling Stones and 'other pop Dorians' are seized upon to prop up this premise, but what The Who or Finley Quaye have got to do with the dear old boy is anyone's guess. The genius of Wilde's line, 'One's real life is the life one does not lead', and how *he* dealt with it, are surely intriguing enough *without* any pop-culture context.

It's bad enough inflicting 'It's A Sin' into things, but Neil Tennant's evaluation of Wilde is surely of minor interest. His big theory about the artist's 'imperial phase' is typical Pet Shop Boy bogus intellectualism. 'As in Napoleon's career,' Tennant pontificates, an artist's triumph is followed by 'survival or disaster before 'the whole thing fades away'. (No shit, Sherlock.) 'I'm sick to death of cleverness,' Wilde wrote. 'Everybody's clever nowadays.' Write on.

October 11–17 1997

Sporty types

'**I**'m a different prospect to some dizzy player's wife,' insists Lucy, one of **Dream Team**'s first-team squad of super-foxes. 'Having to talk about blonde hair-dye all day.' A noble sentiment, of course, but one that suggests Dream Team might not be quite be as realistic as it thinks. Actual proof comes in **Cutting Edge**, back to its cruel, cutting best with 'Football Wives'.

By Lucy's criteria, Dean Holdsworth's wife, Sam, and Ian Walker's mis-sus, Suzi, are the definitive footballers' wives/dolly birds. *Hello* magazine houses, Euro-pop singles, pampered pets, Ibiza jeans and blonde manes. Suzi steals the show if only because Sam has to come back to reality when Deano's fling with a rival blonde hits the tabloids. She still manages to recall the night she and Dean first met, explaining, 'Dean had played away all that weekend,' without irony.

Fortunately (for all of us), 'ex-glamour model' Suzi has nothing more taxing than her own cable TV show to deal with. The superlatively titled Hi Ya With Suzi Walker is surely worth the cable fee alone. No one can say the words 'Hi Ya' like Suzi. Her agent David Hahn, like Suzi herself, is a spectacular specimen of vacuous blandness, talking up Suzi's talents with such earnest conviction you'd think he was representing a cross between Des Lynam and Jeremy Paxman, only for his choice of words to give the game away. 'She looks good, she looks the part, she's got a lovely figure.' Only his comment that 'blue-eyed blondes always go down well in televi-sion' hints at something more sinister (not to say libellous).

Besides Hi Ya With Suzi Walker, Suzi's main concern is their '£300,000 love-nest in Ongar'. 'This is the kit-chin,' she coos. 'A bit messy 'cos I've been away.' (Pan to a kitchen that makes the average show home look like a dosser's cardboard box.) Moving swiftly on, she leads us out to the pool, with its 'summer house', which has a bar, jukebox and snooker table. ('S'nice, innit.')

But do not think there isn't a down-side to Suzi's life. Christmas football means she can't go out on New Year's Eve or go away to the Caribbean. Worries about having to put her dogs in quarantine also plague her every waking moment as poor Suzi seems to be labouring under the illusion that Ian Walker might be moving abroad. (Iceland? Luxembourg?)

By contrast, the life of Ann, Jason Lee's non-blonde wife, couldn't be more miserable, even though he's only fallen from playing 'in the Prem' to second-division Watford. 'Not a nice life,' she says, as if she was living the life of your average council-estate prison widow. 'Come and spend a day with me,' she threatens, 'and you'd soon be frightened...' (something of a self-fulfilling prophecy). 'We don't have no Sky.' (Terrifying.) The tour of her house confirms poor Ann really is in a bad mood as she shows us her boys' room: 'This ain't no fun when you come in 'ere in the morning.' Maybe she should dye her hair blonde.

Or maybe Jason should watch **Equinox**, which looks at sports psychology (what they call 'brain research'), namely 'the zone' – the all-conquering trance made famous by the likes of Linford Christie – through which perfect performance can be achieved with utter self-mastery and absolutely no effort. (A bit like Tapehead.)

Sally Gunnell's zone when she won the 1993 World Championship gold was so total that even though she only passed the race leader (who was right next to her) in the final strides of the race, she had no knowledge whatsoever of what had happened. Derek Redmond's zone meant he believed he could limp round and win his race even when he'd pulled up with a hamstring injury. The selection of sportsmen (Steve Backley, Greg Rusedski, Mike Atherton) illustrates why dullards like Steve Davis dominate their sport rather than erratic characters like Alex Higgins. The alpha waves recorded for people who are 'zoning' are the same as those for people doing nothing at all, proving that being boring, bland or incapable of volatility or introspection actually does help.

Leslie Ash's husband, Lee Chapman, is bizarrely wheeled out to demonstrate the problem of trying too hard or thinking too much. Playing as badly as Lee did for Arsenal was, he says, a 'very public kind of humiliation' – good preparation for his recent exploits. Yet when he was scoring regularly at Leeds, he says the goal 'just seemed an enormous area to hit'. Something Lee should know a lot about.

November 8–14 1997

Boy racers

' t goes without saying,' says one of the presenters on **Deals On Wheels**, 'that most Capris have been thrashed to within an inch of their lives' – a disgraceful suggestion and a diabolical slur on the good name of the careful, considerate Capri driver. (Of which Tapehead may or may not be one.)

The deal concerned is a five-speed, D-reg, white Laser Capri with 68,000 miles on the clock, put up for sale by beautician/swinger/Essex girl Debbie. For the ridiculous reason, as the presenter put it, that Capris 'are about as fashionable as a tank top and a pair of tiaras' – which goes to show what he knows. (Nobody mention Ron Dixon.) Debbie has a good ding-dong about the Capri's CD player with the bloke who wants to buy it and even when she sells it still won't let him take it away because she 'wants some emotional space with her Laser'. Another perfectly reasonable Capri owner.

Elsewhere, the programme follows a splendid old buffer selling his 1939 Alvis and an appalling South African hippy flogging an Austin 1100. Neither particularly entertaining or informative. If nothing else, Deals On Wheels confirms two amateur presenters are worse (not better) than one, not least because 'the two presenters' 'needlessly alternate' 'reading the script out'.

An even bigger car dud, **Coltrane's Planes And Automobiles** confirms that any series based entirely around a pun on the presenter's name is going to end up in the graveyard scheduling of Sunday evening. At an hour long, it is ferociously tedious, full of mind-numbing detail about cylinders and lines like 'the German economy was in a shambles and money, especially here behind the Iron Curtain, was tight' – right out of a GCSE essay (failed).

The high points appear to be watching Robbie Coltrane take an engine

109

out of a Trabant (fascinating) and a conversation with a German bike enthusiast who says 'Yes' to every question on the grounds that it's the only word of English he knows (even questions like, 'Where are the gearboxes from?' 'Yes.' Not even people who are interested in cars will be able to sit through it.

At least **Top Gear** has a nifty theme tune and Jeremy Clarkson demonstrating that (raise voice) irritating, (lower tone) nasal (pause for italicised punchline) *Top Gear delivery*. It's also pretty funny how brazenly they get a couple of terrible, token women to do all the boring bits – making it look rather new-mannish when they didn't want to do them anyway.

In **The Car's The Star**, Clarkson-acolyte-in-chief, Quentin Wilson, enjoys doing the Top Gear delivery so smugly it really is (pause) *beyond parody*. Unfortunately, it's also beyond (pause) *taking seriously*. Quentin is particularly authoritative when smugly dismissing viewpoints no one else really has; saying things like 'to merely describe the Corvette as America's only sports car is to miss the point. It's much, much more (pause) *than that*.' His history lessons are also pretty laboured, as when he says, 'By 1968 a localised conflict in Asia had escalated into a war America would never win' rather than just saying, 'Vietnam happened.'

Most of it is padded out with old music and shots of Quentin grinning smugly at the camera as he shows off driving around a lot pretending he can still feel the breeze blowing through his hair. But as hard as he tries to be Clarkson, Quentin will always be Robin to Clarkson's Batman. He's even wrong about the Corvette, as Clarkson recently pointed out. 'Yes or no?' Wilson challenged him smugly. 'Have you driven it?' 'I haven't slept with Judy Finnegan,' Clarkson declared, pausing masterfully before concluding triumphantly, 'but I know she's fat and ugly.'

The best car programme of the week is **Movers And Shakers**' look at the showdown race at the Wood Green Scalextric Club. A bunch of fanatics who compare themselves with sportsmen like Nick Faldo, they have cars customised with lead ('to feel more sure-footed'), pit-mikes to talk to their mechanics and 80-foot tracks in their hallways. They even have their own Schumachering shunter. The moral of it all: all men are boys.

November 15–21 1997

Daylight robbery

First of all, it should go without saying that **The Lost Weekend**, Brookside's movie-length but straight-to-video-style Christmas cash-in is deeply dubious, inherently flawed, and bound to leave Brookside devotees' loyalties feeling decidedly compromised. The makers' defence that the format and more 'explicit' content allow them to do something they couldn't otherwise do is transparently disingenuous (They could just screen it later.)

And the '18-certificate content' merely consists of dismal Dempsey And Makepeace chase scenes and explosions, Our Lindsey getting slapped about a bit and liberal use of 'you fookin' get', 'wanker' and 'shithead' (a distant cousin of Tapehead's).

Basing the plot around an existing storyline (Barry Grant's vendetta with Finnegan) rather than a self-contained, original story (*à la* Damon and Debbie) means regular followers who do not see the video miss out on the climax of a long-running theme. And any future reference to it in the series becomes either a bit of a minefield or off-limits.

The script (knocked up on the back of a Bar Brookie serviette) reunites Barry with Sheila Grant (the splendiferous Sue Johnston) and Our Terry (the evidently thirsty, hungry Brian Regan) and attempts to give Barry's violent tendencies some sort of historical context. All of which requires awkward background explanations for video viewers who haven't followed the series long enough to know about Billy Corkhill, Bobby Grant and Mattie Lad, which just become irksome for the rest of us.

Barry's reasons for turning into an avenging, vigilante superhero are unclear, as one scene, in which Sheila inconveniently mentions that the whole thing has got nothing to do with him but is Ron and Jacqui Dixon's problem, points out. Even Barry seems unsure of his own motives, alternating between doing it (a) for love, (b) to save The Close from Armageddon and (c) for the money.

When Finnegan kidnaps Our Lindsey and Jackie Corkhill cries out, 'What's Our Lindsey done to deserve this?' viewers will surely have to think long and hard before remembering the answer: her singing. (Lindsey, bizarrely, attempts to win Sing For A Star impersonating Cher dressed as the sort of stripper you find doing karaoke in ropey old boozers on Sunday lunchtime.) The fact is, Our Lindsey isn't good-looking enough for Barry to take down the Legion, let alone go to war over. And no matter how much Barry insists Finnegan is 'Premier League' and 'on a psycho scale, right up there' – as gangsters go, he's a midget next to previous villains like Sizzler or Tommy McArdle. (He doesn't even bring any gaffer tape or chloroform along for the kidnapping, while his mobile phone is the sort of thing you see in World War Two movies.)

Nonetheless, war it is. Cue Barry storming around to the strains of some horrible Gary Moore guitar soundtrack, being compared by various cast members to Mel Gibson, Clint Eastwood, Yul Brynner, Arnold Schwarzenegger, Jimmy Cagney, Bruce Willis and, er, Nelly The Elephant (don't ask). 'How big,' demands Sinbad, rather needlessly, 'are Barry's balls?'

There is much soul-searching ('Why is it always us?' the actress who plays Jackie Corkhill cries, not unreasonably, to the actor who plays Jimmy), an alarming shot of Finnegan's backside and, above all, the return of St Sheila of the Mersey. 'Struggling's one thing,' she intones beautifully, 'suffering's another.' (Our Sheila; Proverbs XVI.) These days, by the way, Sheila has her own flower shop. It's called Sheila's Flower Shop. 'Is that yours, Sheila?' asks Jackie Corkhill, looking at the sign.

One brilliant, not to say legendary, long scene between St Sheila and Our Barry near the end almost makes it all worth the £14.99. But ultimately, it only serves to remind us of the standards Brookside set for itself in its heyday – when characters like Barry and Sheila were the norm, rather than the likes of Cassie, Gladys and Elaine. By comparison, the script and storyline of The Lost Weekend just aren't up to it.

November 22–28 1997

Poetic justice

One of the more moving moments of EastEnders in recent years was the sight of Ricky setting off for the Walford speedway final (sponsored by Phil) with the rallying cry, 'Go on Ricky! Do it for The Arches!' ringing in his ears. **Modern Times**' 'Arch People' sets out to prove that not everything going on in London's 4,500 railway arches involves knocking out dodgy motors, as it whizzes through an array of endeavours from S&M clubs to Bangladeshi prayer meetings and coffin-making.

Of course, as a local plod points out, that's not to say there aren't other more questionable activities going on. 'Drug factories, counterfeiting dens, illegal rave parties' and, worst of all, golf. A cheap laugh at a City gent fluffing his practice putts is one of the few to be had amid dozens of dullards who might be working under the arches but are actually still deadly... boring. Two minutes after the first cockney 'character' and you're crying out for a good drug factory or a nice bit of counterfeiting.

And talking of 'arch', it doesn't get much archer than the pilot for Channel 4's discussion show, **The Big If**. 'What if Marx was right?' is a simple, interesting enough issue, but absurdly over-earnest host David Aaronovitch has reduced his guests to suppressed smirking before the end of the intro. 'Capitalism is victorious,' he gushes, 'but as we approach the second decade of its total triumph, *unease* disturbs our sleep. Eastern tigers howl in the night as their miracle growth turns into phenomenal slump...' He keeps calling Marx 'the bearded, jut-lipped German journalist and philosopher' as if he were auditioning to be a Channel 5 football commentator.

The panel of over-opinionated egomaniacs (or guests) includes Ian Angel, Orlando Figes and Susan George (not that one). Only Paul Foot emerges as somebody you wouldn't hate to be stuck in a lift with, although Charlotte Raven has a rather beguiling way of saying she doesn't understand what the previous speaker's point was. Oliver James's enormous ears are revealed as the reason why he's always off-camera on The Chair.

They all stick to the viewpoints they had when they walked in and nod enthusiastically when anyone disagrees with them. 'The rhetoric of false consciousness,' we learn, 'is just the rhetoric of condescension.' Quite. 'You can't ask a historian to look into the future,' Orlando Figes announces, revealing an in-depth knowledge of Chinese fortune cookies. Raven explains that Marx 'isn't fashionable' for the 'obvious reasons that people got distracted by postmodernity and blamed him for Eastern Europe' when Tapehead thought the obvious reason was his beard. Aaronovitch bids us farewell with the summary, 'I think we're in for a pretty stormy century', as if he was doing the late-night weather forecast.

Bring back The Late Show, we say, or make **The Late Review** longer. At least viewers have an idea, or an opinion, of what they're talking about. Tapehead, for his part, simply keeps his counsel until he's heard what Tom

Paulin has to say, then just agrees with him entirely. Paulin is Tapehead's new guru and a kind of unnatural TV natural – in his element upstaging excellent regulars like Parsons, Greer and Suzanne Moore. (Newcomers make the mistake of just *giving their opinion*, without even attempting to be interesting or amusing.)

When his turn comes around, Paulin seems gleefully unaware of the camera or the presenter, but is staring away into space, with rapture, as if he is pondering whether he can see the Star of Bethlehem on the horizon. After a long pause, when he finally speaks, he seems to be morally troubled, desperately struggling, fumbling along for expression before suddenly hitting a note of fabulously forthright, brilliant clarity which can be inspiringly erudite or just utterly emotional. He will describe things as 'very fascinating' (Face/Off), 'very wonderful', or sometimes (if we're lucky) either 'fantastic' or 'disgraceful'.

When he likes something he seems enthralled by it, beaming with childlike wonderment. But when he doesn't, he is so morally appalled by the mediocrity, he just erupts with 'I couldn't believe it' like a kind of intellectual Victor Meldrew. Having dismissed Alan Bennett's writing as 'the most *dismal* clichés soldered together', Paulin then derails Alison Pearson's impassioned defence by quoting Bennett like a heckler barracking a comedian. '"He drove slowly to the gallery at dusk"!' he chortles with derision. Heroic.

November 29–December 5 1997

Big portions

Tapehead has a confession. It's not the pornography, it's the lunch. Channel 4's **Light Lunch** is, ho ho, consuming him. Channel 4's alternative to the dramatic, not to say devastating, world events on ITN's and BBC's lunchtime news, Light Lunch is so frothy, so light, it makes Richard and Judy look like Romeo and Juliet. It's strange stuff to be sure. Just look at the rousing battle cry they give each day: 'Let's Eat Lunch.' They're not joking either. That's pretty much all they *do* do.

Celebrity guests prepare lunch and are asked questions which they then answer with their mouths full. The studio audience aren't listening anyway because, as we can see, they're busy stuffing their faces too. Guests range from Sacha Distel to Terry Wogan's son and Michael Ball's banoffee pie. Kylie (who obviously did not touch a bite) was rather perky and Shane Ritchie's opinion that Robert Carrier's mashed potato 'tasted like semolina' was a revelation. Where else could you see Paul Whitehouse and celebrity chef Galloping Major Ron Ferguson on the same show?

Sue Perkins and Mel Giedroyc, the presenters, seem to wing most of it – like an end-of-term student revue – but are infectiously sassy, happy and natural enough to be strangely appealing. Like all programmes involving cookery, they worry themselves with no question more taxing than the mind-blowing TV pointlessness of asking, 'Does it taste good?' Answer: 'Mmmm. Yes, delicious'. At which point, presumably, a nation can rest easy.

Almost as much fun is to be had watching the genuinely erotic, strangely moving, nostalgic pornography on this week's **Storyville**. Ole Ege, we are informed, is 'the man who invented Danish pornography'. What a legacy. He started taking mucky photos as a teenager in the late fifties, progressing to erotic films and dirty movies. As his strange, toothy picture confirms, Ole (pronounced Ola not, sadly, Olé) 'wasn't exactly the type women would fall for, so I realised I had to find another way of getting their clothes off'. This usually involved plying them with vermouth and getting them to pose naked. (As methods go, let's face it, this one has never been bettered.) His early innocent flicks were six minutes long – 'which was a suitable duration'. One, 'which sold like hot cakes', shows a woman doing the Twist naked. Try it at home and see how much fun that is.

Ole's excuses for his, erm, premature perversity are certainly imaginative. He wanted, he insists, to 'improve his technique' (of photography) and satisfy his curiosity about 'the female shape, the way they moved, *their large eyes*'. As he would, no doubt, have to explain to officers of the law and customs, somehow this required photographing the women naked – all because of a fascination for 'their waists, buttocks, breasts, their small hands and (go on, have a guess) their ears'. (Good one, Ole.)

His first colour film, entitled A Fight In The Hay, had two girls, Gitte and Elise, frolicking in the hay taking each other's clothes off. 'Elise was a great girl,' he muses (not without reason). 'She wasn't good for much, but she thought it was fun.' Tapehead has to admit it does look like fun too.

Sadly, Ole's fascination with rather artistic erotica went wrong when it mutated into hardcore porn films. Initially reluctant, Ole ended up becoming fascinated by a woman known in the business as 'Bodil the Hog Woman' whose speciality was sex with animals. Watching clips of Bodil riding naked on an enormous horse (enormous in every sense), Ole sighs, 'She just lights up the screen with her special personality.' Because the sound failed, Ole ended up putting Beethoven's 'Pastoral Symphony' over the footage – a perfect expression of the essence of his personality. (How Beethoven would feel about this is not discussed.) Regrettably, he says, sounding surprised, the film drew the scorn of the tabloids and her neighbours who objected to her, er, horseplay. The porn industry, as he puts it, 'exploited her' and she eventually committed suicide.

By 1972, Ole started feeling guilty about filming the pain that modern porn required from his actresses, realising too late that hardcore porn is about violence, not sex. 'It undermines respect, the respect that is found in a loving relationship,' he says. 'It was,' the narrator says sadly with some understatement, 'no longer the connoisseurs' aesthetic product that Ole dreamed of in 1960s Denmark.'

Now 64, he has an Erotic Museum in Copenhagen. Whether this can really be as erotic as his strangely beautiful early work remains doubtful. Somebody should probably tell him.

December 6–12 1997

Atmosphere

When you're sick, so sad, you placed your face in the puddle of a lay-by waiting for a lorry to splash it. And when you are inside the infinite misery jumper, pulling it over and over your head with no hope of ending, 'cos it's replicating at the waistband and you never get out... Then E welcome. Then E off welcome. In Blue Jam.'

Thursday at midnight, and anyone who happened to have Radio 1 on in the background would have been forgiven for thinking they were finally going mad. Not only were there strange, disturbed voices talking a kind of hallucinogenic, nightmarish gibberish coming from the radio, but some of us were convinced the radio had turned into the twisted genius of Chris Morris and was talking to us – like an ambient relaxation-tape version of Brass Eye. Crack paranoia was never this bad.

But lo, it was true. It was called **Blue Jam** and it was good. And a heavy blue jam it was too. By the second programme, over a soothing, soft ambient shimmer and slamming doors, Morris welcomed us, intoning: 'When you monged so soft and blacked in cupboard. But other knuckles, knocky, tried to get in. All right? "Hello." While you lie still. Biting Hoover bags... (Musical crescendo). Then blink, emerge at last. And all people gone. Where now? You needy, so needy, like a *mimi mim*... Bending like a mad, angry-with-the-ground absurd man. Shoot him. Then E welcome. Ooh. Ah. Welcome. In Blue Jam.'

As Lloyd Bridges said in Airplane, 'It looks like we picked a hell of a week to give up drink/drugs/sniffing glue.' Seemingly required to play records to get on air at all, Morris favours the soft depressive disco of doomy electro-pop and people like Bjork, Dead Can Dance and DJ Shadow. 'In Heaven Everything Is Fine' from Eraserhead didn't really help, but 'Oh Lori' by the Alessi Brothers was the clincher. Over and around the music, Morris provides Newsbeat-style newsflashes and vox pops, long, depressed sketches and rambling Joycean nonsense: 'You tongue-burst and mouth-juice run gall-bladder hotter.' 'When you're sick so sad you cry/And in crying, cry a whole leopard from your eye...'

A Japanese dream about Bernie Taupin confirms that, played backwards, the new version of 'Candle In The Wind' contains 'a profane message', namely 'Jesus and your bush. That's no titchy marrow.' The soft, soothing music makes it sound like part of a therapeutic hospital programme he's been undergoing and, indeed, friends of his listening must be phoning each other with concern that he has finally flipped.

Most of the 'sketches' are about doctors, hospitals, therapy, babies, drugs (chasing the dragon, a week's supply of codeine, blowbacks) and operations. 'My name is Michael Palmer,' a man announces. 'I am 42 years old and I am an optician. I've always felt I am a baby, trapped in the body of a man. And about six months ago I had a transplant operation to give me the penis and testicles of a baby. I'll show you. There's the tiny white penis.' Architect Suki Previn says she always felt she looks like she's got the body of a woman, 'but inside there's the body of a woman with the genitals of a duck'.

Morris's mini-short stories are mostly parodies about art installations and arch intellectualism, but usually sound like nightmarish extracts of Burroughs and Beckett cut up with Mervyn Peake. 'Any minute now, the blowflies will hatch. They're breeding in a scrap of kidney near my left foot. I cannot bend down or move from side to side in here. And must remain standing with my face pressed to the thick glass.' You can't really remove the disturbing thought that, forlornly, Morris is, for all his parodic intent, writing about how he feels. 'My eyes are watering. There's a lot of dust in the air. I can't see too well anyway 'cos I pawned my corneas two days ago to buy some shoes... Before she ran away, my wife said this would happen. She even got the date right.'

He's obviously been going to the doctor a lot. (Though probably not enough.) Chris Morris, you can only conclude, is in the infinite misery jumper and we, you can't help thinking, are in there with him. The next and probably last programme is on Thursday. Simultaneous drug-use is not advised. Get well soon, Chris.

December 13–19 1997

Swinging both ways

Sex and violence, they just won't leave us alone. They hound us so hard, some days it's hard not to take it personally. It comes to something when **The Natural World** can't even make a film about three groups of cute and cuddly monkeys without turning it into a blood bath. In the Santa Rosa forest in Costa Rica, the question is this (as the question so often is): who is Top Monkey?

The black-mantled howlers certainly make unlikely candidates, sleeping seven hours a day and all night (a bit like Tapehead), with their glum, down-turned mouths making them look like furry versions of Tony Hancock (ditto). 'Completely vegetarian and usually tranquil,' the narrator whispers, as if she was auditioning for the snooker or was up in the trees with them, 'they are often said to be stupid and dull.' They speak very highly of you too.

The black-handed red spider monkeys swing around like a gang of invading raiders who've seen too many pirate movies while the white-faced capuchins are described as 'versatile and intelligent, bright, restless, intensely social' as if we were talking about Geminis.

After some cute mutual grooming and inter-gang horseplay, the second half is pure Tarantino. Things kick off on one occasion because the howlers start barking when the wind gets up. (And they say howlers are stupid.) One monkey ends up with an injured, infected arm dangling by his side, his swinging days over. In a classic ambush, straight out of The Warriors, the females lovingly attend to him while the young attackers, their faces wild and bloodied, gang up to finish him off.

The sex comes from the subtle way that the female 'signals to the male that she would like him to approach her'. She does this by putting her tongue out and waggling it lewdly up and down in his direction, a scene reminiscent of the sort of movies featured in **Louis Theroux's Weird Weekends**, in which Louis tries to get a part in a porn movie. 'There are fewer working male performers in this industry than there are astronauts on this planet,' says the director of Spasm 3 and Anal Witness 4. The problem, apparently, is 'doing it on cue with a woman that you may not be attracted to' – the sort of problem anyone who's been out in London on a Friday night has probably got used to by now. The pay is $250 per sex scene, as long as you come up with 'the money shot'. If you don't, they bring in a 'stunt cock – to pop for you' ($75). On consideration, this might be the better job.

Louis auditions for the makers of movies such as Sodomy 7 (superior to either 6 or 8), Girls On Top ('probably for the feminist market') and Beefeaters (which probably isn't). He ends up working with Troy Halston, a 'straight' gay porn star. Troy smugly points out that while Louis is scraping by working for the Beeb, he has just made $1,500 in four hours. His pride is only slightly wounded when Louis retorts sweetly that he did it by sucking men's dicks for four hours.

All in all, this show will set some men's view of porno back decades, especially the Northampton girl who says her motivation for getting into it was nymphomania. 'Just want sex. Can't help it.' Even when several of his co-stars fail to show up for work, J. J. Michaels, who makes four movies a week, says having unprotected sex never worries him for the simple reason (and it doesn't get more simple than this) that he doesn't think about it. If he thought about it, he explains excitedly, he'd only end up going home and worrying all night. At least that old chestnut about people like J. J. only doing porn to pay their way through college has finally shot its bolt.

At Club Marilyn in Tokyo the Shinjuku Boys in **Under The Sun** are not quite gigolos, do not quite have sex and are in fact not quite boys at all, using chest-binders, hormones and rockabilly hairdos to captivate admirers. 'He is a woman who likes women,' says one of the girls' lovers. 'I am a man who likes men. So we understand each other.' Confused? The Japanese narrator doesn't help, nor does the rather thin nature of her insights. 'Gaish talks tough,' we learn. 'He is the tough-talking type.'

The theme (in the end) is neutral sexuality, jealousy and love between two women wishing one of them was male, love with no hope of marriage or children, or, ultimately, happiness.

January 24–30 1998

Ask me, ask me, ask me

Why are we here? What happens after death? And what does God mean? Don't panic. Tapehead has not become the Guide's equivalent of an early-Saturday-morning-ring-on-the-doorbell by the Jehovahs. In fact, the days of such spiritual, philosophical debate are over thanks to **The Big Question**, where the big news of the week is that Jeremy Irons has the answers. What is God? 'God is in us. God is the love in us. God is all the good in us. We are God.'

There, that's cleared that up. Jeremy's on such a roll, knocking off the questions that have tormented mankind for centuries, that by the time he gets to whether God does exist, he just drawls, 'I don't think his presence can be questioned if you really look.' As for life after death: 'We remain behind in the spirits of those we have rubbed up against in our lives' – a rather unfortunate forecast in the light of his role as the pervert in Lolita.

Still, you can't help thinking that when he says, 'The Church of England is too intellectual for me' that Jeremy is closer to the truth than he realises. Not that this stops him from pontificating about abortion and adultery and acknowledging that his stable home life allows him to 'go off and be magnificent in movies and in plays'. Raised as a 'public-school Anglican' (a fairly new religion if Tapehead isn't very much mistaken), he married an Irish Catholic. Although he has not converted, he admires the Catholic Church's morality and regularly takes Communion, presumably just because he likes the biscuits. The *really* Big Question ('Why are you so pompous?') remains unanswered.

On **Parkinson**, the great uncle of interviewers tackles the tricky subject of Young People Today, with his guests Ewan McGregor (30) and Robbie Williams (37). Parky asks Robbie how his 'battle against drugs' affected his memories of the Great Geoffrey Boycott and gets young Ewan to entertain us with anecdotes of growing up in Scotland during the heyday of the Great Billy Connolly and tell us about the background of his promising new film, Star Wars.

Meanwhile in **Prostitute**, Esther Rantzen's rampant obsession with prostitution continues unchallenged. Esther interviews Jose, pronounced 'Josie' not (unfortunately) like a Mexican waiter, a 60-year-old dominatrix with (according to the BBC) 'a career spanning 30 years' as if we were talking about Vanessa Redgrave. As charm or charisma goes, Jose is no Cynthia Payne. If Thora Hird had been cast to play the modern-day Myra Hindley, she would look like Jose with Dennis Taylor glasses, a short butch haircut and a dinner lady's face.

After so many BBC documentaries, you wouldn't have thought there was anyone left who could wonder how or why women end up in prostitution or what it's all about. Esther's ridiculous questions ('Are your clients seedy men in raincoats?') show there is. We get a tired examination of Jose's 'tools' – the manacles, whips and leather paddles – as if a dominatrix would have anything else. A full-sized baby outfit – complete with nappy, baby bottle and frilly knickers – is for 'Babykins' (oh dear). Despite having lived her life as a mother, wife, prostitute and lesbian, Jose still manages to come over as not only everyday but just plain dull, a tribute to Esther's common touch.

As interviewers go, Esther is not exactly Sigmund Freud. When Jose was young, her mum would punish her – ergo, she now punishes others. When she was young, Jose's mum would shout at her – she now shouts abuse at men. 'So your mother taught you,' Esther says, spelling it out for viewers at the back. 'What would your mum think of it?' she asks – rather a rhetorical question to ask a prostitute at the best of times. 'She'd try to batter me,' Jose says as the interview comes to an end. 'But I'm in charge now.' Her closing smile is presumably meant to suggest that this, this *life*, is some sort of victory, as if she was not paying a price for what she does every day, which of course she is.

From Prostitute, we move seamlessly to Kate Moss, in a sweet, brief interview on **Inside Story**'s look at models. 'Kate,' the first word of the programme whispers, 'Obsession' – two things Tapehead knows a lot about. The sulky, sneery mouth, the fabulous bags under the vulpine eyes, their darting, alien gaze... Mossy, you fabulous fox, Tapehead's here to make one thing clear. Stop ringing me. It's over.

February 7–13 1998

Zip it

'**D**o you *know* him?' one Calvin Klein stud asks another, expertly sucking in his cheeks for extra bitchiness. 'Who?' pouts the other, narrowing his eyes. 'Versace – the king of fashion.' 'His clothes are shit.' 'You don't like him?' 'I hate him.' 'You hate him?' 'I think he's shit.' At first glance, the scene (from the first TV movie about the murder of Gianni Versace) seems like a queer send-up of camp, a mocking rehearsal. But, as **Modern Times**' set report confirms, this is an actual take, the real thing: a Menahem Golan special.

Low-budget film producer/director extraordinaire Golan – a legendary, mad maverick of tat – has made over 200 movies, but regards the Versace murder project as 'one of my most important films'. He works at breakneck pace and is prone to shouting, 'The whole thing should be Speedy Gonzalez!' 'Nobody goes home,' he rants as night descends. 'Never in my movies.'

In a stroke of genuine inspiration, he has cast the awesome Euro-tack God Franco Nero to play 'Gee-arnie' as they call him and Calvin Klein-model and Andrew Cunanan-lookalike Shane Perdue as his killer. 'Naked again,' Perdue sighs, as we see his shiny white backside walking into the sea for no reason. Still, you've got to admire the way Golan insists there is 'no point' in asking Versace's estate for their cooperation because 'he wants to respect their privacy' and then re-creates his murder on their doorstep.

He has written the script himself from press cuttings and FBI press releases and wants his account to be as 'authentic as possible', even though it is so soon after the murder that nobody really knows what's happened yet. Then, when Warner Bros describe his movie as 'cheap and cheesy', he immediately considers suing. Such mad schemes and cheap dreams have their ups and downs. On the plus side, they can shoot in Cunanan's $30-a-night motel room and the actual SWAT team that took Cunanan out have volunteered to be in the movie re-creating the houseboat attack for free. Then again, the museum he is using to pass for Versace's house turns out to be directly under the flight path to Miami International Airport. Such are the trials and tribulations of a master at work.

Versace is one of the stars of **Undressed**. 'Our work is to make people look beautiful,' he says, echoing Irving Penn's view. 'We are selling dreams, not clothes.' What's good about Undressed is that it begins to explain the serious side-effects of fashion, the power it casts, the love and labour it demands, worse than any love. (Hence, fashion victims.) The themes (Fantasy/Sex/Rebellion/Power) obviously overlap, but the history is grippingly illuminating. And at least (at last) we get a real look at the fabulous glamour and drama of the shows, the models – like hunted felines or thoroughbreds in the paddock before a race – parading for their patrons who not only want to be them but want to kill them too.

One of the stars is the choreographer explaining to one model the difference between a model's walk and a mortal's. 'Ordinary walking won't do,' he says, 'unless it's a hunchback show and they want hunchback models'. (Common, in other words.) When model Chrystelle walks, with every stride the hands hanging on her hip-bones move about a foot.

There are too many French fashion *demi-mondaines* for British screens: waffle dressed up as rich, sexy philosophy but which might as well be David Ginola (just because they're French), until McQueen comes stomping along in his own inimitable way. 'Why do women always 'ave to look like fairies?' he spits. He reckons 'women get a raw deal out of fashion', which is a bit like saying men get a raw deal out of football. Which, as any football fan knows, they do.

An example is given on **Premier Passions**' study of the suffering of Sunderland's fans and management. Peter Reid sails through the managerial clichés from 'If you don't stick the ball in the net when you're at this level, you get beat' to confidence-boosting half-time team talks like 'Fookin' men against fookin' boys, all over the fookin' park, fookin' weak as piss.' The fans are so passionate that when the new stadium goes up, bricks with their name on go for £25. And they say money's tight up there. Watch out for the groundsman who bears an uncanny resemblance to the Geordie handyman in I'm Alan Partridge and the Number One Fan with one ear bitten off who sums up how all football fans feel as their players come running out on to the pitch: 'Howay, ya bastards.'

February 21–27 1998

New York stories

No wonder **The Jerry Springer Show** has scandalised half of America. There isn't a great deal of competition. Saturday Night Live is rank. Only the gag that Clinton was changing his campaign slogan from 'The President For The New Millennium' to 'Kiss It Bitch' raised even a chuckle. But then if you can't satirise the Prez, you're in the wrong game.

Letterman and Leno are still getting by making jokes about O. J.; Dave has gone in for some disastrous old-age-pensioner's glasses, seemingly left over from The Waltons; and by the time the audience has finished whooping every time he or any of his guests are about to open their mouths, he hardly has to bother with anything more arduous or humorous than those deadly Top Ten lists that get more laboured the higher they go. The best

Tonight With Jay Leno could come up with was a sketch interviewing Jacko's new baby and the gag that not only was Jacko absent for the births, he wasn't at the conception either. 'Did he bring any of his favourite toys in?' Leno asked the 'baby'. 'No, Macaulay Culkin wasn't available.'

The good thing about **Howard Stern**'s show on the wonderful E! channel is that if you watch it long enough, something will actually shock you. The first two shows of the week (televised transmissions of his morning radio show) featured tired TFI Friday rubbish like 'guess the virgin' phone-ins and Paul McKenna hypnotising Stern's team into believing they had lost their penises.

By midweek though, Stern was warming up nicely, probably as news of his new CBS deal broke. At a live press conference, a lesbian news reporter, who had obviously crossed swords with Stern before, made the mistake of confirming that she and her lover had become parents. 'Did you use one of those turkey basters to impregnate her?' Stern snapped without missing a beat. 'Lesbians equal ratings,' he reassured her, to placate her accusations of prejudice, promising to have her on his new show – if her cup-size met the necessary criteria. The outrage peaked with the appearance of the Guinness Books of Records' tallest man in the world (seven foot four, 300 pounds), a poor guy whose body was oddly distorted, buckling under the sheer size he had to carry round. 'What condom do you use?' Stern asked him straight away. 'Do you double up?'

Then he moved on to bowel movements (not the irritable kind). 'Is it unusually large?' he wondered, eagerly. 'Does it fill the whole bowl? Do you pile it up above the water line?' The world's tallest man took it in his (enormous) stride, but remained pretty much speechless as Stern went over his penis-size, farting and difficulties masturbating. 'All you need,' he concluded sympathetically, 'is to meet a seven foot four chick somewhere.'

MTV still courts controversy, in a pathetically half-hearted, PC-approved way – fussily covering up all those Nike signs in rap videos and beeping out all the 'ho's' and 'bitches'. Not content with offering us those terrible real-life sitcoms more nauseating than Friends, now, once a week, America has **True Life**, launching with 'Fatal Dose' – a look at heroin problems in Piano, Texas that have resulted in 17 kids OD-ing. 'It is in no way gratuitous,' affirmed an MTV producer in the phone-in debate that followed.

Their gorgeous reporter drove around Piano with Joe-Six-Pack teenagers like Allen and Eric as they went to cop nine caps of cheeba and four of cocaine to get them through the afternoon. The dealers' faces, as their clients rolled up to score with an MTV film crew in tow, remained disappointingly off camera. A shaky handheld camera followed them into a grim, grimy bathroom to shoot up as the long blonde reporter watched on eagerly, the first people to shoot up on MTV – a peculiarly American kind of fame.

To compensate, of course, they dressed it up as a warning to us all and talked to the poor parents. 'We found out Matt was using,' remembered Matt's distraught Mom, 'because Matt told us he was using.' But Piano's cheeba (black-tar heroin cut with antihistamine) was too strong – particularly when the rehab his parents sent him to reduced his tolerance. The pay-off line told us '23 people were arrested in Piano for dealing' – presumably just as the MTV crew were leaving town, having salved their conscience by turning everyone in.

Amazingly, this lesson in how to/how not to shoot heroin was sponsored by Old Navy cargo shorts and by Sony, 'making things for every kind of imagination'. Every kind, presumably, except the kind that needs heroin.

April 25–May 1 1998

Our Lindsey

Apart from romance, it's worth noting that the favourite mainstay of our soap operas is (significantly) illness – not least because, with these two elements in tow, everybody's suffering.

In **Brookside**, the exploding parade has left the cast in tatters. On Tuesday, the screaming fireman has his spine 're-flexed', Kylie is (wisely) pretending to be in a coma and, strangely untraumatised by the gruelling memory of having his legs chopped off, Sinbad is going back to his window round, despite being on crutches. Peter, meanwhile, is seemingly suffering from amnesia. Either that or he has come back from Zimbabwe with some sort of debilitating tropical disease – the sort that makes Lindsey look like an attractive proposition.

There are several reasons why Tapehead must remain wary of saying what he thinks about Lindsey. (He doesn't want her to turn ugly on him.) After all, the right-hander she landed on Peter's Posh Spice lookalike at the party would have floored Naseem Hamed, and the way she went for Tin-Ed by the hospital drinks machine, Tapehead swears she was practically rabid. The memory of her looking for Kylie, charging around the parade like a bull on a Spanish public holiday, squealing like a pig about to be barbecued, keeps Tapehead awake at night more regularly than the memory of her version of 'It's In His Kiss' or the outfit she nearly managed to get into in the Brookside Christmas video.

Obviously the whole traumatic coma experience has left its mark. (The sight of Lindsey without make-up has left us all emotionally scarred.) 'The doctor says he's 100 per cent sure there's no damage to the brain,' she reassures Peter. 'So that's definite?' Peter reiterates later. 'Absolutely no brain damage.' (Tapehead has his doubts too – but shouldn't they be worrying about *Kylie*?) Lindsey is left comforting herself with the thought that it was her tender screeching at Peter that woke Little Kyles from the coma (proof that her nagging would wake the dead once she gets going). This loving breakthrough had become her *raison d'être* for getting back together with Peter. 'It was like fate!' she simpers to Jackie. 'We were bickering together like a proper couple!' (And they say romance is dead.)

Watching her thinking about snaring Peter again is a bit like watching one of those hopeless male spiders about to get his head bitten off by the female after mating. (The way she grins at him and licks her lips when they're about to go for a wing-ding is more frightening than Seven.) Even though she doesn't love him, Lindsey has decided 'Kylie needs a proper Dad' – namely Peter (a man who, in Chris Morris's immortal phrase, is clearly as gay as a window – hence the attraction of a gruesome old drag act like Our Lindsey's). Elsewhere, Mad Marcus (the David Icke/Rasputin of The Close) is on the loose. Mick is having a period party for Gemma. And lovely Ron Dixon celebrates the fact that his rug remained unshaken by the explosion by stitching up Sinbad.

Love and illness also sway in the decidedly poorly **EastEnders**. A clearly disease-ridden place the East End, what with Mark Fowler's HIV, Smiley Susan's Multiple Sclerosis, Bianca's baby's meningitis and now an outbreak of Hepatitis B, not to mention the almost endless bouts of alcoholism and depression. Mark and 'Roof', Grant and Tiff, Phil and Annie, Maffew and Sarah… the whole lot of them are, somehow, more miserable than ever. (It looks like Nigel, Grant and Kaff got out while the going was good.)

This week, Lenny suffers 'a health scare' (a bad attack of acting) and Roof goes for an HIV test – 'at least me and Mark have more in common!'

she beams, looking on the bright side. Along with Peter the hairdresser, EastEnders' gay couple are having a rough time of it too, and not even with each other. Tony has gone back to being heterosexual while Simon's new man doesn't want to move in with him on the grounds that 'I want to see other people'. 'Other men you mean?' Simon says, sharp as a razor.

The toll is high in **Coronation Street** too. Another baby has bitten the dust, Zoe is about to be sectioned and Jim MacDonald is still in a coma, with intravenous Guinness and Jameson chasers the only thing keeping him going. The state of the NHS these days. They could at least have taken his parka off.

May 2–8 1998

Love and hate

It's all very well to let lifelong Man City fan Colin Schindler maintain that **Manchester United Ruined My Life**, but he doesn't know the half of it. Hating Man United is a Man United fan's prerogative. The decision to support Man United (based entirely on George Best's dashing good looks) ruined Tapehead's childhood. A combination of Gary Birtles, Bobby Stokes and Big Fat Ron ensured that for the best part of 15 years, they won precisely nothing. More recently, Alex Ferguson's decision to persist with Brian McClair rather than buy a real midfielder helped lose them the league – leaving the money to pile up for the PLC.

Still, Schindler and the rest of the nation can rejoice that Arsenal's Franco-Dutch alliance have won out over United's home-grown youngsters. Schindler, like Hunter Davies's J'Accuse Man United, brazenly panders to the nation's hatred, predictably chucking in all the so-called 'issues' like Old Trafford's marketing, rather than wondering why his own club hasn't managed it as well as United has. Why so many fans of other clubs care so much about United fans being ripped off or whether they really come from Manchester is anyone's guess (55,000 fans on Boxing Day suggests they probably do still come from Manchester). On this evidence it seems that forlorn old City fans are becoming as sentimental and lachrymose as those soppy old Scousers.

Two things to hate almost as much as losing the league are Chris Evans and golf, making **Tee Time** a pretty lethal combination. A 'fascinating new six part series', according to Channel 4. An excuse for Chris Evans to show off, flying around the world having golf lessons, according to Tapehead. Golf is, frankly, a girls' game, played by people with too much time or money and nothing better to do. The fact remains there are still no George Bests of golf. Golf cannot be played coolly. This is because of things like the way golf carts make you look senile or because anyone doing their practice swing (and pretending it has anything whatsoever to do with the subsequent shot) looks like a berk, as Evans helpfully demonstrates.

Then there's all that male-bonding bollocks about 'a nice little par three' and shots that 'call for a nice seven iron'. Anyway, Evans goes to Florida to get a free golf lesson. We see him laughing a lot (that silly giggle which reminds you he is just a small boy with no actual talent). But he seems to think seeing him having a great time is the same thing as the viewers having a great time, so he never even attempts to do or say anything entertaining.

Hating Jeffrey Archer is of course even more *de rigueur* than hating Evans or Man United, but even Tapehead is not so contrary that he's going to pretend **Omnibus**'s profile of Archer is in any way even remotely tolerable. People talk about Archer's 'extraordinary' life being worthy of a novel but everyone's life is extraordinary in one way or another, and Archer's is only really fit for a novel as banal and simplistic as one of his own.

The only good thing about Jeffrey Archer is he is so hopeless at covering up how odious, self-satisfied, supercilious and nauseatingly pompous he is. Archer's true awfulness has yet to really dawn on the ever fragrant Mary Archer, though she remembers the time of the regrettable prostitute at Waterloo Station incident, describing it as 'an absurd tara-diddle'. 'And that's exactly what it was,' she says now, defiantly. And who can argue?

As for Archer's knack for a story, he insists earnestly, 'It's a myth to think smoking a cigarette or drinking a whisky in Hampstead will produce one of the great world novels.' (Thank God he's cleared that up for us.) No, when it comes to the ability to come up with stories as good as his own – 'that's the God-given gift'. Alternatively, there's always plagiarism, most notably that short story in *A Twist In The Tale* in which it turns out the narrator is a cat. (God came up a little short with that one.)

This was remarkably similar to the winner of an amateur short story competition which Archer had coincidentally adjudicated. 'I did my own version of it,' he grins, challenging us to 'find two words together that are the same as hers' and insisting it was not plagiarism because 'plagiarism is when you write out line after line after line'. Well, no, it isn't, actually. Plagiarism, according to Tapehead's *Oxford English Dictionary* is to appropriate (ideas or passages) from another work or author.

Still, Omnibus confirms we can sleep easy, safe in the knowledge that Jeffrey Archer has as much chance of becoming Mayor of London as, well, Alex Ferguson.

May 9–15 1998

Hiding the salami

Another earth-shattering event, so vital to our lives it can only be dealt with delicately and under threat of a BBC embargo: the **Junior Masterchef Final** is with us, at last. Georgina (aged 13), Serena (11), Emily (14) battling it out and remarkable, resourceful little bastards, er, beauties, they are. After all, most kids given £10 to spend on an evening's nutritional diversion would get a couple of £5 bags of smack heroin and a tube of Uhu.

Not these! Georgina knocks up smoked haddock in cream and lemon sauce, savoy cabbage colcannon and blueberry and mango tart with strawberry sauce, while Serena tempts us with pheasant breast in a cream and brandy sauce, apple and celeriac purée, mixed winter salad and blackcurrant mousse with langue de chat biscuits. Only the third candidate, Geordie-girl Emily, has gone for something slightly less mature – namely fishfingers on toast ('burnt edges with shitloads of marmite'), alphabet spaghetti on the side and a McDonald's apple pie and custard. If nothing else, it shows that the government is right to cut down on unemployment benefits if we can all live off pheasant breast and langue de chat biscuits for less than a tenner.

The three girls are so gormless and desperate for people to like them that they've obviously spent most of their lives (rightly) locked away in the kitchen. Sweet-talking French superchef Raymond Blanc is particularly taken with Serena's pheasant breasts, swooping for *une* kiss when Prue Leith makes do with shaking hands. As always, a discussion on the role of modern feminism ensues and Prue comes up with the view that 'through the centuries, women have learnt to be obedient' – which goes to show what she knows. 'I can be very boring on this subject,' says Leith, before going on to prove it.

Raymond, meanwhile, despairs of the collapse of family life and commends cuisine as its saviour. 'The table is a natural medium to 'ave ze fun, to laugh, to celebrate, to be angry, to play ze footsie under ze table. We are losing ze baseek knowledge of dialogue, of communication, and from communication you get love.' The French, eh? What are they like? But then that's Junior Masterchef for you – food, philosophy and fucking. A bit like Close Relations, really. First, a word about **The Italian Kitchen** – the word 'useless' being the most obvious one.

It is presented by the River Café's Ruth Rogers and Rose Gray – natural candidates for such a show, notwithstanding the fact that they are not Italian and have all the charisma of a plastic spatula. More wooden than a small forest in Tuscany in fact. At least it should be easier to get a table there (though not possibly for Tapehead) once customers have had to listen to their thin, querulous commentaries and seen the bug-eyed Rogers and goggle-eyed Grey in, erm, action. Rose is so coy and self-conscious, she spends most of the time looking up at the ceiling as if she's worried it's leaking. 'Everybody loves and cooks pasta in Italy,' says Ruth, reading (if you can call it that) from the autocue. 'And so do. We. Here! At the River? Café!' At least if they were Italian, you could tell them to fuck off back to Italy. Fuck off back to Hammersmith anyway.

They are all at it in **Close Relations** – worse than The Lakes or anything with Amanda Ooms in it, though the revival of the word 'bonking' is a bit of a let-down considering that writer Deborah Moggach is meant to be so shocking and such a sexual expert. (What they're doing in this series looks unmistakably to Tapehead like 'fucking'.) It would be even better if *any* of the illicit relationships were even remotely realistic and if billing it as 'A Bouquet Of Barbed Wire For The Nineties' didn't only make you pine for the original, but still. In fact, it's a sort of nineties version of Rock Follies, only it's the women's turn to be on top, though none of them are as nasty as Gavin and Frank Finlay. It's funny how you knew sex-maniac Amanda Redman would dump her lover as soon as he lost his job.

Anyway, Maddy has been cured of men, Keith Barren has been cured of racism and lesbians in Land Rovers are rampaging across the nation like nineties medallion men, leaping into bed with anyone that tries to stop them. Sadly, the sexiest person in it (Sheila Hancock) is pretty much the only one who hasn't got laid so far – but then, it's only Episode Three. 'It's amazing a marriage can last 20 years, let alone 40,' says Sheila's son-in-law.

True, especially in this series. The rate they're breaking up, 20 minutes would be pretty good going. 'Wild Is The Wind' is right.

May 30–June 5 1998

Afters

After weeks of waiting, debating and anticipating, the nation's favourite recreational obsession finally launches into full frenzy. Yes, Gardeners World Live is with us. The rest of the schedule has been taken over with tennis, cricket and something called 'the World Cup'. It starts on Wednesday with a goalless draw between Brazil and Scotland (Tapehead has a preview tape), building up to that clash of the Titans: Cameroon vs Austria.

As if this wasn't enough, virtually every other programme has a football angle too – even Panorama (World Cup corruption). This week's Jazz Heroes features Ella Fitzgerald singing a selection of football theme tunes through the ages and after the controversy over the programme challenging the guilt of mass-murderer Jeremy Bamber, Clear My Name tackles the taxing task of absolving the footballing reputation of Brian McClair. In **Euroballs 98**, top-heavy/topless model Lolo Ferrari demonstrates her lung power by taking on World Cup hero Martin Peters at blow football – a one-sided contest if ever there was one.

Thank God, then, for **The Italian Kitchen** which, it transpires, is not a programme about how to cook Italian cuisine at all but is actually about two novices trying to learn how to present a TV cookery show. (No wonder the theme music takes off Mission Impossible.) Ruth Rogers and Rose Gray's private contest to be the worst presenter in TV cookery rages on.

Rose's latest tactics include her beguiling, permanent smile, even while she's talking, and suddenly SHOUTING in the middle of her sentences ('Push in a piece of SCALLOP') as if she's developed some sort of culinary Tourette's Syndrome. At least this livens up the otherwise dreary monotone of her totally hapless autocue-reading. 'To prepare the fish,' she instructs us, smiling, 'I'm going to. Put? Some SEA SALT! A really strong gutsy. Fish!' As you watch her, sweetly smiling in her white coat, carefully and with almost childlike concentration, burying a turbot in an enormous mound of sea salt, Rose looks for all the world like a mental patient under-

133

going some sort of recreational therapy.

To counteract Ruth's whiny, dry American accent, Rose has started advising us that what 'we wanna use' is 'plenny of sea salt' and 'beaudiful red tomaddoes'. *The New Yorker* magazine thinks the River Café makes the best Italian food in the world (it's not even the best Italian food in Hammersmith, let alone Italy) but still can't make words like 'mezza-luna' or 'Luciano' sound even vaguely Italian. Ruth's pronunciation of 'Piombino' and even 'Pisa' can only be deliberately hopeless, though to be fair, her voice is so horrible she can make even a word like 'fillet' sound withering. In the end, Ruth wins Round Two hands down for the sheer dreariness of her speech about 'Saline water round the Malvern estuaries' which has the droning monotone of a 12-year-old girl forced to read something out at school Speech Day.

Elsewhere, the **Close Relations** are getting closer, leaping into bed with each other and converting to lesbianism as if there was no tomorrow. The only character not getting laid is the pet pony (though there is next week) now that, as predicted by Tapehead, Sheila Hancock has joined in the debauchery. 'What a muddle, isn't it? I'm sick of lies,' she sighs – evidently in the wrong series. The moral of the series seems to be that lies are the only thing keeping most relationships going. The truth is hell. The rawer the truth, the heller it gets.

The other moral seems to be: we are all lesbians under the skin (Tapehead certainly is) with sex-maniac Amanda Redman poised to join in with sister Maddy (played with impressive ease by Coventry manager Gordon Strachan). To liven things up, a randy, foxy foreigner (from Holland) joins what must be the most fucked-up family since the Mansons, dispensing wisdom about 'experiencing the childbird' (childbirth?) and 'you being the gassed' (guest?). There's sex in graveyards, loads of drugs and all the mistresses getting in touch with their lovers' other halves. Marvellous.

Speaking of dirty macs, after 10 years we bid farewell to the most famous mac in television since Columbo as the improbably named Tosh Lines makes his final appearance in **The Bill**. Ironically, the storyline features a policeman deciding to quit his job only to die with his mistress. The conspiracy theory starts here.

Tapehead is still reeling from the revelation that Tosh's real name was Alfred.

June 6–12 1998

Hobby-horses

This week, we return again to that age-old question – the one that has taxed great sages throughout the ages besides football: what does life have to offer?

The answer, of course, is nothing. Just football and sex (preferably together). As this week's TV confirms, the other leisurely pleasures we have invented just do not compare: fishing, cooking, gardening, painting. Tapehead's heard of them, and now he's seen them in, erm, action. Tragically, final tapes of Hannah Gordon's **Watercolour Challenge** have been delayed. (They are waiting for the paint to dry.) Suffice to say, Tapehead will meet the challenge and is metaphorically sharpening his pencil as we speak.

Screaming Reels confirms Tapehead's long-held belief that fishing is the smack heroin of leisure activities – the sporting equivalent of nodding out (only with water). As for **Real Gardens**, the programme's novelty is the constant monitoring of how certain gardens are progressing. It is literally like watching the grass grow. Gardening shows are basically the outdoor version of cookery programmes. The problem with watching the experts show us how it's done is clear: they can do it and we can't. At least with cookery we can buy the same ingredients, but no two gardens are the same, so all their best advice is wasted. Most of it is just rambling. 'It's all about plants that are *comfortable* in their environment, isn't it?' As for iris *innominata*: 'They are such fun. They are a lovely plant.' Such fun indeed. 'What's pigeon manure like?' a presenter asked one gardener. 'Very smelly.' No shit.

Admittedly, there is something gratifying about watching them toiling away, working up a sweat, then surveying the acres of half-formed lawns, borders and flowerbeds and saying things like, 'We're getting there, aren't we?' To which we can only say: yes, you are.

The nation's obsession with cookery shows has surely reached some sort of nadir with the BBC's **Let Them Eat Crisps**, and with only three classes to go in the River Café's course in Learning How To Present A TV Cookery Show (**The Italian Kitchen**), you have to wonder whether they can ever get there. Rose's Andy Warhol hairdo is growing alarmingly out of control and her autocue-reading continues to sound like some sort of abstract beatnik poetry. 'I don't want to drown the taste of the ASPARA-GUS!' For her part, Ruth continues her quest not only to plunder Italian villages for their recipes but to massacre their lovely language into the bargain. It takes real skill to fuck up the pronunciation of *antipasto*, especially when you've spent so much time in Italy cooking Italian food, but this much at least Ruth has mastered. Her *bruschetta* with *fagioli* is quite revolting. By the time we see Rose 'sifting through the beans for any broken beans, bits of skin or possibly the odd stain' you have to wonder what on earth she's trying to tell us.

Compared to The Italian Kitchen, Satanism seems pretty harmless. Though we may be prevented from seeing The Exorcist on video, **The Fear Of God: 25 Years Of The Exorcist** has clips, screen tests and scenes that didn't make it. The most noteworthy of these is the notorious Spider Walk sequence, which looks more like the French and Saunders version. Director and madman/maverick William Friedkin still maintains, 'It's a film about people who live up the street; about a real street in a real town with real people living in it' – which shows you what sort of (Los Angeles) street he lives in. We learn how it was all done, including the vomiting scene – using hot pea soup (from the River Café). It turns out the scariest, most demonic of Linda Blair's voices was meticulously created in post-production using a lesser known actress who insisted on method-acting. 'I should swallow raw eggs,' she told an alarmed Friedkin. 'I should smoke cigarettes constantly. And you gotta give me some booze, which is gonna make me nuts. I'm getting off the wagon to do this, so I want my priest around to counsel me.' Almost exactly the same words Tapehead says to his editor every week.

Finally, the end of **Close Relations**. More fun than a naked game of Twister (and not that dissimilar), the moral of the series is we fuck around and then we die. As good a hobby as any.

June 13–19 1998

Unprofessional armpits

Female revenge for the World Cup gains apace. Besides their own feminist history, *Big Women* (or Big Fat Women as Tapehead calls it), programmes about cooking, dresses and even ironing proliferate.

As far as **Why Men Don't Iron** is concerned, Tapehead could have saved Channel 4 the trouble. It's because they *don't want to*. And they can get women to do it for them. 'Ironing is one thing women are better at,' one man explains. 'They can manoeuvre the iron in a good way' – the type of comment that shows you how far male ironing technique has to go.

Kevin is about as tidy and able at housework as men get, having learnt to cook, clean, sew and iron in the air force. Kevin insists he 'could keep the house spotless, as long as nobody came into it'. 'When you bring children in,' he complains, 'they start to mess up all the work you've done!' Poor lamb. Brain scans and neurochemistry analyse 'how men and women's brains are organised' and come to the conclusion that 'the human female is built for this job'. (Amen.)

A group of male guinea pigs are given 10 minutes and challenged to wash up, iron a shirt, pack a briefcase and make toast, scrambled eggs and coffee. (It's amazing what scientists can train guinea pigs to do.) Only one man manages it. The last, a London taxi-driver, blows it when he stops cooking to shout abuse at a cyclist driving past his kitchen window too slowly.

Looking Good is an unfortunate title considering it's presented by Lowri Turner, a woman who makes the Poison Dwarf in Dallas look appealing. Lowri has obviously had lessons in television presenting from the same person who taught (pause, grin smugly from the side of mouth and lower voice before punchline) *Jeremy Clarkson*.

Some journalists will do anything to get on television. Stand up and take a bow Angela Buttolph, Jean Crouch and Liz Savage, who does the ironing in her pyjamas. Her must-have for the summer is a white shirt. 'Buying a white shirt,' she reveals, 'is a great investment.' (The Hang Seng is overrun with people screaming, 'Sell November pork bellies! Buy white M&S womenswear!') 'The thing about shirts,' Liz instructs us, 'especially white shirts, is they bring out the whites in your eyes' (urgh), which Liz is alone in thinking is 'incredibly flattering'. As for trainers, we learn that 'according to Wayne Hemingway, cool labels include Reebok, Nike and Adidas'. (No shit, Wayne.)

Lowri's tip for looking good viewing the World Cup includes eating carrots instead of pizza and watching TV while working out on your rowing machine. For the Looking Good makeover we meet Deborah. 'My name's Deborah Gallagher,' she announces crisply. 'I'm 28. I'm a computer consultant. Each day I meet roughly between five and ten people.'

(Seven and a half people then.) Her summer office outfit of a black sports bra, baggy black shorts and white cummerbund stretched round the waist is this summer's mustn't-have.

Deborah is restyled by Morag Iona Young, seemingly from the *Girl Guides' Gazette*, who orders her to stop showing so much flesh and wear her hair up. 'Cap sleeves are marvellous, yes? Because they don't show armpits.' 'And armpits aren't good?' asks Deborah, worried. Morag is in no doubt. 'Armpits actually are quite unprofessional.' Women, eh? You never know what they're going to decide next.

By Wednesday at 8pm, as the World Cup semi-final gets underway, it will finally be sinking in. After weeks and weeks of fabulous viewing, the end of our delight is nigh. We must face the fact that **The Italian Kitchen** is nearly over. Rose and Ruth – who, for this episode, Channel 4 have rather unfairly labelled 'puddings' – end the series with a panna cotta with grappa and 'a raspberry sorbet so full of flavour it's gonna knock you out'. (Even on television.) Rose's apple-juggling tricks may be rather limited but her aggressive abstract jazz poetry is sublime.

'I want to catch THE LEMON ZEST...
Now it's reached boiling point I'm going to turn
Down the gas to the lowest. I possibly can...
Cream upon cream. Stir it TOGETHER.'

They were pretentious, preposterous, totally hopeless TV presenters. They've made us laugh. They've made us cry. They've made us hungry. And now they're going. We bid them farewell and say 'good luck' with the cookery.

July 4–10 1998

Dream on

There is nothing more boring than other people's dreams. So Tapehead will spare you details of his dream about BBC press officer Kate Crowe riding a bicycle in China playing 'Play That Funky Music White Boy' on a ukulele.

In **I Dream Of Diana** members of the public who have had Diana-related 'premonitions' learn there is 'more to dreaming than they ever imagined', not because of what dream analyst Sarah Dening calls 'the golden rule of dreaming' (Tapehead's golden rule of dreaming is to stay asleep.) Diana herself was 'haunted by a recurring nightmare' which was 'always the same in every detail'. (In the nightmare, she was trapped by marriage to a big-eared chump and his family of socially-deficient monsters.) The bizarre Lady Colin Campbell points out, 'Diana had a great deal of experience of therapy' (i.e. was A Complete Banana.)

For the most part, of course, the dreamers are all insecure, self-deluded, socially-aspirational victims of that old Diana myth that she was Just Like Them or (chortle) 'classless'. They dream about Diana *insisting* on coming round to see them/going to Thorpe Park/taking them on holiday with her. Steve Thorn – the managing director of a property management company in Ladbroke Grove you'd be well advised to stay clear of – denies his dream proves how lonely and inadequate he is on the grounds that 'Diana was somebody who figured very prominently in my life'. (No, she *didn't*, Steve.)

Having read that they had the same dream once, Elaine of Manor House, N4, concludes, 'I was experiencing exactly what she was experiencing' (in N4!). 'It was definitely not a coincidence.' (It definitely *was* a coincidence.) Oliver, a hairy hippy violinist from Lewisham describes a dream in which 'Diana came to my party – unexpected but not unwelcome.' *(Unexpected*! In *Lewisham*! You're bloody right it would be unexpected, not least because, he adds, somewhat unnecessarily, 'I hadn't invited her.') Oliver – the ungrateful git – complains that in his dream 'Diana made a rather snide remark about my flat' and Steve recalls that while he, Diana and Dodi are 'playing in the sea', they 'send Diana to the bar to get us some drinks' – which only suggests what a couple of sad chauvinistic social-climbers they both are.

'Diana fulfilled a lot of different roles in a lot of people's lives,' the programme maintains, but the fact is, she didn't. Diana was a car crash even as she was living: titillation for voyeurs. Now that she's dead, it seems that, to people like these, all she is is a symbol of their broken dreams.

Dream analysis, meanwhile, really is money for old rope if **In Your Dreams** is anything to go by. (Send your dreams to Tapehead, London EC1 and he will analyse them.) Premonition experts include Chris Robinson (aka Walken), a Dead Zone clone who has helped the anti-terrorist squad by predicting 'everything the IRA have done on mainland Britain'. He is now 'addicted' to this gift – the peace process notwithstanding. Then there's Cav Clerkin who foresaw his girlfriend betraying him and never recovered. In the dream, he caught her 'wiv some bloke and she kept laughing at me, laughing and laughing. So I started to strangle her,' Cav says, demonstrating and getting agitated. 'And my fingers have gone straight through 'er neck an' I've started pullin' out 'er veins, pulling and pulling and pulling, like I'm a magician.' Cav, we've all been there mate.

Dreams of gay monogamy in **Bedhopping** as a certain Michelangelo Signorile takes on gay activists like the weirdo from SexPanic who says the call for monogamy is 'so disturbing' because 'gay culture may become as dull as straight culture'. When he asks Ian and Michael whether 'there can be something detrimental in monogamous relationships' Ian says, 'Absolutely, I don't think there's any doubt about it at all' – the detrimental aspect being: 'you can't go out and have sex with someone else'.

Certainly, you've got to admire the way Signorile says 'Hi, it's Michelangelo' into the intercom with a completely straight face (well, not completely straight). The couples in openly promiscuous relationships have an impressive array of justifications, blaming drugs, pressure from the gay media, basic testosterone and the fact that 'as gay men we're taught to cruise all the time' (at cruising school). Personally, Tapehead blames Glenn Hoddle.

All in all, it seems that the people most reluctant to accept that gay men can have a loving, respectful, monogamous relationship are still gay.

August 15–21 1998

Burn this

Readers' dreams come pouring in, to benefit from Tapehead's new-found talent for dream analysis. Robert P., a solicitor, obviously fears failure. As for Isobel in Northampton, Tapehead is sorry to have to remind you there is a law against sending pornographic letters through the Royal Mail. You are very talented (though not at writing).

Moving swiftly on, this week's **QED** features one of Tapehead's favourite subjects. Anyone who doesn't believe in Spontaneous Human Combustion obviously hasn't seen Tapehead celebrate a last-minute winner from Andy Cole. With Exorcist music playing in the background, we see photos of Helen Conway from Pennsylvania. Or what's left of her. Immaculate white legs stick out from the unholy black mass that was her corpse. Investigator Paul Haggerty has been haunted by the possibility of spontaneous combustion ever since, though he may be less haunted if he stopped spending so much time looking at photos of it for the BBC.

In New York State, Kendall Mott's father died the same way. Here too, the heat from this almost entirely self-contained fire was so fierce a nearby TV set melted. (Now that really *is* upsetting.) 'I noticed the odour,' his son says. 'A real sweet, sticky smell.' We see 'a shot of the bed where Mr Mott expired', most of which was left intact. 'There was nothing left of Mr Mott.' The spooky part is that Mr Mott was a fireman – that and the fact that all that was left was a bit of skull and a piece of foot even though the wallpaper and curtains were barely singed. Even in the most modern crematorium in Britain, at 1000°C, the bones are not reduced to dust like this and have to be ground up in a 'cremulator' (a kind of metal tumble-drier). It seems the body had 'literally burned from inside out'. A good trick if you can do it.

One other thing almost guaranteed to have Tapehead spontaneously combust with joy is a movie-length version of **The Bill**. Better yet, Tuesday's 'Deep End' continues during one-hour specials on Thursday and Friday. (Can you smell burning?) It starts with plenty of mentions of 'moody VCRs', junkies, pimps and toms. Do you think the makers of NYPD Blue realise just how tame New York is compared to Sun Hill? Sun Hill has more dealers than Vegas and more pimps than, er, also Vegas.

It starts with a dead prostitute washed up in the shadow of the Millennium Dome, which now gets a bit-part in almost every drama on television. 'I fink she's a gonner,' says PC Polly Page, rightly suspecting she has been killed by the sheer splendour of the Mandelson Dome. From then on, it's an Odd Couple pairing of wide-boy PC Santini and a new WPC with an MA in Religious Studies (someone call Martin Scorsese). They all go on about how much they fancy her – even though she's no looker, dull and dumpy, even for a policewoman. In any case, this one, as they say, will run and run.

Daily Mail film critic Christopher Tookey is famous for spontaneously combusting with rage at films like Crash and what he calls 'Nab-Oh-Kov's' Lolita and thus makes a delicious target for Jon Ronson's sly character assassination in **Critical Condition**. With a narration so limp and withering you wonder whether poor Jon is going to make it to the end of the pro-gramme, he watches the way Tookey has alienated himself from other film critics – a strange preoccupation of Ronson's that has run throughout the series. His main theme though is, 'I fear that Chris is being type-cast.' (Mainly, of course, by Ronson.)

Tookey spends most of the film with a self-satisfied, self-important smirk on his face, laughing at virtually everything he or anyone else says – presumably to create the illusion of popularity or, indeed, happiness. When his juvenile tirades against Lolita fail to excite anyone, even less than the movie did, he is left pontificating that 'Lolita's harmful consequences will, of course, be felt *way* into the future.'

The highlight is Tookey – for once without his yellow anorak – at the London Film Critics' Awards, especially his dancing to Donna Summer's 'Hot Stuff' – the chump. 'Tonight,' Ronson whispers, understandably bare-ly able to contain himself, 'Christopher can socialise with film stars, rather than just call for their movies to be banned.' Having offered Michael Caine some stage direction and advised him how to relax for an interview on Sky News, the hapless opportunist attaches himself to Caine like a lost dog, only to find himself consumed by the thing he seems to fear most (silence) when it matters most. An object lesson in humiliation.

August 22–28 1998

The very Bad Lieutenant

ame, fame, fatal fame, as the good bard said. After previous, scur-rilous assaults on talents such as Liz Hurley and Patsy Kensit, **This Wonderful Life** turns its stalker-like attentions on a more worthy target: Chris Evans. Incredibly, this achieves the unlikely effect of securing some sympathy for 'the Ginger Whinger'.

The DJ's crimes here include 'surrounding himself with a loyal gang', earning too much money and, in particular, having horrible ginger chest hair. Petty personal grudges and perennial professional jealousies are lined up like ducks at the fairground, making the array of witnesses for the prosecution suitably dismal: the newsagents who gave him his first job; his old agent; Ian, 'Chris's best mate 1982-88'. Simon Bates ('radio legend') offers us the benefit of his expertise. Rob, a 'rival DJ' from Evans' days in

Warrington, remembers him as 'a nonentity', which even Tapehead thinks is rather galling. Local radio presenter Tim Grundy recalls a typical Evans tantrum which ended with Evans leaving the station, complaining, 'I'm your best DJ' which, Grundy maintains, 'was patently untrue', although history might say otherwise. 'I suppose that's what they call charisma,' grumbles a bloke at GLR, 'but then I wouldn't know.' Probably the truest words spoken in the whole programme. What we must never forget about Chris Evans is that this is a man whose mentor used to be Timmy Mallet. (Suddenly everything is clear...)

The credits for **Kirsty Young Interviews...** include the likes of Tony Blair, Noel Gallagher and Madonna, but in fact this week's star is Noel Edmonds, 'Britain's highest-paid television presenter'. (Strangely, she does not say, 'Britain's best' or 'most popular'.) From his 850-acre estate in Devon, Kirsty promises he will reveal 'what his enormous wealth really means to him' and 'talk about his reputation as Britain's wealthiest star'. (Yes, Kirsty, we get the picture.) 'Find out what he really thinks of Chris Evans.' (God, not him as well.)

Kirsty starts the interview with that perennial give-away of the dire hack interview (asking him how he feels about interviews) and what he thinks of the way people perceive him. ('I really have no idea' predictably being the answer.) If only to help him out on this point, Tapehead must say that Edmonds is as vile and unreal as ever, vociferously objecting to the description of him as 'a businessman' ('a ghastly term') when, in fact, this is probably the nicest term anyone has ever applied to him. Later, Kirsty sucks up to him with the absurd assertion, 'You were Mr Street Cred in the seventies.' 'Being cool,' Edmonds considers earnestly (seemingly oblivious to the notion that such a preposterous question can only be a set-up), 'doesn't actually last very long. What I've tried to do is recognise that times change and you change and people expect you to change.' (Are you still awake?)

He is probably the only man in the country who can be pompous about Noel's House Party and then launch into a tirade about Australian soap operas being 'superficial' (which is a bit rich) and corrupting our children 'when they could be outside, playing with their ponies'. It's bizarre to consider how genuinely unfunny both Edmonds and Evans are, and how annoying it is that, although we were spared Tracey Ullman, Edmonds's failure to conquer America cost us dear. More than once, he reminds us he has been at the BBC for 30 years next year. So, appealing to him personally, Tapehead begs the question: *haven't we suffered enough?* As Kirsty herself seems to be asking, can't you please go to Channel 5 where none of us will ever be bothered by you again?

Finally, we say goodbye to **Maisie Raine** who this week attempts to fit up her own brother (sorry, bruvver). Once again, most of the episode is taken up with background information on Maisie, suggesting the writers truly thought there'd be a second series where some actual storylines would appear. This week, despite 'no evidence of murder', the whole force devotes itself to investigating a coroner's open verdict on a young girl's boyfriend's rooftop suicide six years earlier. (It's a myth that the police have a heavy workload.) 'Is that Daniel?' Maisie says, in the girl's bedroom, looking at a wall covered with photos. (Doh!) The girl and Maisie go through at least seven or eight more rooftop suicide attempts. If only Maisie had jumped – put us and poor Pauline Quirke out of our misery.

August 29–September 4 1998

Indescribably boring

The most priceless moments in the **Cutting Edge Special** about former *Independent* Editor Rosie Boycott's time in charge there include a features meeting where one section editor reveals an impending cover story on (wait for it) Steve Harley and one of the stars of Bramwell. After declaring himself (rather unwisely) content to 'toddle on as normal', he is eventually fired, lamenting that the days when he could run 2,000 words on how Restoration comedy treated marriage in comparison with modern-day theatre are obviously over (Amen).

Tapehead has a soft spot for Rosie Boycott and not only because her time at *Esquire* included pimping him out to escort the likes of Pamella Bordes on blind dates around London. (For which he can only say: thank you.) An energetic maverick, radical and manic, she inevitably found the somewhat stilted standards of the office there frustrating, despite her best efforts to chastise its more dithering members of staff for displaying 'a massive lack of cool'.

This is where the programme is at its most illuminating, giving us a glimpse of the hideous listlessness of the people she was up against. When Andrew Marr addresses the staff, they are lined up before us – rows and rows of tired, white faces and grey suits, one token black bloke standing out amongst dozens of Oxbridge blondes and spineless, middle-aged liberal wimps. Rosie even feels the need to advise one editor not to meet the much-feared budget-cutter without her being there to protect him. Her determined entreaty for them all to 'have fun' continually runs into a wall of permanent unresponsive mumbling.

The **Omnibus** profile of Creation Records boss, Alan McGee, meanwhile, is so unquestioningly sycophantic, you start to wonder if it isn't the subtlest condemnation you've ever seen. Examined with anything like a critical eye, the moral of The Man Who Discovered Oasis could only be that the music business really is Like Punk Never Happened. McGee and Oasis have succumbed to all the old rock 'n' roll clichés of the 1970s supergroups and Supertramps, with their country mansions, jet-set, dumb-blonde wives and embarrassing back-slapping champagne lunches with the Prime Minister. (Welcome to the Establishment, I'm All Right Jack.)

McGee parades his 'millionaire lifestyle', his office in Primrose Hill, his executive box at Chelsea and rediscovered 'ardent' support of Rangers. The programme-makers seem to think we're meant to forgive him because he's nice to his dad who was once working-class. Artistically, his legacy should be that Oasis have joined the Primals, My Bloody Valentine and the Mary Chain on the long list of bands whose potential as any kind of lasting subversive force has been sadly wasted. From Screamadelica to Rocks was certainly some kind of demise. Compare the shaky video of the Oasis gig where McGee discovered them and Noel's mangled 'Ticket To Ride' guitar against the complacent claptrap of 'All Around The World'.

It is left to Malcolm McLaren to express confusion at how McGee, 'this supposed punk rocker', came to be 'this friend of *Tony Blair* [he says with great distaste]... Tony Blair being something *of a religious fanatic*.' The editor of *NME*, Steve Sutherland, also questions whether McGee is a good businessman, suggesting he only 'has great ears for a certain type of music'. On this evidence, they're certainly big enough.

David Bailey's three-part study of models, **Models Close Up**, just about survives the fact that Bailey chortles his way through it all, wheezing with laughter (mostly at his own jokes) as if he's auditioning for the part of Ratty from *Wind In The Willows*. As professions go, modelling is of course about as unrespected as you can get – worse than prostitution or even journalism. Models are despised when they play dumb (dismissed as bimbo playthings), condemned when they stand up or speak up for themselves ('making demands'). They cannot win. But anyone who thinks they should hate Naomi Campbell should watch her hugging Nelson Mandela.

Most of them, of course, were discovered in launderettes, airports or on the bus home from school, which means they didn't actually ask for it. It is not their fault they're beautiful and anyway, as Bailey says, 'I've never known a beautiful girl who *thought* she *was* beautiful and that is kind of appealing.' We see them all – a parade of funny ears and wonky noses, alien gazes, ill-positioned moles and gaps. (Between their *teeth*.) 'Everyone wants something from them,' observes the ever-fabulous Lauren Hutton. Look into their eyes, the likes of Kate or Naomi, and you will see what it's like to be hunted.

September 12–18 1998

Everyone's a fruit and nut case

TV's obsession with all things dietary and culinary seems to have reached a rather blunt conclusion with the peak-viewing Carlton series, Fat. Following suit, and going back to basics, we now have **Delia's How To Cook** in which the original doyenne of domestic cooking shows us how to boil an egg and even, if we're lucky, cut our bread into little soldiers. (Say what you like about Delia Smith, she knows how to boil an egg.)

Delia starts the series perched somewhat precariously on her soapbox, making New Labour-like speeches about modern values, doing a pretty fair impersonation of Harriet Harman. The plethora of fussy (foreign) cooking shows (i.e. the competition) she says, means 'we are in danger of losing something very precious – a reverence for food in its simple form'. In her own small way, she simpers, she hopes this series will 'provide a springboard for a lifetime of learning'. She is only inches away from saying that it's 'time to put something back' and dabbing at her eyes with a hankie. Even while insisting she is reverting to something very simple, she manages to obfuscate everything with patronising double-speak. 'The egg is, after all,' she says sweetly, 'the symbol of new life and new beginnings.'

Delia knows a lot about eggs. She could bore for Britain on them. What she doesn't know about them is literally not worth knowing. On the subject of eggs and their air pockets alone she could (and does) talk for several hours. 'First of all,' she instructs us, for about the nineteenth time, 'you've got to buy your eggs.' Delia, it turns out, has strong views about how to buy eggs, where to keep them (not in the fridge: controversial), how to crack them open, not to mention what sort of saucepans you should use to boil them in. ('One that holds the eggs comfortably.')

She even manages to be patronising when she (finally) gets on to boiling up the water. 'It's quite interesting,' she announces, idiotically, watching the bubbles boil. It's hard to imagine what sort of sub seven-year-old the series is aimed at. (She's making things even Tapehead can manage.) Anyone who knows anything about cooking will be totally infuriated by being talked down to in this way, while anyone who doesn't probably won't be watching anyway and, if they are, will be just as irritated.

Better surely to just reach for the chocolate bar (a Flake, a Milky Bar or a gently chilled Orange Aero will do it). **Hooked** looks at women's hopeless obsession with the stuff. 'When chocolate was no longer rationed, I went completely berserk... I ate chocolate constantly – non-stop,' remembers one customer from the early days when Ye Olde Mars bar and Kit Kat original were launched. 'It took over my life. It controlled how I behaved,' several women say. 'You just feel a warmth, a glow, as though you were being wrapped in velvet...' Someone should tell them: those little packets of brown stuff... they're not chocolate. (Just say no, ladies.)

On **Health Farm** this week, chocolate-addict Sophie is hoping for a cellulite miracle. 'How much walking do you do?' asks a fitness trainer. 'None.' Diet? 'Terrible.' Sophie then has her fat measured: '42.5 per cent of your body. The recommended would be 20.' 'Whoops!' she giggles.

Chaos reigns when, after an elaborate face-lift, the Forest Mere health farm finally reopens. Apart from the phones, the lecky, the gas, the water, the fire alarms, the restaurant and the building work, everything is faultless. The staff all seem to be useless alcoholics and nymphomaniacs – either pissed or taking the piss almost permanently. On this basis, Tapehead has taken up their invitation and is moving in shortly.

Fresh from her return to Casualty (as Duffin), for the first episode of Sarah Ferguson's new Sky chat show, **Sarah... Surviving Life**, they have at least somehow managed to find someone almost as bonkers as she is. Come on down Eileen Drewery, Glenn Hoddle's favourite spiritual plant pot: the guru's guru. Tapehead hopes Fergie asked her if it's true that the

England players have nicknamed Hoddle 'chocolate' because he loves himself so much he could eat himself. (Chocolate links, we got 'em.) Sky say that Sarah's 'understanding and warmth' (i.e. body fat) and 'infectious sense of humour' (laughing at practically anything) make her a natural hostess. (*Chat show* hostess.)

The second episode is scheduled to be about anorexia. It didn't take them long, did it?

October 10–16 1998

Narcodicks and pharmapseudicals

Channel 4 continue to peddle bad programmes about drugs under the auspices of their ingeniously titled, rocket-fuelled 'Drugs Uncovered' season. Certainly you'd have to be on drugs to make programmes as bad as **Fatal Embrace**. Contrary to popular mythology (i.e. the mythology perpetrated by bad writers banging out too many drugs), this is another example of how drugs can unlock the subconscious to allow truly awful, unfocused writing to pour forth.

Former *NME* journo, Ian Penman, ponders 'the me that I used to be', intercutting his predictably nebulous musings with a truly excruciating Young Romance sub-plot that suggests he still hasn't escaped the thrall of every clapped-out, drug-related cliché known to man. (The Man?) The worst of these is that hoary old notion that drug-taking operates amidst what he calls 'the night-side of life... beneath the crust of the everyday...', 'the other side, the dark side', 'the subterranean elsewhere, the night-side of pleasure...' This sort of renegade status has become the bogus badge of honour that wasted talents like Penman's need to feel they have somehow survived. Likewise, Penman predictably personifies drugs as some sort of evil Mephisto, capable of seduction: all a pretty transparent way of diverting attention from the weaknesses that just make drug-takers weak.

Then there is that tired, old, romanticised idea that lovers on drugs are somehow more exotic than other lovers – 'lighting up each other's sky'. Drugs plus love equals more bad descriptions of emotions than bad D. H. Lawrence (i.e. pretty fucking bad). Worst of all, kids, even Penman has succumbed to drugs' most evil influence: the impression that bad hippy folk music like the shit in this film is in any way OK.

The lurid lure of these dark, drug-related clichés claims another victim in Nick Broomfield, who always has been pretty easily titillated. **Kurt & Courtney**, his compellingly voyeuristic, ultimately hollow sniff around the conspiracy theories hanging over Kurt Cobain's suicide, sees Broomfield consistently falling for fake frissons such as the 'drug-dealer who has an Uzi' (ooooh!), 'a friend who is Divine Brown's pimp' (woooh!) and going 'to meet a woman called Chelsea late at night' (wow!).

Nothing makes Nick happier than the chance of mentioning 'narcodicks' or chasing up 'pho-dos' of Kurt 'shood-ing up'. Broomfield says he is looking for a mystery but when he finds one (the hefty one and a half milligrams of heroin found thrilling round Cobain's veins; a private eye's claim that there were no fingerprints on the trigger of the gun or the shellcases), he decides only to rattle Courtney's cage rather than dig up anything juicy. The problem is that we all know Courtney ain't no fairy and will very probably be the Frances Farmer of her generation but no one can really blame her for not helping Broomfield with his film or letting him use Nirvana's songs for BBC peanuts.

Characters like the loony tune who claimed he was offered $50,000 to kill Cobain are red herrings and Broomfield *knows* it but, *à la* Tarantino, they tingle his middle-class juices. He interviews the nervous nanny, Cobain's best friend, Crispin Glover lookalike Dylan Carson and Courtney's father – a real piece of work who can't help wondering if Courtney 'didn't have that extraordinary sense of commitment and determination' to Kurt. The electrician who found his body says at first he thought the body was a mannequin, as if rock stars are prone to leaving mannequins lying around instead of their own pretty white corpses. Cobain's first love shows us some of his early paintings, pictures of 'diseased vaginas', pieces of meat and a self-portrait – a reasonably well-drawn skeleton ('A very skinny skeleton at that', she says). Numerous images of fetuses allow Broomfield to wonder limply, 'Was he fascinaded with feeduses?'

Underneath all this, though, is the feeling that Broomfield never did get an idea of who Kurt Cobain was or what he represented, as indicated by statements like 'Kurt Cobain popularised punk rock'. The only person amongst all these wackos that he can relate to in any way is Kurt Cobain's Aunt Mary who gave Cobain his first guitar and has kept recordings he made when he was two that are, eerily, reminiscent of Nirvana. Nowadays she uses his demise to teach schoolkids about the danger of falling for drugs. 'All of us go through painful things in our lives,' she says. 'It's just part of life. Nobody is exempt from pain.'

A home movie of Cobain used as the, presumably pertinent, ending, confirms what most of us would have known all along: he was isolated. He was miserable. He was out of focus.

October 31–November 6 1998

Black power

If the BBC had any kind of sense, it would have scheduled this week's painstakingly thorough Malcolm X documentary together with its look at white supremacist terrorist organisations as part of some sort of season. They make a fine contrast: the sober with the sensational; the noble history with pathetic prophecy.

The Everyman Special, **Heart Of Darkness**, begins with the murder of James Byrd in Jasper, Texas earlier this year by three fuckwits whose level of military planning included leaving a KKK lighter behind at the scene. (Another one of the KKK morons has WHITE and TRASH tattooed down his arms. Doh!) His face had been sprayed with black paint to underline the fact that he was killed because he was black. His body was dragged until the road became a two-mile blood trail, scattered with more than 70 body parts. Amazingly, the demonstrations that took place in Jasper after the crime included some by the KKK which the BBC dutifully film, showing them posing in their hoods and shades and Armalites and setting fire to 30-foot crosses in their back gardens.

The programme groups together the successors of George Rockwell's American Nazi Party, the Aryan Brotherhood, the National Alliance, the Church of Christian Identity (which has a bust of Adolf Hitler on its altar) and, of course, the cretinous KKK Klowns. Even collectively, the feeling that they are being over-aggrandised begins with the very premise that they are 'part of a large, growing, white supremacist movement' no longer isolated to a few states in the South. In fact, as soon as they open their mouths, you remember the KKK are generally recruited in prison, being mostly ignorant, desperate and criminal. The more they tell it – 'It's all in the history books' – the more you realise a little knowledge is a dangerous thing. 'Grand Imperial Wizard' Charles Lee uses the platform the Beeb have given him to protest about the white man's unfair 'reputation' for 'persecuting and enslaving other races'. (*Hello?!?!*) 'To be a Klansman in America,' he whinges, 'is to be hated and ridiculed by your own people' – proving they haven't even got the sense to claim popularity.

Scheduling **Malcolm X: Make It Plain** at 12.20am is some sort of insult. Assassinated in 1965 at the age of 39, on this evidence you can't help but wonder how high he could have gone eventually. In the years before his death, his influence had already reached a global stage, visiting 14 African countries as a kind of UN envoy. 'Once you heard him speak, you never went back to how you were before,' remembers one Harlem resident. 'Even if you kept your position, you had to rethink it.' 'He had a beautiful sense of humour,' smiles one of his friends, 'especially when he was kidding me about pork.'

This is a more complex, illuminating biography than Spike Lee's film, especially on his break from the Nation of Islam because of their reluctance to make a stand on civil rights. The breaking point came with the news that JFK had been shot ('He's dead – that devil is dead,' Malcolm said straight away), after which Elijah Mohammad banned him from making speeches or giving interviews. Having left the Nation, he was branded a Judas by none other than Louis Farakhan and had already survived a fire-bomb attack on his family when three Nation of Islam members assassinated him.

The conventional shorthand on Malcolm X always spells out segregationist, set against Martin Luther King's message of unity and peace, etc., but one of the most illuminating aspects of this film is the way the word 'segregation' seems to be a negotiating stance, a *signal* of his readiness for militancy. Above all, it seems to have been more of a metaphor for the need for black self-sufficiency and pride. 'The angels are white,' he would warn his audience. 'You have to fight your battles.' 'Besides,' he told one interviewer when he was young, 'no one was more thoroughly integrated with whites than I', and it was true. The only black kid in his class, when he and his friends would play Robin Hood, Malcolm would always be Robin Hood.

In his final years, his pilgrimages with 'white-skinned Muslims' in Saudi Arabia had made him reconsider even the stance. His speeches here were righteous and piercingly lucid, built on a kind of beautiful confidence that you could not deny. 'Better than the white man?' he proclaims. 'That's not saying anything. Who is he equal to? You can't compare your skin with his skin. Why, your skin looks like gold beside his skin.' 'In honouring him,' reflects Ossie Davis, 'we honoured the best in ourselves.'

October 24–30 1998

Buongiorno salami

Yes! They're back!!! Our old friends from the River Café, the strangely alien Ruth Rogers and the positively potty Rose Gray, with their new series, **Italian Kitchen Two**.

Sadly, though, some of the innocence that once made them seem so beguiling has gone. Ruth's pronunciation, for example, almost sounds vaguely like Italian – as if General Pinochet had been helping her while he lunched out on her risotto. And Rose, God bless her, has stopped blushing furiously and coyly looking up at the ceiling and now occasionally looks at the camera. Her Andy Warhol party wig is more or less on straight.

Luckily, though, her terrifying, strangely affecting abstract haikus are as sublime as ever. 'I cut off/The tough stalks/Cut off/At the base' has a kind of doom-ridden Ted Hughes quality that makes her a worthwhile outside bet for the new Poet Laureate. Alarming outbursts of madness still strike. '*Beautiful* capers!' she shouts suddenly, like some idiot savant who's knocking out crates of the stuff down the market. Watching her tossing salad leaves or endlessly, contentedly chopping things up like a sweet (possibly disturbed) child is still the most tender thing you will see on TV this week.

'I'm making this recipe for six,' she says simply, like a kid making a speech about her school project, 'and I'm cutting four fennel bulbs and this pan is hot.' She finishes, gushing with childlike triumph, 'I'm very proud of it and it-does-look-very-beautiful-and-it's-also-very-very-good-for-you.'

Delia, for all her winning ways, doesn't come close. As **Delia Is Mad For It** (or **Delia's How To Cook** as the BBC prefer to call it) confirms, she is simply far too sensible. Tapehead's jest about Episode One (that soon she'd be instructing us how to cut soldiers for our boiled eggs) cruelly came home to roost when Episode Two saw her lecturing us on how to make toast. Like those of an overly opinionated cab-driver, her views on toasters will have the bureaucrats in Brussels rocking when she publishes her manifesto.

She's at it again here – emphasising the difficulties she has had to overcome in her mission (to give us 'foolproof recipes'), railing about the fact we haven't all got the same ovens ('fan-assisted ovens should be avoided', she admonishes), revealing a hankering for some Stalinist state where identical ovens are issued to everyone at birth. Her views on the scandalous state of eight-inch-diameter cake tins become a tirade (some are eight and a half inches, some are seven and three-quarters) whilst others border on pure paranoia. 'If your cake base browns too much on one side, it may not be your fault. Your oven may need checking.' As if she has been cooking for some culinary Brave New World, Delia seems to be advocating a Stepford Wives-esque universe where every household is the same – all built on her philosophies like 'A home-made cake has a lot going for it on days when life seems to lack that special edge.'

In the ever competitive world of TV cooks, Delia seems to be canvassing not only our votes but our devotion as the Dalai Lama of TV cookery. 'Home baking,' she states, with that sinister simplicity familiar to the Moonies, 'transports you psychologically into a world of comfort and wellbeing. Even a simple sponge cake can be a wonderful way of making family and friends feel really special.' By the time she pleads, 'Let me transport you to another world with this very moist layered coconut cake,' she is only inches away from advocating levitation.

But it is all a blessed relief compared to watching Keith Floyd – now languishing in the Beazer Homes League of cookery on Channel 5, with **Floyd Uncorked**. Watching TV cooks showing off, making things you can't is fairly futile at the best of times, but wine-tasting on TV is right up there with radio ventriloquism. 'Yes,' Floyd and his mate, JP, tell us repeatedly, 'that one tastes delicious.' Floyd himself has added being charmless and pompous to his repertoire of self-indulgence. 'If you've got time,' he says, luxuriating in some of the best vineyards in France, 'do visit some of them.' (Some of us have got nothing but time.)

There is nothing entertaining or edifying about watching Floyd anymore. 'It's a-long-way-to-Tipadrinkdown' is as close as he gets to wit. He has become a clown, a bore. The only possible reason to watch him is to see whether he'll mess up, or to see how pissed he'll get. He is the TV cookery equivalent of Gazza.

November 14–20 1998

Hanging out

This week, the sheer volume of naked flesh adorning the nation's screens becomes so overpowering we have virtually no alternative but to avert our eyes. Channel 5 have been bombarding Tapehead with consignments of free pornographic material for months now in the hope that he will mention **Sex And Shopping** (as if that's going to work!). But, rather like being pestered by some overexcitable teenager showing off about how shocking they are, anything remotely hardcore is, in the end, all mercifully fairly subliminal – with any overinflated organs or German porn star's testicles appearing on the screens for no longer than two trilliseconds.

Witness, though, is another matter. 'Acting Natural' is an exhaustive, not to say *exhausting*, study of the history of Britain's naturist communities and the hot controversies and secret antipathies raging between them. 'Nudism', for example, is 'a dirty word' as far as most naturists are concerned, although the suspicion remains that some naturists are 'secret nudists'. There are, Witness claims rather ridiculously, '40,000 estimated naturists who regularly take their clothes off all over the country'.

Tapehead, it's safe to say, is not one of them. Nakedness should be confined to bathing and (preferably) having sex, and even then there are certain benefits to having your clothes on. What you *don't* want to be doing is what (on this evidence) the naturists do: playing ping-pong or the violin naked; exercise classes, knitting or gardening naked. (Even sunbathing naked is, frankly, not advisable – too risky; while mowing the lawn naked is just ridiculous.)

This is the problem with being naked. It just doesn't look right. It's just not natural. It is the opposite of natural. It is perverse. And yet those who love it disagree. 'It's a great feeling to be naked,' argues Gary. 'In woodland, for example.' Gary, an enormous fat skinhead, is naked as he says this, of course – his dignity spared only by the net of a ping-pong table. (He's a strange shape, is Gary.)

The rest of the advocates seem to consist of old buffers in the buff, nutters in the nuddy, whose observations look like sketches of old gentlemen from The Fast Show, only naked. 'We are absurdly modest in this country,' mutters one old boy. 'We must not expose our genitals! But why not? Why not?!' Actually, his own genitals answer this question rather aptly. Other controversial contributors include: Mark Nisbit, editor and publisher of 'the outspoken and radical nudist magazine', *Starkers* – who we see typing away (naked) in his shed. And Norman Tillett who, they say, has been 'a practising naturist for over 70 years' (and still can't get it right – besides his walking stick, he's got shoes on).

Naturists' president and splendid caricature, Gerry Ryland, makes a stand against 'the maverick nudists of the left' who, he insists, are 'hell-bent on everybody getting their clothes off, which in my opinion is a nonsense and tends to frighten the horses'. The main division ('which threatens the future of the entire movement') seems to concern the question of rules: 'no photography, no dogs and no erections, of course' being the best of them. Issues of class, sex (i.e. having sex), hetero- and homosexual single males, 'the philosophical side of naked body culture' and whether women should keep their thighs together are the other contentious, erm, areas. Some naturist clubs have so many rules they become self-conscious, thus defeating the whole point of the exercise. All very messy.

Lucy Blakstad's **Naked** is, you might say, a different kettle of fish altogether. It starts with a perfect pair of (silent) breasts. From then on, though, it looks at ageing, or rather middle-ageing (sagging, wrinkling, drooping, etc). One woman laments that, between the ages of 38 and 45, the average woman puts about 42 pounds on her 'mid section'. 'A grey pubic hair,' she asserts with conviction, 'is one of the most sobering sights there is' – a statement her husband for one probably agrees with. For her, the menopause did not involve 'hot flushes' so much as 'episodes of intense sweating, like catching fire from the inside'. For men, not only does your girth inevitably grow fatter – *as* it does, it makes your willy look smaller. 'I don't think about the willy any more,' one man says. 'It has done its work. It is just an organ to, you know, pass water.'

All very worrying, and although Ms Blakstad dresses everything up in her usual pretty pretentiousness, slow-mo and music, all in all it's a programme you'd be well advised to steer clear of. Never grow old.

November 21–27 1998

Licking the mirror

I n the endless universe of nauseating, inescapable celebrities there is smug (Jeffrey Archer), there is very smug (Robbie Williams) and then there is Richard E. Grant, a man whose principal achievement has been to be so superficial and affected that he makes the Pet Shop Boys look like Chas and Dave. Just as we thought the burden of his sickening, preening features had been passed over to Hollywood, R. E. G – whom for the purposes of this column we shall refer to as Reg – has popped back to haunt us with the BBC's lavish production of **The Scarlet Pimpernel**.

Even in the opening credits Reg raises up his handsome chin in self-admiration, looks elegantly down his nose at us and flashes his eyes excitedly: an exhibition of vanity worthy of a princess's peacock. Even before the opening theme music has finished we are longing for the Pimpernel to get captured. Instantly, we are reminded of the years we have suffered watching him showing off on chat shows – singing Swaziland's national anthem, luxuriating in his perfect parenthood or out luvvying luvvies at the same time as revelling in the frankly facile controversy of his film-set diaries. Straight away, in his first scene, Reg heads for the mirror – more out of habit than direction. Only self-restraint stops him from licking it, opting instead to fluff up his ruff.

Needless to say, this three-part extravaganza is swimming in the familiar historical detail the BBC just dusts down once in a while: dirty-faced urchins in brown smocks and triangular hats mingle with elegant beauties wearing frills, petticoats and powdered wigs. Not to mention the women. It is not just drivel but lavish drivel. Carry On Pimpernelling. Dangerous Liaisons meets The Onedin Line, only as done by the school art department when they produced the fifth form play. There are stunning fires burning in every street for no reason – the backdrop for the Equity quota of trusty steeds, lusty wenches and a host of sweaty extras who have based their performances on Mrs Bridges from Upstairs Downstairs. The idiotic monarch is the traditional amalgam of Robert Hardy and Christopher Biggins.

Most out of place is poor old Martin Sheen – Doyle from The

Professionals – reprising the role as Robespierre's chief detective Chauvelin. While everyone else is mincing around in horse-drawn carriages, he is the only one driving a three-litre, fuel-injection Capri. The period detail is undoubtedly spot-on. But who would have thought that the Scarlet Pimpernel had a Swaziland accent?

Modern day peacock/pimpernel RuPaul doesn't fare much better in the second episode of **The RuPaul Show**, Channel 4's new, imported chat show. At least this week's guests work in the porn industry. Last week's special guest was Pat Benatar ('Oh boy, I'm so excited about Pat,' gushed our host. 'I *live* for Pat Benatar.') Porn stars Tom Chase and John Doe fail to illuminate though. Considering RuPaul's potentially challenging/risqué persona, the questions are Wogan-esque they're so obvious. 'Do you have to be attracted to the person you're in a scene with?' ('It helps.')

RuPaul towers over all the guests like some sort of modern-day Land Of The Giants. The Truman Show in reverse as if a full-size person has fallen into a TV set occupied by tiny starlets. It is all about as 'alternative' as Letterman or indeed VH1, where it's from. The studio audience fill half of the screen-time up by whooping and clapping. The patronising host roars with laughter pretty much regardless of what anyone says and even signs off with a phoney pay-off wisdom: 'Learn to love yourself. 'Cos if you don't love yourself, how the hell can you love somebody else?' The luvvie factor is worthy of Reg at his worst. 'I really wanna say – and this is on behalf of every porn star that's ever lived – you guys are really doing a great service for the whole... *world*.'

If 'subverting' the American chat-show format is pointless it's even more thankless trying to parody British boy bands. But that's what **Boyz Unlimited**, wedged unhappily between Friends and Frasier attempts. Although predictably it falls hopelessly short of anything remotely as funny as the BBC's documentary on Upside Down. 'You're shit, you fucking stink and you're all poofs,' squeals a 10-year-old boy when their manager takes the Boyz to a Welsh holiday camp to meet their public. He is closer to the truth than he realises.

January 30–February 5 1999

Passé

The continuing popularity of John Peel in certain sections of socie-ty/the media is one of modern life's more enduring, perturbing mysteries. These days Peel is so busy doing commercials for multi-national oil companies and building societies it's a wonder he has time to bolster his flagging credibility by listening to any music. Then there is the minor fact that Peel not only has terrible taste in music but hopelessly anti-quated criteria for even considering what he might play. Major labels are, of course, an anathema while hip-hop or jungle remain basically alien to him unless a member of The Mekons is in there somewhere playing the guitar (badly). The only chance that he might play the new Mobb Deep monster is if they set up their own label in the Hebrides. (And give up hip-hop.)

Tapehead would like nothing more than to be proved wrong by Peel's new series, the modestly titled **John Peel's Sounds Of The Suburbs**, but, from the first episode, wouldn't necessarily bet on it. (The excruciating closing pilgrimage to Bill Shankly's birthplace sealed it.) Peel can bore for Britain talking about indie bands or himself and now, with this series, he seems determined to prove it *in situ*.

Claiming to be curious about where the peculiarly British style of cre-ativity that has given us everything from, say, The Fall to, er, The Mekons comes from, Peel announces he 'decided to take a round-Britain trip to find out'. (The lucrative Channel 4 commission was, presumably, just a coinci-dence.) His mission: 'To try to unearth the social, cultural and economic influences from which all of these good things flow.' This consists mostly of him plodding around Lanarkshire with Major Talents such as 'Sean from the Soup Dragons, who took me on a tour of his teenage haunts – the places where his musical career had begun'. (It's not exactly Al Green but still...) Our excitement at such a tour is capped by a rare TV appear-ance by Sean from the Soup Dragons's Dad. (A Channel 4 exclusive.)

We are then privy to a tour of some of East Kilbride's finest underpass-es in the company of the lead singer of God's Boyfriend: an obscure/irrel-evant band even by Peel's standards. But her efforts to stop herself nodding off/out while Peel drones on and on commend her. 'I'm lost for words,' Peel sobs ludicrously in front of Shankly's memorial. If only.

Close Up's 'LA Stories' follows four wannabe British screenwriters of varying success pursuing the American (British) dream and being among the 200 scripts that get made every year in Hollywood (out of 40,000 registered). Novice Tina Jenkins 'gave up a career in factual television' to try to write Nine Lives, an idea she had when her cat was dying of cancer. The fact that she feels the need to explain it doesn't bode well for her. 'I thought… there's a human being there,' she gushes, excitedly, as if she was writing the script for Chinatown. 'I thought, "What if a guy gets turned into… a cat – reluctantly."' As if we might have assumed otherwise. This guy is, of course, a serial seducer who (as a cat) has to 'learn how to be a decent human being' and only has *Nine Lives* to do it in. Given that the consensus here seems to be that being a writer in Hollywood 'is about waiting to be fired', Tapehead can only hope that a major studio doesn't buy her idea and turn it into something really commercial and pathetic.

From Lanarkshire and LA, this week's final destination for documentary-makers to patronise the local inhabitants turns out to be Moscow as **Trouble At The Top** follows the launch of Russian *Vogue*. Unfortunately, just as the party hats have arrived, the rouble collapses, bread queues start forming and unpaid miners occupy Red Square. (Don't you just *hate* it when that happens?) *Vogue*'s staff, luckily, remain undaunted. 'Russia just can't live without a party,' they determine, coming out in solidarity by declaring, 'We're doing it for the Russians.' Russia's women are 'beautiful, clever, wise women who deserve *Vogue*' pleads the editor, who got the job by cunningly styling herself as Anna Wintour (Anna Wintourski).

Ultimately, their triumph is achieved by adapting to the sudden demise in Moscow's demand for Bulgari and Versace and running pieces on old stand-bys like furs, long skirts, fur hats and fur gloves, with only a couple of ads for potatoes.

February 27– March 5 1999

Shoot-out

Spin-off series are all well and good unless – as in the case of the fresher, racier Holby City – they usurp their precursors so thoroughly, they make them suddenly look rather dated or, in **Casualty**'s case, infirm.

Celebrations intended to commemorate Casualty's 250th episode only look set to seal things. A daytime quiz – 'What's Up Doc?' – between cast members gives the Holby City whippersnappers the chance to humiliate the Casualty veterans, while the closing episode of the series on Saturday (the conclusion to 'Casualty's first ever two-part special') seems surprisingly sedate compared to former, more explosive climaxes. One bank-robber ends up with one of those scary yellow wheel clamps on his head and a youngster gets impaled on an antler trap ('we need the antler *in situ*'). But it's strangely dull fare, most notable for blonde Doctor George leaving, complaining, 'I'm just tired of being tired' – a steal of Aerosmith's classic 'sick and tired of feeling sick and tired' line.

The basic bank-robbers/hostage drama story with a salmon-poaching sub-plot (Tarantino it ain't) limps on with Josh joining the hostages. Josh, who only just survived being blown up a couple of weeks ago, has enjoyed a torrid time of late. His whole family were wiped out in a fire, plunging him into alcohol-fuelled, gambling-addicted debt and misery – not, in short, someone you'd want to hang around with.

In its prime, the staff at Casualty represented shining proof of all that was great about the NHS, but they've really deteriorated recently with most members of staff going bonkers, copping off with one another or fending off malpractice suits for killing their patients. Now it's more like anti-NHS propaganda for going private. Saturday's episode ends when one of the most popular characters bites the dust. It crosses your mind that it's a shame it's only one.

There's a disappointing, surprising lack of fireworks in **Cutting Edge** too, with 'Shot', a classic case of a good idea (the psychology behind being shot/shooting people) wasted. Even the interviewer seems to have been expecting more dramatic answers, naively probing – to no avail – for members of the military to have more feelings for the other person involved in the shooting. 'The army trained me well and the aim was to neutralise the person trying to kill me and... I neutralised him.'

Despite so much (deeply pretentious) in-depth photography, even the presence of an arms industry salesman fails to explain how guns work. How does that little trigger cause the bullet to move at speeds of 3,000 feet per second? 'It's designed to do a job and it does it very well' doesn't really explain it. Throughout, shooting the screen out of sheer boredom is, sadly, always an option.

Targets of a different kind in **The Football Millionaires**, presented by the magnificent Alan Hansen – namely the 70 Premiership millionaires booed, abused and despised by millions every week. Several are interviewed – the likes of Shearer and Beckham, Adams, Clayton Blackmore – by a predictably envious, penny-pinching Hansen whose first boot deal back in 1978 made him £600-a-year compared to Beckham's £600,000 (surely not enough). In his day, Hansen would do five or six interviews a year, which is what the millionaires can do in a single day. Beckham's footage – coaching schoolkids, making Adidas ads – contains rare film of him not being booed and accompanied by chants of 'Does she take it up the arse?'

The flip side of the footballers' gilded lifestyle is offered by the likes of Jamie Redknapp (mobbed in his car either by fans or by Scousers trying to have his hubcaps away) and Dwight Yorke who misses both his family (in Trinidad) and his old friends in the Midlands (John Gregory). Yorke's hotel room is littered with clothes – both men's and women's, presumably the aftermath of one of his famous cross-dressing parties with Mark Bosnich. 'Interesting' Alan Shearer and 'Quick-witted' Michael Owen dazzle us with their insights. Owen gives Hansen a beating at golf, snooker and Battling Tops.

Their affluent lifestyles – adequate remuneration not just for their football skills but for their diving – is contrasted most touchingly with that of Norman Whiteside, who is shown turning Hansen inside out before scoring against Liverpool at Wembley. Since a career-ending injury Norman has gone back to college and trained as a physiotherapist. 'With their money do you think Michael Owen or David Beckham will go back to resume their education?' Hansen asks. As if their primary schools would take them back now.

March 13–19 1999

Watching the wildlife

Sometimes you can't help but wonder if the nation's programme-makers are getting paid in air miles. Just a quick flick through the schedule will get you from Brixton to Virunga via what **Supernatural** rightly calls, the 'Outer Limits'.

Legions of holiday programmes and travel shows have now been joined by a mutant hybrid that has a token dollop of docu-soap thrown in.

At least Sky's Miami Uncovered is slick, but watching Viva Espana and Was It Good For You? you have to wonder if People From England Who Now Live In Spain are really that interesting. More mundanely, John Peel is still trundling around Britain looking for unlistenable indie demos with which to persecute us when he could just be at home listening to the mighty Nas or trying to decipher Juvenile. As for Russell Grant's Postcards In Switzerland, surely even featuring this odious ex/non-celebrity contravenes Channel 5's remit.

Thank God then for the animal kingdom making foreign places not only more appealing but so foreign we will never comprehend them. **The Natural World** on Iran has crocodiles that you can swim with and a fight between two male mud-skippers that is like something out of Star Wars. It has yellow-bellied sea snakes that are so poisonous 'one drop of venom can kill three men' – a pretty neat trick if you can do it (snakes being able to swim really is the last thing we need, isn't it?)

'Wild Tales' introduces us to Virunga, an epic national park in Central Africa named after its active volcanoes that create what the narrator insists on describing, in a doom-ridden, sonorous boom as 'great rivers of fire', as if he was a Red Indian. He then suffers an outbreak of Brass Eye disease as he presents us with 'a vegetable kingdom seemingly gone berserk!' It is here (and not Sainsbury's) that we discover 'the big game of the vegetable kingdom, real-life triffids, like monstrous cabbages on the march' (except, er, stationary).

The animals, though, are fantastic: 30,000 hippos lounging around in the mud as tightly crammed as sardines, male deer parading like street walkers, being expertly cruised by females. Then there is the weirdest cemetery you will ever see, littered with 'bones and bodies' (old and fresh), 'bats, birds, butterflies and buffalo' – victims of an indiscriminate killer more elusive than the Pimpernel. (You'll never guess it.) Finally, we see a group of gigantic mountain gorillas studying a delicate chameleon as fascinated and attentive as any anthropology class, folding their arms, frowning and virtually stroking their chins with interest. Ace.

Only a series as stupendous and psychedelic as **Supernatural** could top this, though sometimes you can't help thinking they're just making things up. The *fantastic* Thorny Devil, for example, has surely been knocked up in the studio – a mechanical, multi-coloured toy covered with spikes, made out of Lego. One bacteria (in South Africa), they claim, 'can live for 1,000 years, eating nothing but rock'. Fire beetles will travel miles to get into a fire, while migrating bar-headed geese fly so high, at temperatures of minus 55, that 'only the heat from their exertion stops them from freezing solid'. (It's a goose's life, as they say.)

One little red desert frog survives, entombed under the sand for seven years only for an old aborigine to come along, dig him up and squeeze a drink for himself out of the water it has stored in its bladder, crushing it like a tin can. Do not miss the thousands of red-sided garter snakes racing out of hibernation to mate, like a valley full of spaghetti. One tardy serpent freezes in the cold ('like an ice sculpture'), only to be resurrected the following day thanks to the anti-freeze round its vital organs. (Result!)

It would be unfair to expect Vincent Osborne, would-be Brixton entrepreneur, to compete with all this (no matter how exotic he is), but **Electric Avenue** stands out from the week's documentaries in that it makes its subjects *human*. Mistakenly labelled as a docu-soap, the four forthcoming episodes treat its characters with enough respect to give them each their own programme – more like an *anti* docu-soap. It politely, courageously resists resorting to the Brixton bad bwoys and girl gangs but instead gives a patient, unobtrusive and rather poignant picture of the Brixton people trying to make a life for themselves against the odds. It makes a change to see a series that, instead of relishing the chance to stitch its subjects up, for once manages not only to show some love but actually *represents*.

April 3–9 1999

London calling

Unlike the rest of the country, Tapehead's expectations at the prospect of the adaptation of yet another literary classic are never really that great. Sure enough, despite a script by the creator of the seminal Holding On, the start of **Great Expectations** is weighed down with hordes of winsome, dirty-faced urchins, overacting extras dressed in bonnets and country-bumpkin types in enormous brown skirts doing their Mrs Bridges from Upstairs Downstairs. Bernard Hill wades in with a West Country Yosser Hughes, 'oooooh-arrr'-ing away like one of the Wurzels, reducing it all to a French and Saunders sketch.

Things pick up – as they generally do – with the arrival of a spectral Charlotte Rampling as Miss Havisham, looking as pale and haunted as

John Hurt, sitting mentally and physically unbalanced on a throne in a tiara and wedding dress covered in cobwebs. For a while it looks promising – The Turn of The Screw styled as a Visage video – until you realise that Charlotte R. is so good, so mysterious and off-kilter that when she's not in it your interest wavers.

Tony Marchant's script turns the chocolate-box, period-piece details down to a minimum until his protagonists are so dark, so self-centred and sadistic, the interplay becomes emotionally rather stilted. Amidst this, Pip is too shining and spineless (Jude Law with lipstick) to care less about. The BBC maintains that it 'explores the nature of guilt and desire, money and capitalism' but Marchant's interpretation of Pip's obsession to be middle class makes him as shallow and unlikeable as any New Labour clone.

The second part of the easy and engaging **Electric Avenue** – Stacey and The Buff Bay Crew – is actually a more convincing and more touching rite of passage (Brixton 1 – Charles Dickens 0). The night before her Child Development GCSE exam, Stacey Monroe, the junior queen of the South London ragga scene, is out on the town, an explosion of colour and PVC, tearing up the front row of the Scare Dem Crew dance. A Channel 4 film crew has generously come along to help out. No wonder she lets her poor mum open her exam results. When one of the fuckwits from Reclaim The Streets, who have invaded her high street, tries to chat her up by campaigning to her about the bus fumes she just mutters, 'I'd rather smell buses than smell your BO.'

This is a neat, non-judgmental portrayal of the way teenagers like Stacey are torn between being grown up enough to want to do the right thing but young and foolish enough to mess around and mess things up. When the Crew take Alton Towers by storm, mayhem ensues and Stacey is stuck between the two. Somehow you knew straight away they should never have left Brixton. She walks away from the Crew declaring, 'I have things to do. I have to get on.'

Still only 16 but sounding 60 at the christening for her 14-year-old friend's daughter, she comes out with the view, 'You have to look out for the young ones. People like to take liberties with you if you're young.' Sadly, as the footnote confirms, the ring of Self-Fulfilling Prophecy is unmistakable.

If they had any decency or sense Channel 4 would give Stacey a job – preferably presenting **She's Gotta Have It**, their supposedly happening version of The Clothes Show. In fact, more or less anyone younger, hipper or less frumpy than Liza Tarbuck would do. This week, wearing the sort of pink cardy much favoured by Margot from The Good Life and obviously suffering yet another bad hair day, she spitefully introduces the colour yellow to the previously safe, black and white world of Newcastle. 'I'm gobsmacked,' says one local lassie clad against her will in yellow from head to toe, looking like a large banana. 'I can hardly speak.' Why-aye bonny lad, you will have a fishy on a little dishy, etc.

Yellow, we learn, is 'the colour of the summer – it's the colour of the sun for a start' and Bobbi Brown bronzer to go with it can give us 'a nice healthy glow which is *very* this season'. 'Girls with olive skin,' Liza trills merrily, 'should wear red-gold yellows' while 'if you have dark or black skin any yellow looks great'. (The white girls in the programme seem considerably more fussy.)

Finally we encounter Sadie The Bra Lady, 'a woman who knows women's busts like the back of her hand'. According to Sadie, '80 per cent of people are wearing the wrong-sized bra' which, if nothing else, shows you the men of Newcastle are more broad-minded and egalitarian than we all realised.

April 10–16 1999

Ask a stupid question

Rarely can so much out-and-out twaddle have been written about one programme as the nonsense churned out about the demise of News At Ten. One MP was so outraged he claimed it signalled 'the end of democracy in this country as we know it'. All just so that we could see Trevor McDonald uttering the words 'and finally' before telling us how some hamster infant has survived an hour in a tumble drier.

The cancellation of News At Ten has coincided with a severe decline in the standard of serious news. Jon Snow's interview with Monica Lewinsky was just an embarrassment while both Channel 4 News and Newsnight have been panicked into unnecessary style over content re-designs.

The launch of **Tonight** and exclusive interviews with the five youths suspected of murdering Stephen Lawrence provoked only dismay. Having failed to lure Jeremy 'Mad Dog' Paxman, the show, 10pm on Thursday, found Uncle Trevor McDonald still sitting there intent on proving that, unlike his American contemporaries, he has spent too long reading autocues rather than doing any serious reporting. 'We subject them to the interrogation they've never had,' he purrs, inadvertently contributing to what he calls 'their image as a *swaggering gang*'. He places bewildering faith in the fact that the five men 'were prevented from speaking to each other' in between interviews – brushing aside the fact they'd had six years to get their stories straight. 'We unearth a surprising admission,' he boasts, even though the admission was casually offered up voluntarily.

For a 'hard-hitting current affairs series', it is alarming that Martin Bashir's entire line of investigation seems to be based on the idea that there's no smoke without fire. His faith in anonymous tip-offs and the suspicion of one ex-girlfriend is so naive it is almost touching. 'Why on *earth* would so many people suspect that you were responsible?' he demands, even though he has himself been banging on about their rep for ages. 'Why would you *want* to take a knife out with you? It's not like a watch or a bag,' he moans, as if he has never been on a London council estate.

Gradually it becomes clear this programme is going to be about *him*. Questions like 'Am I what you call a Paki?' are purely self-aggrandising, a transparent display of fake bravado which predictably fails to rile them. Getting nowhere with the murder, he starts lecturing them about morals instead like an ineffectual headmaster, clutching at so many straws he even drags up their comments about Cameroon vs Germany. He pompously harps on and on about their spitting and swearing, making the ludicrous statement that the way they sarcastically blew kisses at the crowd 'was *not* the behaviour of an innocent man at a public inquiry'. (Actually, of course, criminals rarely behave as they did.)

Bashir's 'investigation' is so poor that they are able to challenge his assertions about the police cautions they had received or the trouble they'd got into at school without him being able to produce anything with which to contradict them. Despite weeks to prepare, he completely failed to bamboozle five yobs whose combined IQ barely reached double figures or dent their ring of support around whoever did the stabbing. In fact, they barely broke sweat. 'Why don't you enlighten me?' mocks Neil Acourt, contemptuously sealing Bashir's humiliation, clearly bored and amused by Bashir's (irrelevant) displays of moral outrage.

Tonight succeeds only in giving the suspects a platform with which to revel in the fact that no one could touch them. The only food for thought it gives us is the notion that five people as ignorant as these morons had managed to confound not only the Metropolitan Police but the media's finest and probably got away with murder.

Many of their rivals in the media enjoy looking down their noses at Sky, but ironically the time it most comes into its element is often precisely when the news is at its most important. This week's most compelling viewing will probably continue to be the Ministry of Defence briefings that **Sky News** has been airing live with Robin Cook's impersonation of Captain Mainwaring in particular growing more and more alarming. Flicking round the other channels, while Sky News had live coverage of news conferences, breaking news of Serbian rape camps and other atrocities taking place in Europe, Channel 4 and the BBC were showing a choice of Going For A Song, Sesame Street or The Munsters. ITV was showing Richard And Judy.

April 17–23 1999

Richard Madeley's Millennium Cupboard

Reputation is everything as they say, but Richard Madeley's reputation as the inspiration behind the creation of Alan Partridge is surely unmerited. To be fair, he is far, far weirder than that. This week, Richard and the estimable Judy are presenting **The British Soap Awards** with many of us hoping Richard will seize his chance to tell the nation's (night-time) viewers all about the concept that has gripped Tapehead for months, the sort of genius that not even Steve Coogan could come up with – Richard Madeley's Millennium Cupboard.

Anyone who has seen Richard's occasional (Partridge-esque) musings on This Morning will know that his obsession with the implications of 31.12.99 is such that he has been preparing to hunker down, stocking up his Millennium Cupboard with enough supplies of powdered milk, tins of baked beans and walkie-talkies to survive the impending meltdown. Richard has even talked (with the kind of passion that only he can) of filling the bath up with fresh drinking water. (Judy's despair is understandable.)

The morning that he combined his Millennium Cupboard with that other passion of his, poetry, was, as one of Tapehead's many Madeley monitors put it, a moment 'bordering on insanity' – especially when he invited viewers to ring in with suggestions of words that rhymed with (wait for it) *millennium*. You couldn't make it up. According to his press officer, Richard's cupboard is simply equipped with items 'appropriate if law and order break down', to be 'prepared for all eventualities'. So when the shit goes down, Tapehead's heading over there straight away.

The soap awards, meanwhile, pale into insignificance as the 'Viewers' Vote' section goes to show what kind of damage regular viewing of soaps can inflict on the minds of what was obviously a fairly deranged bunch of social inadequates already. The presence of Ashley from Coronation Street as one of the nominations for 'Best Performance', or of Tin-Ed as 'Most Attractive Man' is the kind of mystery even Mulder and Scully would shy away from investigating.

Still, at least the endless endeavours of Lindsey Corkhill have been recognised in the 'Most Attractive Woman' category, meaning that the long-overdue appearance on the cover of *FHM* surely can't be far away. Tapehead's votes went virtually entirely to Coronation Street, though the category for 'Best Exit' went not to Tiffany but to the road out of Brookside. For example, just look at their nominations for 'Sexiest Female' (Leanne, Maxine and Natalie) as opposed to Brookside (Lindsey and Jacqui) or the dreadful EastEnders candidates Lisa Shaw (who she?) and Nina Harris (huh?). 'Best Dramatic Performance', 'Best Comedy Performance' and 'Best On-Screen Partnership' should all go to Roy and Hayley.

Tapehead's own awards include:

Best Male/Female: just Hayley.

Worst Male/Female: Margi Clarke.

Sexiest Female: Janice Battersby/Alma Baldwin.

Sexiest Male: Greg Kelly.

Best 'I Was Blind But Now I Can See' Miracle In Soap: Jim MacDonald.

Best Human Cartoon Character (for his tireless work as Foghorn Leghorn): Fred Elliot.

Maddest Storyline: Jack Duckworth's spell as Lusty Jack Johnson, a nineteenth-century innkeeper.

Scariest Children: a tie between Kylie Corkhill and Rosie and Sophie from The Children Of The Dummy (Coronation Street).

Best Child: The Wonderful Tyrone from Coronation Street.

Best Suggestion For A Child's Name: Calvin Corkhill.

Best Criminal Record: Martin Fowler, the one-man crime wave.

Best Underage Fox: Emily Shadwick.

Best Overage Fox: Emily Bishop.

Best Token Black Man Working In A Caff: Mick Johnson.

Best Orange Man In A Soap: Nick Tilsley – by a whisker from Lindsey.

Worst Hairdo (deposing long-term holder Gail Tilsley): Jason Shadwick.

Most Miserable Person In A Soap (showing experience pays): Mark Fowler, pipping The Entire Cast Of Brookside at the post.

Best Foreign Soap: obviously Planet Brookside.

Our excitement will – like Richard Madeley's Millennium Cupboard – be uncontainable.

May 15–21 1999

Huge swingers

I n television, as in life, there are few things worse than professional wackiness, the kind of curse that for some reason continues to afflict grown men in particular. Think Noel Edmonds. Think Timmy Mallett. And now think **Big Kevin, Little Kevin** – the BBC's latest exercise in scraping the bottom of the TV cookery barrel, licking the spoon and screening what's left.

This series is based on the brilliant premise of taking two chefs *both called Kevin* and having them patronise the hell out of each other. No opportunity to bludgeon any racial or regional stereotypes to death is wasted. The professional Northerner/Little Shit (Kevin Woodford) enthuses about eeeh-bye-gum brass bands and curries while the big black American (Kevin Belton) obediently ends all his sentences with the word 'baby'. It is, to coin a culinary phrase, tripe.

The implicit problem with giving Louis Theroux's otherwise excellent debut series the burden of the title, **Louis Theroux's Weird Weekends**, has quickly become clear with Series Two. His obvious intelligence and charm notwithstanding, Louis has now fully succumbed to the all-too-easy TV temptations of wacky/wacko Americana, much like Clive James and

Jon Ronson before him. Programmes about 'colourful characters' making infomercials or this week's dip into the American suburbs swingers' scene are instantly devalued of any serious 'weirdness' simply by virtue of being about America where such stuff passes for cliché. Next thing you know, he'll be doing weddings in Las Vegas.

As his style becomes more familiar, Louis' bashful awkwardness and vain displays of gawky nudity appear more mannered than endearing. Just as Michael Moore is prone to exploiting innocent receptionists with his bullying, watching Louis benignly baiting nice American women with his brand of knowing irony, gives you the uncomfortable feeling this series is more about Louis than anything else. The swingers episode is thin compared to the wealth of characters in his porn escapade, depending almost entirely on only a couple of fairly average sources with Louis teasing married swingers Gary and Margaret and a pretty vacant hostess, Cara. Where, we cry, is the swinger who wore the diver's suit/penis nose-mask at Gary's last party ('She was a lot of fun', asserts Gary with some authority) or the woman who has been massaging Gary in the jacuzzi? 'You're never going to meet another woman like Jennifer,' Gary recommends. 'She'll do anything to anybody at any time.' Sadly, we will never know.

The supposedly serious science series, **Equinox**, looks at the widely-held view that breast implants can leak, rupture or cause 'chronic fatigue syndrome' but bizarrely messes this up by falling for the transparently wacky ways of California. A horribly zany title, 'Storm In A D-Cup', is accompanied by a bewildering array of gratuitously groovy tunes, pointless scenes of two enormous implants hounding young women in the street (à la Woody Allen's Sleeper) and a frankly unnecessary number of shots showing us what women's breasts look like. (Strangely, they are virtually all attractive, well-endowed young women too.)

Interviews with a prerequisite array of fruitcake American 'scientists' selling their diagnoses for compensation cases predictably follow, along with anti-implant activists like actress Sally Kirkland. Kirkland claims that she was so affected by her implants she considered having her left arm amputated and was only healed by carrying 'the love of a little doggie' around on her arm, becoming 'so filled with love I felt the life-force energy coming back'.

Against this, an independent serious scientific review for the British government has concluded 'breast implants could be positively beneficial' – and not just for the husbands who pay for them. There is even compelling evidence the implants can prevent and even remove tumours. Instead, the producers have ingeniously decided to bury this intriguing possibility amid more gratuitous top-shots than Hugh Hefner's holiday snaps. The use of footage like one model cooking two fried eggs or 'R-E-S-P-E-C-T' on the soundtrack is not so much 'irony' as just further insult to our intelligence.

May 22–28 1999

Hearing voices

The last time Tapehead wrote about Richard E. Grant – in The Scarlet Pimpernel – the big puffed-up thespian responded with an abusive phone call, describing the experience as 'like being sprayed with hot shit'. 'Shame on your head really,' he declared, adding, rather less chivalrously, 'I hope you get some life-threatening disease very soon.'

Expectations were high, then, when Tapehead saw **All For Love** (another costume drama starring Mr Grant) in the schedules, only this time to find that he was back on form. There was none of the pompous pretension, the ridiculous posturing and hackneyed, ham-fisted overacting that usually makes him so excruciating. Instead, there were subtleties in the performance, a wry, wickedly witty underplaying of the social snobbery of the time. He was flamboyant but amusing, he was eccentric but entertaining. He was... oh come on, you didn't think that was serious, did you?

Poor R. E. G. (aka Reg) has long been reduced to pantomime dame stuff and here is aptly cast as 'a bumbling Major' in what purports to be a semi-farcical 'romp' – i.e. it's neither funny or dramatic. It's a farce, but it's a shit farce. The laboured slapstick and hor-hee-hor French accents are positively Michael Winner-esque. There is a duel within the first five minutes ('I demand satisfaction'). The swordfights are like children's TV. The quality of the acting is sub-Rent-a-Ghost (except worse), worse than The Flashing Blade (which was dubbed) thanks mostly to lead Jean Marc Barr who gives Reg lessons in seduction, a prospect akin to being seduced by a giant oily fish. (By the by, in an apparent breach of her contract that demands otherwise, Anna Friel mysteriously keeps her clothes on throughout.) It is (hopefully you're sitting down) more of an embarrassment than the recent two-parter, Nantcheroo. (And that was on ITV.)

173

Reg plays Major Farquar Chevening, a sexually-confusing/confused officer, yet another in a series of Reg's cuckolds (why is that?) and a right big Farquar he is too. Once again, Reg appears to be playing himself (yet again, it starts with Reg admiring himself in the mirror), a self-important dilettante who walks around as if he's got the wrong end of a hairbrush up his arse, looking like a kind of startled, fat-faced turkey – about as dashing and handsome as Charles Hawtrey meets Brett Anderson with Reg Varney sideburns on. By the time we see Reg on horseback, charging across the horizon, chanting 'rumpety, rumpety, rumpety-rump/Here I come on my charger', a surge of pity sweeps across us.

All For Love is based, apparently, on an unfinished novel by Robert Louis Stevenson. Presumably he realised how crap it was and gave up.

Speaking of things beyond parody, the difference between **Silent Witness** and the French and Saunders sketch, 'Witless Silence', is so minimal they had obviously had a sneak preview of this week's juicy two-parter, 'A Kind Of Justice'. 'The second area of major injury is the head,' the pouting Amanda Burton deduces shrewdly during her autopsy of someone who has been nearly decapitated with a garrotte and then had their skull bashed in with a brick. 'I'd hate to assume anything,' said the F & S version, 'until I've gone back to the scene of the crime and needlessly talked to the family and put their lives, and mine, at risk.' 'If something happens to me,' warns the only witness in this one, 'I want you to go and see my daughter. I'm scared.' 'Don't be,' Burton soothes. 'Do Be,' we shout back, enjoyably.

Finally, we bid a fond farewell to **Psychos**, which is surely about to be sent away, sectioned in fact, until the cast get better. As if things weren't bad enough on the ward, it's Friday the 13th. 'It's the end of the world, I'm telling you… Someone's gonnae die,' cries another paranoia-filled, apocalypse-addicted, nerve-frayed nutter and, for once, it's not one of the doctors. Your heart goes out to the Scottish Tourist Board who have only just got over Trainspotting.

This week's case is a mathematician (a naked mathematician) auditioning for a doctor to treat him. 'I need you to settle an argument for me – I want you to find out if I'm mad.' Nash plumps for a 'borderline manic' diagnosis. 'Interesting,' considers the patient. 'The way I see it, I'm just an eccentric.' That's what we all say.

June 5–11 1999

A marriage made in Heaven (the nightclub)

Competition for the honour of worst programme of the week is, in the absence of anything starring Richard E. Grant, depressingly intense. Dalziel And Pascoe is certainly original – mostly for having a title that viewers can't pronounce – as is Channel 5's **Young, Hot And Talented** which has, bizarrely, chosen to feature subjects like Jordan and her boyfriend from Gladiators, Ace, who are in fact none of these things.

Jo Whiley meanwhile is still gamely showing how it's done, generously giving viewers an idea of the rubbish ahead by prefacing her show with intros like 'Hi there, I'm Jo Whiley exploring the *intoxicating* sounds of the orchestral jungle' as if the big words are particularly exciting. 'Helping me to fight my way through the thickets this week are my guests…' Mind you, she'll have a job to better the moment she followed a clip of 'Back To Life' with the immortal statement, 'Soul II Soul wanted to achieve world domination. Shirley Manson… do you think they failed?'

As usual though, when it comes down to intelligence-insulting, stupor-inducing mediocrity, the royal family are predictably leading the way. **Edward And Sophie: The Making Of A Royal Marriage** is Sky's aptly vacuous precursor to Saturday's 'low key ceremony' in, erm, Windsor Castle. Calling it 'the most important royal wedding of the decade' (not to mention the only one), Sky's publicity had, inadvisably, promised much, threatening to 'reveal what kind of man Edward really is' with (sinister) 'revelations about Edward's charity work' and the answer to 'the most closely guarded secret in Britain' – no, not that one about Sophie's dress.

The much-touted 'never-before-seen footage' presumably referred to never-before-wanted footage featuring neither Edward nor Sophie but people who had been to school with her, worked with her or, in the case of one Australian surfer, shagged her senseless. Growing up in a picturesque village in Kent ('known as the garden of England'), Sophie ('Edward's English rose') is, Colin Brazier declares bluntly, 'a commoner'. She fought her way out of the ghetto to make it to Dulwich Preparatory School. 'She was very good at sport,' says one of her Dim-But-Nice friends. 'Swimming, tennis – that sort of thing.' (Yes, we know what sport is.) Over a picture of what is perhaps the most respectable, middle-class family in the whole of Kent, a voice informs us her parents were 'secure, not wild… Her mother made good cakes.'

Edward, for his part, 'hardly shone at exams' but somehow – God knows how – nonetheless 'managed to get into Cambridge'. One thing Tapehead didn't know is that one year he 'took part in The Crucible', losing in the first round to Stephen Hendry. He played rugby but was singled out for (gulp) 'special treatment', 'rough treatment, which forced him to give up the game'. (And rugby.) He joined the marines but left because of the same thing. ('Mud was pushed in his face'.)

Edward was pilloried by the press and, the programme speculates, 'perhaps this treatment at the hands of the media is why Edward later became so secretive about his private life.' Then again… perhaps it isn't. Edward and Sophie, the programme reveals, 'met in the most unexpected of circumstances'. The front row of a Mobb Deep show? The dole queue in Toxteth? A tattoo parlour in the backstreets of Caracas? Seeking an environment where people wouldn't keeping beat the shit out of him, Edward had turned from the marines and rugby union to the only slightly less masculine world of real tennis. His patronage has given the sport 'a modern high profile', helping it to bloom until there are now as many as *forty* real tennis courts all over the world. A 'perfect match' (ho-ho), it was playing real tennis, participating in a charity event that Edward 'had a hit with Sophie'. Afterwards, presumably, they played tennis.

In the only truly revealing moment of the whole programme, Edward explains that, with rules that virtually no one can comprehend and courts that are walled on all sides, real tennis offers the very real benefit that he doesn't keep hitting the ball out. Lawn tennis, on the other hand, he continues with perhaps fatal enthusiasm, is too difficult because 'the courts are too small and the net too high'. Apart from that, though, it's easy.

Cheap jibes aside, Tapehead wishes them luck. Especially Sophie.

June 12–18 1999

Loss of innocents

'**T**he Lost Children', the **Witness** investigation into the political crisis and human tragedies surrounding the case of Belgian child-killer, Marc Dutroux, is a disarming combination of being both utterly unmissable and, at the same time, virtually unbearable to watch. As a film about hell and modern horror, it certainly shows up Thomas Harris and his Hannibal as the sham that it is – as nonsense – with the added dimension of an insight into the nature of human courage that the likes of Harris could not approach.

Parents, politicians and even one survivor of his attacks are interviewed, alongside news footage from the investigation at the time and the national outrage that followed. At first, you wonder why the parents would want to appear so willingly – why they would risk keeping the torment in their lives so fresh? The sheer scale of the police ineptitude soon makes it clear that their pain and anger will probably never go away, no matter how many times they vent them. For example, Dutroux's neighbour, Claude Thirault, a police informer, explains how, long before the killing started, he had told police that he had seen Dutroux staring at little girls in the street and that, later, Dutroux had offered him 150,000 francs to help abduct one. Working on one of Dutroux's houses, Thirault asked about two old water tanks Dutroux had and what they were for. 'He said it was a good place to keep children.'

When 17-year-old An Marchal disappeared, despite her parents' certain dread, the police didn't even investigate. Neither did they do anything when two more girls, 8-year-olds Melissa Russo and Julie Lejeune, vanished. An's mother says that the police told her not to watch so much Miami Vice. Then one day, when they turned on the television to see police digging for bodies, Melissa and Julie's parents started their own campaign. They gave out leaflets all over Europe, made sobbing appeals on TV ('Melissa, my little baby, my treasure, if you can hear me...') and offered a large reward but, mystifyingly, not one phone call was made.

Meanwhile, Dutroux, already under suspicion, had been arrested for car theft. While he was serving four months in prison, the police searched the cellars under his house and even reported hearing children's voices, but they didn't pursue them. The voices were Melissa's and Julie's, who were locked in cages 1.6 metres high and only 80 centimetres wide. Dutroux had paid an accomplice to feed them while he was in jail, but the accomplice had reneged on the deal. The girls starved to death.

Just as you are despairing of this seemingly unending catalogue of depravity and misery, a ray of human hope arrives in the shape of Laetitia Delhez. Bright and lively as you like, she describes how Dutroux, released from jail, dragged her into his van, shoved some drugs into her mouth and gave her a can of Fanta. 'I spat them into the drink and it started to fizz up,' she laughs, making you assume that this had effected her escape. But it did-n't. She woke up 10 kilometres from home, caged with another girl, Sabine Dardenne, who had been missing for two and a half months.

Eventually, Dutroux was arrested and led police to the girls, but the police couldn't even get this (the rescue) right, making Dutroux coax the girls out. 'I could hear voices and thought they were coming to kill us,' Laetitia says brightly. 'I was so terrified as I put my shoes on, I was trem-bling all over.' Her breezy fortitude seems even more remarkable when her mother destroys our hope that Laetitia may have emerged unscathed by saying, 'She told me how much he hurt her. Her hips were crushed.'

Just when you thought a parent's pain couldn't get any worse, it does. Watching Sabine and Laetitia's release on TV, the parents of the other missing girls grew suddenly hopeful. Julie Lejeune's mother even tidied up her room and got her clothes ready. The four parents were together when, days later, the police rang and said Julie and Melissa had been found. 'They just said they had found a leg – and put the phone down,' one of the par-ents says. An Marchal was also found. Dutroux had abducted her and 'given her to a friend. After five weeks of abuse, she had been suffocated and buried in his back garden.' Julie's parents went to see the cages three times – probably, you feel, to try and take it in. The whole of Belgium will never really recover. It was a time, An Marchal's father, struggling to explain, says 'of losing a lot of things. Because it was possible in our coun-try that children became toys for monsters.'

June 19–25 1999

Call the cops

The moral of the story in **Homicide: Life On The Street** seems to be that Baltimore is beyond help. In Baltimore, there is so much lawlessness – so much homicide – even the cops are killing people. In last week's Vietnamese restaurant massacre ('What do you think, doc? MSG rage?'), they were killing each other. 'You want the call?' the awesome Giardello asked jazz hipster, Detective Meldrick Lewis. 'A multiple homicide? On Friday night?!? All-ways!'

His ex-partner, Kellerman, is feeling the heat for feloniously wasting Baltimore's baddest drug-dealer, Luther Mahoney. 'Have we met?' Luther's sister wondered. 'No,' Kellerman snapped back, 'but I once had the pleasure of shooting your brother.' Pathologist/sex-vamp Dr Cox is monitoring signs of Kellerman cracking up (and taking her and Lewis with him), which perhaps explains her own malaise. 'Sorry,' she carped during a particularly cold-hearted autopsy, 'I always get a little giddy doing an entire family. I start to fixate on the resemblances.' Still, when it comes to autopsies, she makes Amanda Burton look like a novice. 'She's been beaten, strangled, possibly sexually assaulted.' 'What caused the head wounds?' 'I'd say she was beaten with a rock, maybe a brick.' Your heart goes out to the Baltimore Tourist Board.

Tapehead has always thought that if the American networks knew the rubbish we have to put up with over here, they might give the likes of **Oz** and Homicide (which has itself recently been bumped off) a longer run. Then again, if they knew the type of no-hope graveyard slots Channel 4 were giving them, they might not.

Tapehead struggled with the first series of Oz on the grounds that it has a worse title than Dalziel And Pascoe, one that alludes (wrongly, thankfully) to Australians or hippie publishers from the 60s. It also has a spurious narrator whose monologues bear the unpleasant echo of Street Theatre and no obvious characters to rival Homicide's Giardello ('the G man') or Sipowicz and Fancy from NYPD Blue.

Still, faith in the Levinson–Fontana ticket is rewarded. Series Two, Episode Four and Oz is brewing up nicely with the same dark, deep/mad, chaotic melting pot of violence, paranoia and retribution that Homicide thrives on. The investigation into who killed Ross in the riot that closed

Series One, for example, was diminished only slightly by the fact that he was, as one inmate put it, 'a low-life scum fuck'. Some of the wackos and thugs are right off the scale. Anyone remotely half-decent gets shanked and you've got to respect any series where one prison gang-leader goes down on another and ends up biting off more than he can, um, chew.

The prison's hi-tech surveillance desk gives the game away: Oz is basically brutal, urban, *sci-fi*. The prison is operating in its own *space*: a contemporary Escape From New York, full of violent aliens. As a statement about the racial divisions ravaging the US, it couldn't get much bleaker. The prison ('Oz') has been carved up into 10 groups – the Muslims, the gangsters, the Latinos, the I-talians, the Irish, the Aryans, the bikers, the Christians, the gays and one called 'The Others' – and never the twain shall meet. (As if to prove this, this week even has a guest appearance by Elaine Stritch). After the (black) prison chief's daughter has been raped, for instance, a (Latino) gang-member is ordered to tell him what he's heard. 'That she's a lousy lay?' he mocks. Once in a while you get a flashback of a naked prisoner chained upside down by the ankles with the word JEW scrawled across his chest: Oz is not taking any prisoners.

By contrast, these days **NYPD Blue** is looking more and more like the Blue Ridge Mountains of Virginia PD. Bobby Simone's replacement, 14-year-old Detective Sorenson (Ricky Shroeder) is getting nicer and nicer by the episode and helping Diane with his own particular form of grief counselling, ensuring that the traditional ending where we get a glimpse of her in the shower and see a male detective's backside carries on.

Sorenson is so young (or so stupid), 'he doesn't know who Norman Bates is', which has rightly given Sipowicz the hump. 'Elvis was old when he was born,' he grouches. 'The Beatles had broken up!' Diane points out. 'Yeah, well I don't care less about that.' Maybe when he grows up Shroeder will be fine. Until then, maybe they could just transfer some of the cats from Homicide (Lewis, Giardello and Pembleton, Munch and Kellerman) over to New York.

July 3–9 1999

Badgers vs ducks

Anyone doubting whether the gulf between the quality of British and American television is as bad as Tapehead keeps saying, need look no further than this week's schedules.

The BBC's new offering on Sunday nights, for example, is the worryingly titled **Badger** starring the glorious talents of Robson And Jerome reject, Jerome Flynn, who appears pictured in the promotional material for the programme looking as gormless as ever, but this time with a spiteful-looking ferret perched on his shoulder (presumably to replace Robson). The 'action', such as it is, 'follows a wildlife liaison officer's fight against wildlife crime'. The justification for this as a valid idea for a drama seems to be that 'wildlife crime is now the fastest growing area of crime after drugs' which, as far as Tapehead is concerned (given that the alternative is crime against humans), can only be a good thing.

Meanwhile, in the American corner, we have **The Sopranos** – already described as 'far superior to virtually anything seen on television or in the movies today'. To be honest, this description just won't do. The Sopranos is, frankly, much, much better than that. In scope and style, for the classy quality of the writing and acting, the humour and violence, it is probably the most original and powerful TV drama since Hill Street Blues started. It is like Homicide meets GoodFellas, David Lynch does Get Shorty, Godfather Part II on crystal meth. (In other words, much, much better than Badger.)

Creator David Chase's pitch to HBO must have been simple – a New Jersey mobster has to go on Prozac and see a therapist. 'Whatever happened to Gary Cooper!' he complains uncomfortably. The strawng silent type. That was an American. 'He wasn't *in touch with his feelings.*' Effortlessly likeable, the key to its success is the way James Gandolfini as mob boss Tony Soprano (combining all the lumbering charm and brutality of a black bear) makes the anxiety attacks he has started suffering so funny and distressing. Even as a made guy, Tony's mid-life crisis is palpably human. For a start, as he says to his shrink (the estimable Lorraine Bracco), 'To be honest, I'm not getting any satisfaction from my work.' The 'waste management industry' (i.e. the mob) is in recession. The stress and irritation of having to go out to a pay phone every time he wants to make a call that is safe from the FBI is wearing him down. His teenage kids are too PC to sympathise with the pressures he's under from running his crew, his wife Carmela (Edie Falco) is a pain and he feels guilty about putting his Mom into a home.

At the same time the old battle-axe is too close to his Boss, 'Uncle Junior' Soprano. 'It's none of my business,' whispers one of his goombahs, 'but down at the club, word is: your Uncle Junior is going to whack Pussy Malenda.' 'I can't go into detail,' Tony shrugs to the psychotherapist, 'but I will say this: my uncle adds to my general stress level' (i.e. he's possibly going to have him whacked). On top of all this, a family of ducks has been living in his pool. Their departure fills him with an overpowering sense of melancholy. 'Yeah I could be happier,' he grudgingly acknowledges. 'Who couldn't?' 'But do you feel depressed?' his therapist insists. 'Since the ducks left... Yeah.'

The dialogue sparkles with the sort of rough casual charm you get in Mamet at his best – like the conversation between mob guys sitting around talking about cloning ('I'm not talking about cloning cell phones! I'm talking about fucking sheep. Science'). This leads seamlessly into speculation about 'whether the royal family had Princess Di whacked'. 'Not only does he shit on us,' one aggrieved crew member complains about Uncle Junior, 'we're supposed to say "thanks for the hat."'

The violence, when it comes, is exemplary: sudden, casual, upsetting, funny and brutal. (Like Soprano himself, goons like Paulie Walnuts have a penchant for battering victims over the head with whatever is handiest – items like the telephone or the bell on a hotel reception desk). It is utterly seductive. 'A genuine fucking pleasure,' as Soprano puts it. Television at its most challenging and charming. When Tapehead saw the first two episodes had been paired into a two-hour pilot that runs straight into an hour of Oz, he practically spontaneously combusted. All we need now is for David Caruso to come back to NYPD Blue.

July 10–16 1999

Badger-baiting

Public outcry has convinced Tapehead that he might have done the new BBC series **Badger** a disservice. It might – readers insist – really be as good as The Sopranos after all.

To re-cap... in Episode One, Northumberland wildlife liaison officer Tom McCabe (played by Robson And Jerome reject Jerome Flynn) got off to a flying start by smashing an illegal ring of poachers, wrestling an enormous plastic crocodile to the ground and discovering a daughter he didn't know he had.

By Episode Two, with no real animals left to worry about, McCabe had moved on – diverting valuable police resources away from Triad turf wars, burglaries and drug-dealers into catching the spate of dodgy taxidermists sweeping Northumberland's panthers. 'Sir,' he complained in the manner of a typically aggrieved, overly idealistic TV detective when his boss won't give him the back-up, 'if someone like *me* doesn't look after these animals, then who will?' – a good point hindered only by the fact that the panthers are already stuffed, in more ways than one. Expertly manipulating a reluctant informant, he came up with the classic, 'Tell us what we need and maybe, *maybe*, we'll go easy on you.' Finally, he threatened the hapless taxidermist with the warning, 'If one bird so much as comes down *with a nasty cough*, I'LL HAVE YOU!' before screeching off in pursuit of Mr Big.

Having cleaned up taxidermy, as the publicity tantalisingly explains, this week 'McCabe has been accused of police harassment, but this does not stop him from investigating a national carp-fishing competition.' It turns out (and who could've known Northumberland was so ridden with this sort of criminality) that the Mr Big of carp fishing has not only killed a cormorant but an otter – a crime that leads to forensics being called in, a door-to-door search for witnesses, CCTV, DNA, you name it. 'I don't need a search warrant for outbuildings, sir,' he tells his boss with the dogmatic, heroic authority of one of The Sweeney, *'someone's killing otters.'* 'And cormorants,' chips in his partner.

The killer touch behind the series' loyal following is obvious: the title is a mystery worthy of The Prisoner or Twin Peaks. The key is: *the badger hardly features*. The enigmatic badger is glimpsed briefly only once in each episode – in a cage at the bottom of the garden – and never helps solve any crimes. Inevitably, conspiracy theories are already emerging. Is the title a cynical device to trick viewers into thinking they'll be tuning in to another cuddly nature programme? Or is it meant to sound like the sort of idea for a series ('One Detective And His Badger') that you might expect from watching Reeves and Mortimer?

Or is it playing on some sort of subliminal pornographic level – badger/todger, that sort of thing, a theory that grows further with dialogue such as the moment this week when a young child suggestively asks, 'What do you call your badger?' The more you say it, the more 'Badger' sounds like the title some sort of exotic porn mag: *Badger Magazine*. And certainly, the promotional picture of Jerome Flynn gormlessly posing with a wicked-looking ferret perched on his shoulder grows more and more fascinating every time you look at it. Besides possessing a chin the size of someone you normally only see on Mount Rushmore, our ingenious detective seems completely oblivious to the fact he has a live animal living on his shoulder. And – the mystery deepens – why is the series called *Badger* being promoted by a man with a *ferret* on his shoulder? (Or is it, as some say, an otter?) Positively Cantona-esque.

In this light, by comparison, series like **The Sopranos**, Homicide or Oz look dismally one-dimensional. Even if they do have guest stars of the calibre of James Earl Jones or John Heard, they're missing one crucial element: they don't have a badger. Instead, they resort to wise-guy wise-cracks; superior American irony; knowing references to Martin Scorsese; darkness. This week, for instance, as his inner turmoil increases, Tony Soprano adds an industrial staple gun to the series' highly innovative list of weapons.

Oz goes one better – featuring a bunch of Nazi prisoners crucifying a convicted child molester to the gymnasium floor by hammering large nails through his hands and feet. Later, a prison officer has his eyes stabbed out. No wonder Channel 4 stick it on after midnight. After all, who's going to watch this when they can watch Badger?

July 24–30 1999

Regnail and I

It's important to have a hobby and this week Tapehead's constant vigil against the forces of evil continues – namely the Ku Klux Klan, Richard E. Grant and **Badger**.

In Badger, the mystery of the series' enigmatic title deepens. On the cover of the *Radio Times*, Badger star Jerome Flynn continues to remain heroically oblivious to the fact he has a small furry animal living on his shoulder. In a new development from last week's picture (when the little chap seemed to peek cheekily over the top of his shoulder), in this week's, although it appears to be gazing fondly up at its master, you can't help thinking the little blighter is about to sink its teeth into his jugular. (Wishful thinking?) True, it now looks more like a small grey seal than the ferret/otter hybrid of last week (a little fotter?) but fools no one into thinking it's a badger.

This week, badger-addict Tom McCabe (Flynn) blithely abandons his post during a surveillance operation mounted to protect the public from a violent protection racket. 'As Wildlife Officer I had to respond,' McCabe pleads to his boss, before uttering his superhero catchphrase, 'Someone's baiting badgers!' ('And cormorants!' adds his partner). His badger-baiting sting climaxes with an exciting, Sweeney-style raid during which McCabe drives his Range Rover through a barn door, runs after the bad guy and shouts, 'Protection of Badgers Act 1992! You're nicked, sunshine!' into the villain's face. 'I *like* animals,' the culprit pleads – inches away from insisting 'some of my best friends are badgers.'

Twin Peaks fans continue to speculate that the badger in a cage at the bottom of McCabe's garden is being kept there for McCabe's personal sexual gratification and that the title, Badger, symbolises something more sinister: for example, Jerome's daughter asking, 'Can I stroke your badger?' His daughter is nicknamed 'Wilf' but the way McCabe says it, it sounds more like 'Woof!', which makes you wonder if, in the end, perhaps the Badger is McCabe himself. (A giant human badger.) Rumours that McCabe grows his fingernails and starts living off earwigs are increasing.

Badger-baiting is all well and good, of course, but nowhere near as much fun as Richard E. Grant-baiting. Yes, R. E. G. ('Reg') is back, with several contributions to Channel 4's **Withnail And I Weekend**. Interviewed against a black background, wearing a black polo-neck, Reg appears to have had his head impaled on a stick (more wishful thinking) – a sort of Talking Head/Talking Reg apparition. He is on truly oleaginous form in what is ultimately a rather embarrassing luvvie extravaganza. Dozens of bohemian actorly toffs/tossers involved with Withnail go on about the creative process and how wild they all were, staying up late, getting drunk, *improvising* like a load of punk rockers who went to RADA. Even the crew gets a mention. ('Marvellous!')

Reg's insight into Withnail's nature is that 'he's got the vanity of a bad actor' – a subject that, let's face it, he speaks about with some authority. 'It has become this huge cult,' someone says, summing Reg up rather nicely. The simmering hatred between Reg and the man who made his career (writer/director Bruce Robinson) is rather fascinating. 'Fatty Grant!' Robinson chortles. 'With his great jowls drooping.' (Tapehead's always liked Bruce.) Reg – the old porker – gets very upset about this. 'I've got pictures to prove it,' he sniffs. 'I've never been fat.' Sadly a picture of Reg as a rather chubby youth suggests otherwise.

The clips of Withnail are testimony to Reg's Carry On Overacting style, a sort of amateur dramatics version of The Rocky Horror Show. 'Mind you,' Bruce says about Withnail, 'Richard was brilliant in that film' – a series of words you will probably only ever see expressed once in your lifetime.

The Nazis in **New Klan**, Jon Ronson's film about the Ku Klux Klan, have a sorry time of it too. The dumb fucks don't even know how to light their burning crosses or keep their pointy hats standing up straight. And the hood linings are so scratchy. Klan members wearing glasses get very confused about which to put on first.

When Klan moderniser Thorn Robb tries to explain to them that using the N-word creates negative connotations and only attracts racist morons, they look genuinely bewildered. They obviously thought that was the whole idea and, let's face it, who can blame them?

July 31–August 6 1999

The outlook is grim

Looking back, if Tapehead could have his time again, he would probably have chosen to be a weatherman. ('My advice for tonight? Stay in and watch videos.') As jobs go, being a weatherman or woman (depending on what suits you) is probably about as cushy as it gets. You can make it up as you go along, talk complete nonsense and get it wrong almost indefinitely. The more money spent on equipment for weathermen to play with (radar and satellite pictures, pots to catch the rainfall in), the less it seems to help. A smiling sun or black cloud will do.

Masters of rhetoric and ambiguity (i.e. lying), weathermen are basically the Used Car Salesmen of the sky. Although what the public wants to know is quite simple, they will use any amount of fancy patter to avoid telling us. What we want to know is: (a) is it going to rain – thus ruining my new jacket and spoiling my hairdo? and (b) will I need a jumper? That's basically it. But they never say. (They never say, 'Jim, you need a jumper.')

What we get instead is a mind-blowing bombardment of irritating irrelevance from a bunch of pathological trainspotter types, most of whom are suffering from the delusion that we are in any way as interested in the weather as they are. So we get endless info and insights into isobars, atmospheric pressure troughs and south-westerly winds moving in from the Atlantic. Sometimes they even get into 'sea temperatures' ('only 12 or 13 degrees') – presumably in case there are any fish watching. The mass of arrows they show moving in from the coast look as if the black plague or Armageddon is approaching.

Their idea of thoroughness is just to tell us more and more things that we don't need to know – telling us where the weather has come from and where it's going. Even more mystifying is when they go back, not only telling us but *showing* us what the weather was like earlier on. Or they inform us that, after midnight, 'the clouds will start to clear' or that 'it's going to be an overcast night' (it's dark for Chrissakes, who cares?) when we're all asleep or indoors anyway. As if having to sit through the weather in East Anglia or the Hebrides wasn't bad enough (most of us pretty much assume that the forecast for Scotland, Wales or Northern Ireland is that it's raining), they insist on filling us in on 'the low mists over the Balkans' or Scandinavia ('that's getting some heavy rain right now'). 'We could well see temperatures over 40 Celsius over parts of Saudi Arabia later,' said the BBC lunchtime weatherman. (No shit.)

The satellites, global info and show-off science are all designed to distract us from the basic fact that mostly they're either going to get it wrong or hedge their bets so profoundly we'd be better off just looking out the window. 'Sunny spells with showers later' just about covers it. Why they do 'long-term forecasts' or 'forecasts for the week ahead' when they don't even know what's going to happen that afternoon is anyone's guess.

ITV don't even bother half the time. Their weather forecast nowadays is just a line drawn unsteadily across half of Britain with words 'mild' on top and 'breezy' underneath. If you want a proper forecast, you have to call their 60p-a-minute 0800 number. Their other decoy is to get personal, telling us to 'sleep well', 'drive carefully' or what factor sun-cream you should put on and how long you're allowed to stay in the sun. This week, Isobel Lang even claimed showers were going to 'make driving difficult – with spray and standing water'. (What, everywhere?)

They've also started offering their opinions on sporting events –

whether the cloud cover means England should bowl first, or how the overnight rain and good-to-soft ground for the big race will affect the favourite's chances. Then they tell you that they themselves are going to be making the most of the dry weather, spending the weekend in the garden.

The exception to all this is former GMTV weather queen, Francis Wilson, now purring away on Sky News. Like a softly spoken, ultra-casual cross between Des Lynam and David Hunter from Crossroads, Francis keeps his hand in his pocket and chats away using a series of smooth elliptical phrases – 'that rain will linger, I think' – pausing suavely to pout at the camera, and generally treating reading the weather forecast as if he's making love to a beautiful woman: smooth but authoritative.

As for the rest of them, they should bear in mind that the only time I have ever had any faith in any of them was when Michael Fish read the forecast wearing a short-sleeved shirt. Good clue. Maybe when it's going to pour down, he could wear a cagoule. Then we'd get the picture. If it's going to snow, he could wear a ski-mask.

August 21–27 1999

Bringing out the beast

' I looked at her and she looked at me,' sighs an American hillbilly coyly, virtually blushing with affection, 'and all my resolve just went. I realised I couldn't deny it any more. I lurved her, I was in lurve with her, and I told her.'

After last week's Adult Lives, the relentless crossover of programmes about sex from the salacious tackiness of Live TV and Channel 5 onto the more 'respectable' channels reaches an inevitable nadir this week with **Hidden Love**'s boast that it is 'the first film to examine a subject which many find disturbing'. 'I love my animals,' Mark, our besotted hillbilly continues. 'Sex, clearly, is an option, but I don't have to have it all the time. I've got my dogs – a male and female dog and of course I've got my female donkey.'

Yes, Channel 4 are at it again, returning, belatedly, to their roots trying to fulfil their government mandate to antagonise the *Daily Mail* with 'Animal Passions'. This mostly involves hanging out with Mark and three other 'zoos' in their trailer home, watching them surf the dreaded net and cruising with them for wildlife in their car. 'Wow! Look at her!' one of them purrs, as if they had just passed a girl in a bikini, but actually ogling a field full of horses. The son of a preacher, Mark is locally most notorious for his appearance on The Jerry Springer Show ('I Married A Horse'), having married his pony, Pixel, five years ago in what the programme refers to, somewhat gratuitously, as 'an unofficial ceremony'.

A misguided attempt to gain some sympathy for Mark and his suicidally sad life, or the children he never sees, proves futile. Besides being visually impaired, and probably abused, when Mark was young, the girls he asked out consistently turned him down, 'saying "some other time"'. 'But,' he whines, 'some other time never came.' Mix in the coquettish wiles of the animals themselves and, ultimately, what choice did he have? With a grubby inevitability, we arrive at the moment when he describes the first time he became aware of his desire – as a boy, wiping down a friend's pony. 'And she had her tail up in the air' (the little hussy) 'and something just went ker-ching!' The question of consent is, even he concedes somewhat unfortunately, 'a slippery issue'. But, like paedophiles, the logic of his viewpoint requires that the blame for their predilection is shared and, in part, absolved by the belief that the victims 'can walk away' or resist if they want to.

Sarah, a middle-aged supermarket check-out worker in Nebraska, goes even further. When one of her animals 'wants sex', she explains earnestly, 'it's as clear as a tall blonde stepping out of a negligée before your very eyes and saying, "Come here baby".' (In other words, pretty clear.) She was 36, the narrator inform us sonorously, 'when her husband began to suspect her relationship with Miles, the family dog.' Obviously deciding Miles hadn't suffered enough already, the husband had him castrated. These days she has a pony stallion – 'a baby', she coos, 'but he will grow and then will be able to show me certain behaviours.' What use or interest any of this is seems debatable.

Several, transparently bogus justifications are piled up to try to bolster the validity of the film, starting with the argument that 'it is not known how many zoophiles are out there'. Attempts to cover up the prurience with a more scholarly approach result in several sound bites and elementary psychobabble from a variety of therapists, reference to Darwin, the Bible and, inevitably, the Ancient Greeks who had a thing for swans. A great deal is made of some rock carvings in Sweden from 3000 BC depicting 'animal human contact'. The point of all this seems to be to prove that mankind has a history of fascination with the subject of animal–human sex, as if it was a condition *other people* suffered from rather than the programme-makers themselves.

It veers into Brass Eye territory as Mark announces he would 'love to have children with Pixel' and starts weighing up the advantages of having a human child, a cross-breed or 'a regular foal'. Mark's story was 'too controversial' even for Springer. A studio executive explains they cancelled the show after they started to ask themselves 'if anyone really needed to see this on TV'. Perhaps Channel 4 should have taken the hint and thought about that too. And anyway, what time is the watershed for any pets watching?

September 11–17 1999

(Everybody's looking for) Last gang in town

Life Without The Sopranos Week One, and Tapehead's depression has reached Italian mobster-sized proportions. To cap it all, **Homicide** is now counting down to its own violent death. Rather than hanging its head in shame, Channel 4 (prime suspects behind its execution) have started running it in double bills as if they can hardly wait to see the back of it. The problem, as demonstrated this week by 'Secrets' and the superlative 'Strangled Not Stirred' (The Black Dahlia meets American Psycho with stun guns) is that, even running it after midnight, Homicide still makes the rest of their schedule look rubbish. In 'Secrets', for instance, as members of Georgia Ray Mahoney's crew are still dropping, Detective Meldrick (along with Kellerman, possibly the culprit) admits, 'This one here, I don't get at all. This guy here, he's *supplier*. He's like... *neutral*. He's like *Switzerland* or some place.' Getting Detective Munch started on the Swiss – as with a lot of things – is a mistake. 'I don't like their chocolate. I don't like their cheese. I don't like that little knife that folds out into cutlery. Don't go talking up the Swiss to *me*.' The next two episodes are directed by Kathryn Bigelow and Steve Buscemi – though, presumably, Channel 4 are waiting for them to prove themselves.

The tone of the Blondie **Omnibus** is, sadly, pretty much how you would expect any Omnibus/South Bank Show punk documentary to be: superior, cutely nostalgic, unexcitable. In her fierce early finery, shifting the band's gear around in her old Camarro, Deborah Harry was quite something: Angie Dickinson doing Patti Smith. The pedestrian pointlessness of their recent reunion – illustrated as they duly murder the inspirational 'Union City Blue' at some dodgy festival – is conveniently ignored. They split up – as bands do – because they couldn't stand the sight of each other but, in retrospect, Chris Stein realised, 'I've spent more time with more irritating people than them.' The highlight is seeing them on the way to a benefit gig for Tibet in Chicago, crammed into a van rather than a limousine – 'to make it look good'. 'Yeah,' Debbie drawls in that way that she does. '*We* wanted those Buddhist bastards to know how sincere we were.'

If Blondie's film is about reforming, **The Clash: From The Westway To The World** is a programme about not being able to – even though they look as if they wish they could. Looking at them now, without the eyes of adolescent adoration, the Clash seem really strange: their sheer reach (musically), lyrics that are totally bonkers, their inexplicable fury – what Strummer calls their 'lunatic Stalinist overboard behaviour like sticks of dynamite. We could go off at any time.' Their songs seem virtually uncategorisable, oddly timeless: 'Bankrobber' (described by a frowning Simenon as 'like David Bowie backwards'); 'The Call-Up'; 'Straight To Hell'; the lonely, rumbling rampage of 'London Calling' ('I live by the river').

No one ever noticed that Simenon, Strummer and Jones were actually the most handsome punk band in the world – like Dean, Brando and 70s Pacino. Their extraordinary posing looks even better now: James Dean leather jackets and cigarettes, collars up (surely where Cantona got the idea from). Their stories are like they are: funny and fraternal, heroic and slick. Today, though, they all seem slow, defeated, like hollow shadows – especially cut up against the amphetamine rage of the clips. They seem like lovers, still mourning for what they lost or threw away. When they played their last gig in 1983, they had only been going for six years, charging through such a ridiculous number of songs that they did Sandinista in three weeks.

The pain and sorrow in Strummer's voice is heart-breaking because it makes you realise they probably all knew that the longer the split lasted, the more foolish and irreversible it was. They look as if they've spent 16 years continuing somehow, without the heart, knowing what had gone.

But even this – even deciding not to take the money and get back together again as a pale imitation – like everything else The Clash did, still has a kind of magnificence about it.

October 2–8 1999

For real

Potentially a series for all the thugz, **The Hip-Hop Years** has turned out to be nothing more than a consummate example of the white liberal media's continuing quest to appropriate, and dilute, black rap. Writer/director David Upshal made his point of view perfectly clear at the beginning when he stated, 'Hip-hop music has been with us for 20 years now, but what most of us haven't realised is how big it's become.'

You might think any viewers who had bothered to watch The Hip-Hop Years probably had realised this. The only people who *hadn't* seemed to be Channel 4. Whereas entire evenings and even whole weekends have been dedicated to white icons like Elvis, Neil Armstrong and John Peel, Channel 4 granted the most important art form in black culture since Motown three hours. 'The Hip-Hop Minutes' would have been more appropriate, with the subtext, 'Teaching Your Granny What Time It Is'. 'Two turntables,' Upshal explained, 'meant DJs could play music without interruption – mixing the end of one record straight into the beginning of another.' You don't say. *Oxford Dictionary*-type definitions of 'break-dancing' and 'scratching' were almost as embarrassing as the *Sunday Times*' recent profile of Tim Westwood, which translated 'his *cool homeboys*' as 'his friends'.

The series has been distilled down to this mind-blowingly simplistic chronology: Grandmaster Flash–Afrika Bambaataa–Run DMC–Tone-Loc–MC Hammer–Vanilla Ice–Public Enemy and Ice-T up to Snoop–Tupac–Puff and Eminem. Even Episode One – which was supposedly about its genesis in the Bronx – still gave more air time to clips crediting Aerosmith and Blondie with breaking hip-hop than anyone from Queensbridge. Black street culture has been portrayed in terms of funny dancing, awful graffiti art and the usual obsession with gangs and Gangstas. Biggie Smalls was thus a 'former drug-dealer', Snoop an 'ex-crack-dealer' and the Bronx 'rife with savage territorial conflict'.

Ludicrous consideration has been given to student novelty acts and white-liberal 'controversies' like Two-Live Crew, Fuck Tha Police and Cop Killer, which is not even a rap record. Comparing the seriously overrated Tupac to Miles Davis is frankly a joke, whilst the theory that the album, Efil4zaggin by NWA, 'set the tone for hip-hop for the future' is novel if nothing else.

At the same time, the BBC's **Python Night** has three and a half hours of air time devoted to a pathetically pointless series of programmes analysing the Python's horribly unfunny songs or going back to the houses where they filmed their sketches. And Channel 4 have given white music managers like Tom Watkins, who gave the world Bros, an hour of their schedule for 'Mr Rock And Roll'. So, you might think that modern-day moguls like Russell Simmons, RZA or Dre might merit more than the sound bites they get here. To dismiss Def Jam's success as being based on 'packaging hard-core hip-hop as music with crossover pop appeal' is a serious disservice, while the one clip of the Wu, presenting them purely in terms of their capacity for making money, could hardly be more insulting.

The series' concluding judgement is that hip-hop's ultimate achievement is that it has become 'a new rock 'n' roll for the 21st century' – a shockingly *white* criterion by any standards. The omission of even seriously commercial phenomena (from Rakim, LL, EPMD, Gangstarr, Cypress Hill and De La Soul to modern-day mega-stars like Nas, Busta Rhymes, Jay-Z and DMX) is positively Stalin-esque. And as for female acts, sassy role models like Roxanne Shante, Missy, Mary, Faith, Foxy Brown, Lil Kim, Eve, the only female interviewed in the whole series (Monie Love) is billed as 'a friend of Tupac Shakur's'. The concept of *talent* is never mentioned and acts who've never shown any interest in crossing over are predictably overlooked. (Tapehead would like to show some love to everyone from Genius, the Real Live, Method Man, Blahzay Blahzay or the God-like Mobb Deep to Schoolly D, Stetasonic, Jeru and Pete Rock.) Mos Def and Andy 'Most Definitely' Cole are ignored.

And yet, the final part still finds plenty of time to accommodate a string of liberal bullshit from honky, middle-class journos from *Rolling Stone* and the *LA Times*. No wonder they call it Murda Muzik. Word is bond, as they say. Or, in this case, not bond.

October 9–15 1999

Ha fucking ha

Suddenly the reason behind Ali G's popularity on **The 11 O'Clock Show** is obvious: it's because the rest of it is so mediocre. Channel 4 have been marketing the show's return around their very own O. G., even though he didn't actually turn up until the third episode.

Without Mr G, the format of a news-show parody is looking more and more threadbare – crumbs from the cable of The Day Today, Have I Got News For You and even (surely not) Friday Night Armistice. Some of Iain Lee's gags are not so much a parody of an irritating, smarmy news presenter, as just... irritating and smarmy. Iain is obviously one of those people who has been hoarding old Christmas-cracker jokes for years: 'The Booker Prize,' he smarmed, for example, 'is a prize about *books*. Next year I'm hoping to judge (wait for it) the Booby Prize...' Boom, boom.

Remember those old jokes about Michael Jackson blowing bubbles? Iain's got a drawer under his bed full of them. As for topical... The news that Wales was hit by an earthquake, for example, would seem like a gift. 'An area the size of Wales was affected,' came the punchline. (Stop it, Iain, our ribs are hurting). 'The race row at Ford's troubled Dagenham plant continues. Surely it was Henry Ford who said you can have any colour you want as long as it's black.' That was it. All of it. The 11 O'Clock Show is so flawed it's not even worth watching out of morbid curiosity (like TFI Friday). 'Outrageous' means mentioning spunk, tits, shit, etc.; 'controversial' equals randomly lobbing in a mention of Rose West.

It's not a very good sign when the guests they've invited on in order to take the piss out of (Malcolm McLaren, Linda Blair and even Michael Winner) are funnier than they are. The good news is that even the people who make it know how bad it is. Hence the howls of canned laughter they've plastered over the top of it – especially for the vox-pops where Iain patronises the (thick) man in the street. Even the G-Man himself is struggling. Alexander Haig certainly didn't get where he is today without seeing through chumps like Ali G and was laughing almost as much as the audience. But what can we expect from a channel that schedules a show called The 11 O'Clock Show at 11pm, 11.05pm and even 11.30pm. Why don't you just repeat Brass Eye, you pussies.

It must be a source of constant embarrassment for all those trendy 'controversial' comedy shows fronted by veterans of London comedy clubs and the Edinburgh festival that that boring old git, Rory Bremner, is still sharper and politically more subversive than they are. Put it like this: which show do you think Tony Blair feels more uncomfortable watching? The Stand-Up Show compèred by Tommy Tiernan or **Bremner, Bird And Fortune?** The Frank Dobson and Peter Mandelson are so accurate, they're scary. His Prince Edward is camper than Christmas. 'Hi, I'm Ed Wessex, but you can call me "Sir".'

Tiernan also stars in the aptly titled **Small Potatoes**, looking like a stand-up who has wandered into someone else's sitcom and is doing his best to copy Dylan Moran in the marvellous **How Do You Want Me?** which, unlike its contemporaries, is confident enough not to have any laughter at all. Instead it's just well observed and (here's a radical concept) realistic. Instead of wanting to make lots of noise, it concentrates on just being, quietly, funny. 'Did anything break your fall?' Moran's wife asks him when he falls from the roof of a barn. 'Yes,' he frowns, 'I did.'

The likes of Simon Tilly (from Big Train), meanwhile, star in **Hippies** – this year's answer to The Young Ones/The Goodies. To save you 29 minutes, you might as well know the best gag is the first one – where one of the hippies turns up at his local police station handing over a bag of drugs for 'the drugs amnesty'. 'What drugs amnesty?' says the copper on the front desk. Hippies only confirms that, like Channel 4, BBC2 still haven't twigged that sitcoms in which all the characters are implausibly stupid usually means the series is too.

The real jokers of the week, though, are the useless fuckwits at Channel 4 who are still refusing to show a further 16 episodes of Homicide. Not enough people watched it when they stuck it on at one in the morning. They're having a laugh aren't they?

November 6–12 1999

Unhappy families

Tony Marchant is not, as far as Tapehead is concerned, the best drama-writer on television, as some people have suggested. As far as Tapehead is concerned, after Holding On and even Different For Girls, he is the *only* one – certainly the only one worth staying in for.

The estimable Douglas Henshall (the flame-haired nutter from Psychos) finished the first episode of Marchant's new three-parter, **Kid In The Corner**, kicking the shit out of his eight-year-old son, Danny. Defeated by his son's clinical behavioural condition, he raged, 'You fucking freak! You loser! You're no fucking good to us at all!' He then turned to his lovely wife Theresa (Clare Holman) and their best friends who were watching in horror and screamed, 'People say, "he's a boy – don't worry, he'll grow out of it". Have you ever seen a boy like that?! I've seen a *girl* like that. In the fucking Exorcist!'

It's indicative of the brilliance of Marchant's writing that we can't help but feel for him, even though Danny is not only irresistibly charismatic but helplessly ruled by his ADHD (Attention Deficit Hyperactivity Disorder). Like a nitroglycerine version of Zammo from Grange Hill, Danny, it has to be said, is a right little monster, a lovable nightmare – tearing round supermarkets, shoe-shops and the family home, shouting and swearing with an excitable energy that makes Taz look like John Major. Eric Byrne's performance as Danny is so natural and powerful you can only assume he must be some sort of baby-faced veteran/midget rather than a preternaturally talented child star. (He's probably 28.) Marchant makes Danny's ADHD contagious: the only way his parents can keep up with him is to race along at the same speed or be even more manic than he is.

Kid In The Corner is funny and savage and original. As with Holding On, Marchant takes no prisoners. The end of Episode Two will drain the colour from your face. Marchant's work really makes you wish that Alan Bleasdale and Andrew Davies wouldn't bother adapting costume dramas any more and write something contemporary.

'**Oliver Twist**,' announces the opening titles, 'by Charles Dickens.' Despite some pointless tinkering, like changing Bill Sykes's dog, Bleasdale's made a pretty decent fist of it, neatly adapting the novel to fit his own obsessions familiar from GBH: missing fatherhood, the latent evil of women/wives.

It doesn't take long, though, before it simply becomes a sequence of high-quality cameos competing against both one another and the overbearing oboe accompaniment. Robert Lindsey as Fagin is no Ron Moody and Julie Walters might as well be in a panto. Lindsay Duncan, Liz Smith and Mr Bumble enjoy themselves enormously, as does the bloke playing Oliver's epileptic half-brother, looking exactly as if Malcolm McDowell was doing Marilyn Manson in Stars In Their Eyes. As with all costume dramas, a huge amount of time (especially early on, before the story starts) is devoted to minor characters striding around heartily in riding boots, roasting their chestnuts in front of the fire.

For the first few hours, Davies' adaptation of **Wives And Daughters** seems to consist of nothing else. This is a sedate, stately, period piece of the old school – as if brilliantly ballistic productions like Malkovich's Dangerous Liaisons or Blanchett's Elizabeth had never existed. In the absence of anything actually *happening,* it settles for being a lavish confectionery occupied mostly by ladies-in-waiting with heaving bosoms and heart-shaped hairdos, carrying frilly pink parasols the size of lampshades. 'Ah, Molly!' all the elders bark at our insipid heroine. 'Let me look at you!' 'I think I've been here long enough,' she simpers back. 'I'd better go and be a governess.'

All the fields and woods are decorated with precisely placed groups of extras wandering around pointlessly in neat lines. Everyone wears a big floppy hat and has a sun-dappled four-poster bed. The streets were certainly bloody clean in those days and even the bales of hay, being carried hurriedly around by street urchins, were spotless. The tedium is only alleviated when Michael Gambon bursts on to the scene doing his Fred Elliott and Iain Glen strides about handsomely as if he's got a shuttlecock up his arse. The one saving grace is the absence, for once, of Miriam Margolyes as the batty old auntie. But your heart sinks when, just as you thought Davies might have broken the mould forever, there is at least one Ruby from Upstairs Downstairs, followed inevitably by Mrs Bridges.

November 27–December 3 1999

And the loser is...

Looking back, the most important awards are, as ever, the most contested. For **Most Self-Important Arsehole-In-Love-With-Himself (Of The Year)**, there were sterling year-long campaigns by the likes of Richard E. Grant, Melvyn Bragg and Michael Palin's series about what Ernest Hemingway would have been like if he had been more like Michael Palin.

But they were all wiped out by Donal MacIntyre who ingeniously passed himself off to the national media as a humble, hard-working journalist exposing serious issues when actually all he was doing was hogging the soft-focus close-ups and listening to trip-hop with his shirt off. His sensational exposés included the shock revelations that thick football hooligans like talking about violence and lascivious old Italian-Swiss Tonys enjoy boasting about plying young models with fine wines and Belgian chocolates. Donal's tireless self-promotion and blatantly bogus moral pomposity have been quite exceptional.

Tapehead would like to salute veteran nominees (Clive James, Clive Anderson, Ruby Wax, John Peel, Melvyn Bragg, Jeremy Clarkson, Jools Holland, Noel Edmonds, Nick Hancock, Graham Norton and Prince Edward) who, once again, insisted on having their names in the title of their programmes even though no one actually likes them.

The Best Programme Of The Year was Oz, with Homicide and The Sopranos right up there. (Many thanks to Channel 4 for cancelling only one of them.) The worst was... MacIntyre Undercover, miles ahead of Badger, Joanna Lumley's Dr Willoughby, Jo Whiley, The Frank Skinner Show and anything with vets, pets, cooks, gardeners and Nick Hancock.

Tapehead's **Hero Of The Year** was, it goes without saying, Tony Soprano. Uncle Junior, Big Pussy Bonpensiero and cousin Christopher will have to lump it. Runner-up was Dean from The Cops with Munch and Giardello from Homicide and Big Ron Atkinson from ITV's Champions League coverage resting on their laurels.

Respect is also due to James Richardson (Gazzetta), Tom Paulin (Late Review), Ali G, Richard Madeley (for his Millennium Cupboard), The Wonderful Tyrone (Coronation Street), The Kid In The Corner (Danny) and Alan Hansen.

The Commemorative Sheila Grant Award For Punishment And Abuse Of A Much-Loved Fictional Character Beyond The Call Of Duty went to Jim Carver (The Bill) as Sun Hill's version of the Bad Lieutenant, with Danniella Westbrook not far behind.

Pin-Ups Of The Year: David Wicks (Holby City) and Sexy Cindy (Real Women), Tina from Casualty and Burnside (The Bill), Tom Paulin and Caroline Aherne, Carol Jackson (EastEnders) and Tony Soprano.

Young Pin-Ups: Tyrone (Coronation Street) and Sonia (EastEnders), Jamie (EastEnders) and Sarah-Lou (Coronation Street).

Opposite Of A Pin-Up: Troy (EastEnders), Ian Beale (EastEnders), Linda From The Factory (Coronation Street), Donal MacIntyre.

Odd Couples Of The Year: Troy and Irene (EastEnders), Niamh and Joe-weeee Musgrove (Brookside), Maxine and Ashley The Munchkin (Coronation Street).

The More-Interested-In-Themselves-Than-Listening-To-The-Person-They're-Interviewing Interviewer Of The Year (a category from which Donal was excluded only on a technicality): Runners-up: Paxman on Bill Gates, Dimbleby, Clarkson, Oliver James, Clive Anderson, Clive James, Chris Evans and (perhaps unfairly) Jo Whiley. Leaving the winner: Martin Bashir for asking the Stephen Lawrence suspects if it wasn't true that they were Really Quite Unpleasant and Not Likely To Have Been Friends With The Princess Of Wales One Bit.

Most Overrated/Overpaid TV Personality was shared between Frank Skinner (Male) and Ally McBeal (Female/Bones). Disappointed runners-up included David Jason, Des Lynam, Charlie Dimmock, Kirsty Young, the cast of Friends and the Dinosaurs in Walking With Dinosaurs. (And Donal MacIntyre.)

Inexplicable Phenomenon Of The Year was not, as expected, Badger, Denise Van Outen, The Vicar Of Dibley, Gail Porter, Gail Tilsley, A Touch Of Frost, Jonathan Creek, the return of It's A Knockout, or Buffy The Vampire Slayer, but Barry Venison (On The Ball) and his frankly bewildering career as a peak-time football pundit.

The Let's Forget It, It's Not Really Working Award: The Priory. Runners-up: Maisie Raine, Badger, any series based around an ex-soap star.

Worst Title Of The Year was hotly disputed by Women's Bits, Maisie Raine, Dalziel & Pascoe, Russell Grant's Postcards, Jo Whiley, Oz, Sebag and David Copperfield, but carried unanimously by Badger. Sean Bean's Extremely Dangerous (aka Extremely Useless) was disqualified for being too obvious.

Compulsively Deteriorating, I Used Ta Be Somebody/You're An Embarrassment Award: TFI Friday, Michael Buerk (999), The South Bank Show, Davina McCall, John Sessions, David Frost on Through The Keyhole, Trevor McDonald on Tonight, Joanna Lumley, and the winner: Sunday Grandstand (swimming/bowls/show-jumping).

Best Impersonation: Rory Bremner/Tony Blair.

Worst Impersonation: Michael Palin/Ernest Hemingway.

Best Children's Programmes: Pig Heart Boy, Taz-mania, Dream Team.

Worst: The 11 O'Clock Show, Brookside.

Best Drama: Tony Marchant's Kid In The Corner.

Worst Drama: Joanna Lumley's Nantcheroo. Runners-up: Lucy Sullivan Is Getting Married, everything trying to be like This Life, anything in which Joe from EastEnders takes his shirt off (particularly as Jesus), anything with Richard E. Grant, someone wearing bonnets, or a combination of the two (Scarlet Pimpernel).

Unfunniest Comedy: The first 10 minutes of TFI Friday.

Funniest Comedy: MacIntyre Undercover on 'the PRs of Milan'.

Least Real Women: Real Women.

Least Real Doctors: the foxes and hunks of Holby City.

Smug Bastard Of The Year: Donal MacIntyre.

Talentless Tart: Ditto. Runner-up: Denise Van Outen.

Most Miserable Bastards: (Runners-up) Peak Practice, EastEnders, Oz, Christmas Day's Casualty, Boxing Day's Turn Of The Screw. Winner: The Cops (e.g. blonde female cop: 'I've done me best.' Old fat cop: 'Yeah well, your best is shite.')

Best Miserable Person In Soaps: The Jacksons' Very Very Miserable Grandad. (Runners up: Mark Fowler, Gail Tilsley, Ron Dixon/The Cast of Brookside.)

Worst Crying In A Soap: tied between Janine, Frank Butcher and Barry Evans.

Most Boring Soap Storyline: Ken Barlow's history of Weatherfield, the Brookside rape trial, the Di Marcos' grandparents.

Most Stupid Storyline: Ashley being lost at sea, Max Farnham's 'secret'/off-camera 20-year affair and sea-faring business/beard, Jim MacDonald in a wheelchair/Sinbad going deaf, etc.

Fastest-Growing Child Star: a dead heat between Janine (EastEnders) and Sarah-Lou (Coronation Street).

Best Animals In A Wildlife Documentary: Orang-utans, Komodo Dragons, Thorny Devils, those weird fucking hexagonal/three-dimensional bacteria that live in your duvets.

Lookalikes Of The Year: Tyrone (Coronation Street)/Sonia (EastEnders), Troy (EastEnders)/Spider (Coronation Street), Alma (Coronation Street)/Diana Ross (Motown), Sgt Boyden (The Bill)/Angelo Peruzzi (Inter Milan), Frank Dobson (New Labour)/Bill Maynard (Heartbeart).

Best Christmas Programmes: One Man And His Dog Celebrity Special, Match Of The Day Coventry–Arsenal (Sky Sports), WBA–Man

City (Sky Sports 3) – all on Boxing Day – The Bill, Definitely Dusty and Columbo.

Worst Christmas Programmes: The Best Of Clarkson, The South Bank Show on Bing Crosby, David Frost One On One with Elton John, Bob Hoskins and Maisie Raine in David Copperfield, Joanna Lumley's Coming Home.

Predictions for 2000: Donal MacIntyre fails to get assassinated despite 'death threats', Richard Madeley survives the millennium. (Thanks to Millennium Cupboard.)

December 18 1999 – January 3 2000

Doing the okey-cokey

One of these days Channel 4 will Just Say No to the temptation of making 'streetwise' programmes about drugs. Wednesday's 'Coked Up' night is a serious downer with titles like 'Cocaine On The Brain' and **My Mate Charlie**, which could have been pure entertainment but turn out to be cut with rubbish. Channel 4 reckon that cocaine is 'an under-researched phenomenon' despite things like a BBC survey which confirmed that 99 per cent of bank notes contain cocaine residue. (And that's just the ones in the BBC employees' pay packets.)

Liberals like Channel 4 are surely the only people still labouring under the idea that even the very word 'cocaine' is either ultra-cool or scary – despite the best efforts of Richard Bacon, Frank Bough or minor members of the royal family to give taking Class As a bad name. As a result, the Excruciating Embarrassment factor is so high, some of the scenes are worthy of Brass Eye. ('Sam takes cocaine. Chris has never taken any drugs. They live together in Cornwall.')

My Mate Charlie opens with a revelation reminiscent of the still-to-be-assassinated Donal MacIntyre – exposing the fact that cocaine 'does not turn you into a raging monster foaming at the mouth' and not everyone who uses cocaine is 'part of the glamorous elite'. Drug-takers include Unemployed People (Gasp!), Working-Class People (Shriek!!), even mothers and housewives (Oh no!!!). Emma, for example, a very bright secretary in Hampshire, argues that taking cocaine makes her 'a better mother' on the grounds that it gives her some release. 'It's better than drinking,' she announces. 'It lasts longer and you don't throw up. Afterwards, you can just go into mother-mode.' Emma and her friend Claire, a housewife, boast that they 'wouldn't dream of doing coke in front of their children' – not because it's in any way disgraceful but because 'it's so obvious. When you make a line out on the table and snort it, it's just so there. In your face.' (Or up your arse.) 'I work hard,' one of them shouts, 'and I don't see why I shouldn't spend money on myself. My children don't go without. Obviously, if I *did*n't do coke and saved the money, I could probably take the children on holiday. But I'd be depressed and miserable, so it wouldn't be good for the kids.'

Channel 4's Guide To Youngsters On How To Take Coke consists mostly of endless slow-motion close-ups of people snorting lines of coke listening to tinny jungle music. There are (hilarious) explanations of 'scoring', 'getting sorted' or 'getting caned some'. 'Just take a credit card and chop it,' advises the Delia Smith of the narcotics world. People like Sam, the dim Country Bumpkin, insist that he's 'been doing more cocaine lately 'cos my body's told me that I need it'. Matt the welder discusses the deteriorating insides of his nose. ('Thick wads coming out. Gristle. Thick, thick blood.') Paul, a painter and decorator, breaks his mother's heart and makes Channel 4's day by doing loads of lines during his interview. (The makers can be proud of themselves.)

Piers Hernia of sad lads' mag *Front* explains that, like climbing mountains, people take drugs 'because they're there'. Except they're not there, Piers. You have to ring round for them and then wait all night for people to mess you around, and then they don't turn out to be mountains at all, but hillocks, where the views are shit. A girl named Sue claims that she went from taking her first line to doing 15 grams a day in only four months – a kind of Personal Best that Liam Gallagher would be proud of. What goes up must come down though, and Sue, the owner of seven cats, says she would find herself ending the night licking her cats' paws or snorting bits of cat litter in case they'd got tiny grains of coke on them.

My Mate Charlie also features some of the funniest middle-class drug poetry you will ever want to wince at: 'It seems that it's simple / There's no one to blame / For the whole of this nation is taking cocaine / Simply everyone.' All in all, it's so simplistic and idiotic, it could have been made for the schools' schedules – except, of course, the kids would have pissed themselves laughing.

A better class of hallucinogenic experience can be found with David Attenborough on **The Greatest Wildlife Show On Earth** where the great man is seen standing in a forest in Mexico surrounded by 50 million monarch butterflies. A serious trip in more ways than one.

January 1–7 2000

The artist formerly known as...

Spurning the opportunity of capitalising on his royal credentials, **Crown & Country** is, according to the opening credits, 'written and presented by MC-in-the-place-to-be Ed Wessex'. But Ed then opens his searing examination of the history of Hampton Court by announcing that for centuries England's kings and queens (or 'my ancestors' as he puts it) 'have used the river Thames as their principal form of transport' – as opposed to, say, *our* ancestors who have done likewise. From that point on, you can't help thinking that the hapless ham, the runt of the already runt-full royal litter, is strolling around the lavish chambers of The Court as if he thinks he owns the place, or should do.

Luckily, this week's essay suffers from none of the historical hiccups of last week's programme about St Paul's in which he made the astonishing claim that the great cathedral was designed by Sir Christopher Robin rather than Christopher Wren. (Easily done when one bird looks much the same as another.) He also goes on about Jane Seymour (Dr Quinn: Madwoman herself) – presumably referring to an American mini-series that Tapehead must have missed somehow.

We get to see a lot of Ed Wessex and precious little of Hampton Court itself, and there is more lute-playing and soft-focus close-ups of flowers and embroidery than anything since Scorsese's camp classic, *The Age of Innocence*. Edward delivers his monologues lurking sinisterly between the pillars and strolling/waddling awkwardly towards the camera, wearing the same green Polo shirt as last week's episode, with his hands almost always thrust behind his back as if he is handcuffed. (He wishes.) Each time he finishes a segment of his address, he tilts his head to one side slightly (slightly gormlessly), his face reddening, and stares malevolently into the camera. He then suddenly exits stage left as if he's got somewhere really important to get to. (Presumably to get some money off his mother.)

Edward's speech suffers several worrying moments, though none quite as alarming as last week's appearance on a building site when, wearing a green hard hat, he looked uncomfortably like one of the Royal Pet Shop Boys. There is, though, a coffee-spluttering distraction when he starts talking about 'the two greatest gardeners in Europe'. A brave mention of the Cottages turns out, sadly, to refer to Fulham's nearby ground.

This aside, Edward proves that the royals' mastery of the art of small talk is unrivalled. He himself is someone who could bore for Britain. In fact, he is probably not only Britain's most boring presenter but possibly its most boring person. Deadly Edward and his deadly friends know everything that there is to know about topics such as Hampton Court's system of water conduits, for example, and a lot more that is, frankly, not worth knowing at all. They were made from 'three miles of pipes, 150 tonnes of lead' and built 'with doors with extra locks' and 'walls that were extra thick' – a bit like Edward.

As a loyal and devoted subject, Taphead feels it is his duty to say that Edward should be stopped from making programmes like this, not just for his own sake, but for ours. Maybe if we gave him more money he could go back to doing what he was obviously best at: nothing.

At The Sharp End confirms that the only people more desperate than the royals to do anything for a photo opportunity with the public or the chance to get on television are members of her majesty's pleasure, er, parliament. We follow three MPs going back to college to endure three days socialising with students and attending a media studies course. (A real nightmare in other words.)

True to type, the Tory MP is a patronising, Nice-But-Dim toff. The Blair babe is a heartless, joyless, anodyne Labour automaton, badgering the students to make some sort of scary Christian contribution. But most hideous of all is Lembit Opik, the self-satisfied Lib Dem who appeared on Have I Got News For You recently, who ostentatiously takes his tie off, rolls his sleeves up and starts drinking bottles of lager in order to prove how desperate he is to be liked. In the bar, his idea of cool street banter is to ask, 'So... are you interested in politics?' Lembit/Lib Dem even has a go at some ill-advised rapping but, this aside, the show is not remotely humiliating enough. Certainly no more humiliating than being an MP in the first place.

January 15–21 2000

Tossing off a turbot

Judging from the start of her new series, **Delia's How To Cook Innit**, Delia Smith is something of a reformed character compared to the rabid persona of her previous TV classes. Watching the first series, as Tapehead recalls, was not unlike being trapped in the back of a London taxi cab (albeit a particularly fragrant one) and being barked at by the driver about the pressing issues of the day in the world of food, cuisine and wooden spaghetti servers.

In those days, Saint Delia was so ardent about her mission to make us all as great as she was that she had even taken to lecturing us sternly about how to cut our bread up into soldiers to dip in our eggs. She had firm views on issues like making baked potatoes that were actually so complex Tapehead has never attempted to cook one since. Delia must have real problems going into Spud-U-Like. Spud-Delia-Don't-Like in her case.

Delia is – like those other misfits of society, the politician and the football manager – never far away from an opinion. She gets very hot under the collar about issues like 'herb vinegar' (disproportionately so, really) and positively irate about the concept of raspberry mustard. Her views on the benefits of serving fish on the bone would give Beethoven himself earache. 'Take herrings,' she will trill primly, with the expertise of a woman used to cornering innocent passers-by in the supermarket, 'why-oh-why-oh-why do we regard sardines from abroad as a delicacy but not herrings from our own country?' 'Herrings are a perfectly nutritious meal just waiting to be eaten,' she says. 'That's why I'm campaigning for them,' she announces as if she were running for the European Parliament on a platform of herring policies. Herrings, of course, might prefer that she didn't. The way she opens one up on the table and PUMMELS it with her bare fist will give any herrings watching nightmares, especially as she purrs, 'Some people like to use a rolling pin, but I like to give it a few bashes,' while she does precisely that.

Some of Delia's other views are, frankly, cranky. 'Slow cooking is just as good as fast cooking,' she says – though fast cooking is obviously better. 'There's no point in cooking,' she shouts bossily, 'unless you get the maximum amount of flavour.' (Or, unless you're hungry.) When Delia promises that she'll 'soon have your kitchen smelling of a Chinese restaurant', you can only assume she's never been down Tapehead's local – The Golden Pong. As for her recipes, at some point they all seem to involve pouring copious amounts of sauces over everything. Huge amounts of wine, sugar, butter, onions, wine and crème fraîche are usually sloshed in – with a dash more wine to be on the safe side. Some wine to wash the meal down is also recommended. 'Coarse oatmeal is available at wholefood and health food shops,' she advises (whatever *they* are).

Modesty, as Confucius – the owner of The Golden Pong – would say, is not a friend of hers. You'd have thought she'd have had enough recognition not to need to make statements like 'I'm very good at giving you lots of short cuts' and 'I'm a great champion of casseroling' with quite such vehemence. 'I am the princess of the pudding,' she announces. Indeed. Tapehead is the king of the tarts.

It also gives Tapehead no pleasure to see Delia resort to persuading us that she is right by exploiting her famously coquettish wiles – coyly fluttering her eyelashes and swaying from side to side as she beats off an egg, fingers her fondue or tosses off a turbot. 'When it's boned out,' she says with a little pout at the camera, 'it looks like this,' before giving a knowing glance at the mention of her 'tender hind quarters' and 'lovely meaty juices'. We can only wonder what 'my most favourite ways' really are. Everything is 'my' in Delia's universe. 'My saucepan', 'my mixing bowl', even 'my birds in the garden'. Delia, they're not your birds – unless you're baking them. The pornographic food photography is so intimate, meanwhile, it could put Robert Mapplethorpe to shame as the camera lingers in super slo-mo close-ups on Delia's lovely soft potatoes.

In the end, though, you have to hand it to her. The final results clearly suggest she knows what she's doing and could do well if she pursues her cooking career. 'Fish,' she says categorically 'is *the* food for the 21st century' and certainly – whatever anyone else says about her – the fish-in-the-bag she conjures up knocks spots off Tapehead's.

January 22–28 2000

Hippie shits

Our need for heroes is so endemic these days you can't help thinking our choices get rather *desperate* – as programmes on John Lennon and the Kray twins this week make clear.

John Lennon: Gimme Some Truth consists of original home-video footage following the recording of the diabolical 'Imagine' (or 'the making of musical history' as the BBC put it) in 1971. It confirms that, as icons go, Lennon offers pretty poor material and that, after his last, piss-poor, solo album (the hilariously titled 'Woman'), an early death was the best thing that could have happened for everyone. Weak, nasal singing voice, dull haircut, awful granny glasses, zero sex appeal. Unable, in rehearsals, to hold a note, his vocals are almost as bad as Julian's.

His lyrics are standard student politics clichés or excruciating hippy nonsense ('I see the wind/I see the trees/everything is clear in my head'). The song 'Imagine' is essentially the same melody as 'Jealous Guy' or 'A Day In The Life', and is, in any case, a farce. 'Imagine no possessions/I wonder if you can', he drones from his millionaire's retreat.

Admittedly, you have to feel some sympathy for him for having to put up with Yoko constantly chipping in, chipping away at his confidence, like a wasp buzzing in his ear all the time. (No wonder he shot himself.) But, 30 years later, Lennon's most enduring legacy is being responsible for stunting Oasis' chance to become the first truly subversive British band since the Sex Pistols. When it comes down to it, any of the visiting celebrities in the film – Andy Warhol, Jack Nicholson, producer Phil Spector, Miles – were more exciting artists and better icons than he was. The fact is, as any Beatles anorak will tell you, that Harrison was the good-looking one, Paul was both the genius and the bohemian (he wrote 'Helter Skelter' while Lennon was peddling tosh like 'Strawberry Fields'). Watching Lennon caterwaul his way through several painful takes of 'Oh My Love', you realise even Ringo had more talent. Thomas the Tank Engine wipes the floor with it.

Then we have, what has, optimistically, been declared a **Cutting Edge Special** on Reggie Kray. 'What is the magic of the Krays?' asks the odious James Whale. 'Why are the Krays still a legend?' Because of people like Channel 4 mostly, knocking out rubbish like this. Made by hapless wishful-thinkers Norman Hull and Marcus Sully, the programme is basically a PR job for Kray's wife, Roberta, who only met Kray five years ago anyway ('when he needed someone to help him with PR'), and is intellectually aimed at all those idiots who turned up to cheer Reggie when he went to his brother's funeral and reckon he should be released.

It is full of all the same old faces (Frankie Fraser, Tony 'Soppy Nuts' Lambrianou, train robber's son Nick Reynolds) – all still making a living from the Krays' name. Amazingly, the narration even alludes to the fact that the Krays' myth (that they used to look after their own, only hurt other criminals, kept the streets safe, etc.) is a load of cobblers, but doesn't pursue it too far because it underlines why the programme shouldn't have been made.

The Krays were not 'gangsters', they were thugs, bullies, yobs who made a living terrorising local businesses. (That's what 'protection racket' means, Norman.) The Krays were people you or I would not want to meet. (Francis Bacon said Ronnie had the most frightening face he had ever seen and, let's face it, he should know.) 'If Ronnie sent for you,' reminisces hard-nut Johnny Squibb fondly, 'you'd take six pairs of pants with you.' 'I have nightmares from what Ronnie Kray did to me,' says one old lag who was tortured by Ronnie and his primus. 'I'm bloody glad he's dead, so fack him!' 'Reg is still in prison after 31 years,' Whale complains mawkishly. Good. He was sent down for all the things he got away with, not just for doing Jack The Hat. No one cares how old he is or whether he's changed his ways.

In any case, what none of the Kray sympathisers seem to have realised is that if they did let Reggie out, he'd only get done over in the first boozer he went into, by some young thug or local headcase wanting to prove how hard he was. Someone a bit like one of the twins themselves, in fact.

February 12–18 2000

Out of puff

Cigarette smokers literally kill me. They are, in more ways than one, so full of shit. In their mind's eye, they think of themselves as tough and glamorous when the reality is that the most enthusiastic smokers you see these days are not rodeo riders or 60s sex sirens from the silver screen, but ridiculous schoolchildren, women who can't think of anything else to do and grey groups of office workers puffing away in the rain with all the allure of laboratory beagles.

Smoking should be outlawed not because it gives people cancer but because it's boring – so boring that teenagers think it's a way of being REALLY HARD: like having a bum-fluff moustache. Smokers have yellow fingers, brown teeth and throat cancer. They revel in absurd double-standards that allow them to recoil at 'disgusting' smoky pubs or train carriages and complain when you transgress their 'ashtray etiquette' by putting your chewing gum in it. Worst of all, unlike even your average glue-sniffer, they are always missing one of the essential components and wander around dumbly, looking for a light, an ashtray or even the actual cigarette. (Smokers run out of cigarettes so regularly it's as if they expect packs of 20 to carry secret 'bonus' cigs.)

Storyville: The Last Cigarette concentrates on only one of these petty complaints: the way that smokers seek refuge in the delusion that smoking is erotic or, above all, rebellious. We see lots of old American cigarette ads from the 50s and 60s that suggest the hard-sell on cigarettes has always been rather suspect. 'When you change to Philip Morris, you'll *feel*

211

better,' announces one. 'Here are the reasons why. In case after case, coughs-due-to-smoking *disappear.* Parched throats *clear up.'* In another, air-line pilots enjoy a healthy cigarette mid-flight. (Those were the days.) On the negative side, one anti-smoking ad reminds all those macho male smokers 'the more you smoke, the less you poke'. An anti-smoking scientist holds a white mouse in his palm and watches it wriggle and kick as a solitary drop of pure nicotine takes effect.

At two hours long, the whole montage offers only two really great clips. The famous Senate Committee meeting of (lying) tobacco company presidents, is one. You have to admire the cigarette executive who, sitting alongside his (squirming) colleagues begins, 'I am proud to be here today' and defends his product with analogies to coffee, chocolate and even cheese. 'The difference between cigarettes and Twinkles,' points out the Committee chairman, 'is death.' There is a great scene from David Lynch's Wild At Heart. 'When did you start smoking?' Laura Dern asks Nic Cage as they lie, smoking, in bed. 'I started smoking when I was about... four. My mom was already dead by then, of lung cancer.'

If smoking is a crime, so is **Crime Squad** and Sue Lawless's 'investigation' into the way criminals are getting into the gambling industry. Casinos, farmers and bookies are getting ripped off. (Ahhhh! Shame!?) 'Kids as young as sixteen are getting into bingo halls' is only one of their shock revelations. One schoolboy tells of a classmate using his dinner money to buy scratchcards. 'I saw him with, like, two cards a day.' This is a programme that makes the Watchdog team look like The Untouchables – full of exposés of people betting on hare-coursing, 'destroying crops', 'trespassing on farmers' land' and even 'not wearing green wellington boots'. 'Threats were dished out,' they announce darkly. Laundering money, it turns out, has nothing to do with launderettes. One (anonymous) 'senior steward at the Jockey Club' claims that horse racing is 'attracting increasing numbers of undesirable characters'. (Isn't that the whole point of horse racing?)

In their Blue Peter Guide To Cheating Casinos, the most sophisticated scam is someone plonking their chips onto the number that has already won. (Ingenious.) 'My first lesson,' says the show's undercover investigator, PC Sarah Nagle, 'is to learn how to spin the roulette wheel' (Doh!) – something that, incredibly, she gets wrong – irrationally hurling the roulette ball across the room. All in all, this is a programme whose most notable achievement is that, by comparison, it makes Donal MacIntyre look like one of the blokes who broke Watergate. It makes Donal MacIntyre look like someone who gets death threats that are actually serious. (If only.)

February 26–March 3 2000

The agony and the ecstasy

The one thing that the type of people who make the type of programmes that you get in thoroughly commendable, self-righteous seasons like BBC1's Kick The Habit always fail to comprehend is that, fundamentally, we are weak. We smoke, we drink, we take drugs. We run the risks and take the consequences. We invent all kinds of excuses and justifications, but the fundamental reason for it all is that we are weak.

For the next four weeks, **Giving Up For Good** follows a few decent, good-hearted citizens wrestling with their cravings for alcohol or cigarettes. The nice, well-meaning people who worry about not being able to give up smoking are all very interesting, but it's hard to sympathise when they are the type of smokers who get all apologetic and panicky when they find out they have been diagnosed with cancer.

The drinkers, on the other hand, tend to just plough miserably/heroically ahead. Tina, a 19-year-old addict (and, unlike the comparatively lightweight smokers, a serious mess), has been drinking 10 cans of Special Brew and two litres of cider a day. She has 'mood swings, head shakes, hot and cold sweats, bellyaches, head-rushes', whereas all the smokers have is bad breath. Pamela is five weeks off the drink, principally at the behest of her 19-year-old daughter, Merissa. When Merissa goes off to college, Pamela starts keeping a video diary, which she commences by sipping a large glass of red wine. 'I'm a bit gung-ho right now. Because I've had six glasses of wine. In fact... I'm on my second bottle. I feel good. I feel OK.'

Following the problems of Merissa and Tina, the ridiculously titled **Children Of Drugs** makes you wonder if Paul Betts (Leah Betts's depressingly self-absorbed father) really thinks he has the monopoly on grief/parental pain. There are many surprisingly interesting facets to the story of the Leah Betts overdose in here but you have to sieve through the rot. 'Leah's death (in 1995) was a turning point,' booms the doom-ridden narrator, Jim Carter, patently not knowing what he's talking about. 'It showed a new generation had arrived: the Children of Drugs, for whom

213

drugs like cannabis, ecstasy, heroin were part of everyday life – to accept or reject. The choice is theirs.' Never mind all the drugs that were around in the 60s, the 70s, the 80s... or the abject denial of collective blame that such a hollow preliminary statement contains.

Plenty of things could have saved Leah Betts, but fate beat them all. Her father was a police officer – who saw the effects of drug use on a daily basis (but tellingly never talked to her about it). Her stepmother was a nurse. Both were actually there when the effects of the single (uncontaminated) pill she had taken (not, by any means, her first) began to take effect. The ambulance they called came in 10 minutes. In a way, this is more a programme about her father and (less obviously) her younger brother, William, who is the most affecting victim of the affair. While Betts and his wife were going on Kilroy to promote their anti-drugs campaign, William (who at the age of 11 had to cope with the guilt of having actually seen his sister take the pill that killed her) was coping with getting bullied at school because of Leah's death.

Paul Betts is still railing at the drop-in centres which have probably saved the lives of hundreds of schoolkids like Leah by telling them how to take drugs safely. He is still boasting about how his boorish, bullying school lectures are vindicated by that old platitude, 'If it saves ONE life...' when, the chances are, his haranguing is virtually a challenge to provoke drug-taking defiance. His lectures show he has the facts, the stats, the embarrassing 'street lingo' but still no comprehension of the notion that a lot of kids just don't care whether they end up like Leah or not; or that the way he has absolved the pain of Leah's death by submerging himself in the resulting media storm is just as good a way of escaping life's pain as by taking drugs. His self-pity, self-hatred and rage are palpable, but his lectures berating potential drug-takers are all about HIM, not Leah.

Paul Betts looks down on drug-dealers and young pill-poppers making the same choices his daughter made, but there are worse things. They will never never be as low as the press photographers we see, clamouring to take pictures of Leah's friends arriving for their friend's funeral – part of a media pack whose attention Paul Betts still attracts.

March 4–10 2000

Medication

Last week's Casualty ended with the unedifying sight of Holby General's most fabulous super-fox, Tina, running frantically halfway across town to catch swarthy Doctor Sean and propose to him. Looking even more handsome/gormless than ever, Sean (Mark Ramprakash) said nothing. 'Is that a "yes" ?!' Tina panted but, given that he was on a train, pulling out of the station on his way to London to catch a plane to Australia at the time, it seemed unlikely, even though the idea that anyone could resist an offer of marriage from British medical drama's equivalent of Uma Thurman is, admittedly, ridiculous.

At the start of this week's **Casualty** Tina is still, mysteriously, missing (in action?!) and so the proposal situation could go either way. Max – the other doctor she has been seeing – is, of course, forlornly, none the wiser but then he has generally been subdued of late. (Having seen his son, Frank, set alight, murdered by drug-dealers and then – inadvertently – having saved one of the perpetrators' lives, now – just when he thought it couldn't get any worse – Max has lost Tina, who has gone back to Mark Ramprakash: a real bummer of a month all round, in other words.)

The timing or continuity in Casualty this week seems to have gone haywire. All the viewers (even Tapehead) will be vaguely aware that a week has gone by since the last episode, but characters are still talking about Sean having 'left for Heathrow last night'. Last Saturday, his flight for Australia was 'in two days'. This week's medical stories are (for once in this current series) grim and involving, more like the old days. A man with an axe could be afflicted with self-mutilation fantasies or a suspect for a stabbing; the fear of child abuse is in the air; a bloke called Lenny is up to his oxters in grain, having fallen into a silo – though this, it transpires, is the least of his worries once his wife arrives.

All the Special Guest Victims link up nicely. It's not long before one of them is 'tacky-cardic' and, inevitably, the police and the social services are called. Most of our anxieties, though, are taken up with the lovely Tina. Charlie Fairhead in particular starts being nice about her – presumably assuming that, after Max and Sean, it's his turn for a wing-ding. The bad news though – and there's no other way to break this to you – is that, through one plot twist or another, she is leaving. A couple of weeks ago it was David

Wicks leaving Holby City. Now it's Tina Thurman. Tapehead's world is cast into darkness. Playing doctors and nurses will never be fun again.

As far as Tapehead is concerned, the best thing about ER is normally the theme tune: Roger Whittaker at his finest. Without the frankly gorgeous George Clooney, the doctors are so clean-cut and decent it's all too much like The Waltons Go To Med School. Compared to Casualty, this week's double episode is faster and flashier, altogether more emotive and dynamic. In this way, it reflects precisely the differences in the cultures of, say, Carshalton and Chicago. The first episode in particular is so bleak and brutal it makes Casualty look like Teletubbies. In one storyline, 'a choir-bus from Louisville has been hit by a semi' and, in another, the lives of both a ruthless car-jacker and his victim are on knife-edge, with an ER doctor having to sort it out. ('Tell me where she is or I'll let you bleed to death' is not an approach Duffin would encourage.)

The injuries in the programme are savagely unpleasant. ('Abrasions to the external genitalia. Get the camera.') The pace is so hectic the doctors and nurses can barely even draw breath. (In Holby City they're always just standing around talking.) The medical advice is more abrupt and impressive: 'Let's shoot a lateral C-spine', 'Get the rapid infuser', 'Give him a hundred of lardy caine and prep a drip'. No one is mundanely 'tacky-cardic', while 'nasal oxygen' sounds like something we could all do with a blast of.

Above all, though, you can't help but notice that what distinguishes all the women doctors in American healthcare is one shared, essential qualification. They all have lovely hair – all in the same cascading, lavishly curly style (big; brown). Look at Dr Carol, Dr Cleo or Dr Moll Flanders (Alex Kingston). 'Forsooth, he hath arrested! Give me 6.2ccs of adrenaline and, merrily, we shall save him,' she says through her doctor's mask, riding around the ward on horseback. Still, it was nice to see her with some clothes on for a change, albeit with her bosom heaving. Maybe Doctor Moll could replace Tina.

March 11–17 2000

Felony

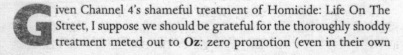

Given Channel 4's shameful treatment of Homicide: Life On The Street, I suppose we should be grateful for the thoroughly shoddy treatment meted out to **Oz**: zero promotion (even in their own

Programme Information), no advertising or trailers (even on their own channel), a transmission time scheduled anything between 12.35 and 1.40 in the morning. (Americans seem to be able to cope with watching it at 10pm.)

If ER can be compared to Hill Street, as some critics have suggested, then what does that make Oz? It's so good, so hardcore, it makes the most savagely real moments in Hill Street look like Hollyoaks. As a portrayal of issues like American crime, race and violence, it makes The Sopranos look like a bunch of carol singers. Written by Homicide creator Tom Fontana, and with episodes directed by the likes of Matt Dillon and Steve Buscemi, Oz, now in its third series, is under private management. They have removed the word 'Penitentiary' and, according to Augustus, its narrator, ditched the whole concept of penitence on the grounds that 'nobody's sorry', and renamed it the Oswald State Correctional Facility instead. ('Catchy huh ?')

In other developments since the last series, the warden, Leo, has grown a beard; Alvarez, in solitary, is existing by drinking his own piss; the cons are jerking off over the woman presenting a children's puppet show. ('Lucky fucken puppets.') O'Reilly's auntie has sent him in a knuckle-duster. ('Next time, tell your aunt to send socks.') The only woman on Death Row (a dark and dangerous, beautiful angel) has been joined by a single male. He tells her he's launching a campaign to protest his inno-cence. 'You're appealing!' she pouts, before a pause. 'Show me your prick and I'll show you my pussy.'

Oz is an unusual series because it is based on a foundation of storylines about brutality, drug-dealing, rape and violence – heavily laced with some serious, seriously clever, funny, philosophy. 'Love is the ultimate half-truth,' the narrator proposed, thus comparing it to a jail-house confession: a half-lie. The theme running through last week's episode was Napoleon: his phi-losophy on war, beautiful (tall) women, plus speculation about the fate of his dick after his death. Oz is still swarming with gangs of tattooed S&M Nazis and bikers, barrio Chicanos and Mean Muthafucka bruthas. Virtually no one in Oz is innocent. Unlike The Sopranos, the series is remarkable because there is absolutely no concession to the concept of anything cud-dly. The violence in Oz is VIO-L-ENT.

Retribution is always being sought by someone. Prisoners get cruci-fied, hung, have their pricks cut off, get injected with AIDS blood. (Things, in other words, that you just don't get in The Bill.) Last week's closest shave was Augustus's as we were introduced to the new barber, a self-professed mass murderer. 'I whacked a whole family. Mommy, Daddy, two little, sweet, adorable kids, sweet old Grans.' 'Why'd you kill 'em?' Augustus asked as the razor scraped his skin. 'Fo' *fun*... I go laying into the little fuckers... Cut their throats.' 'Napoleon once said, "In war, as in love, one must meet at close quarters to get it over with." There ain't no closer quarters than in Oz, baby.' As television goes, it's so explosive, so fierce and feral, Oz is literally the bomb.

Compared to Oz, the kind of dramas we get on ITV, like **The Blind Date**, are rather vapid. Rather than quoting lines like 'Napoleon once said that men are more easily governed by their vices than virtues', The Blind Date instead heralds the return of the word 'bonking'. The plot is based on a rather obvious Colin Stagg scenario: a mother and child stabbed violently; a failed 'honeypot' confession. It is enjoyably unpleasant, reasonably gripping, but rather optimistic if it thinks it can get away with having one character/cipher tell another that it's time to 'call the cliché police'. We have the ruined police officer who is unlucky in love and lives in a stupid house (a church not a houseboat), and whose friends and family are dropping likes flies; we have her photographer ally/suspect with a Comfort of Strangers-esque wall of pictures. And so on. A TV version of Cluedo, several hours go by and the story works its way through so many red herrings that gradually it becomes clear that they have no idea how to end it. Unlike Tapehead.

March 18–24 2000

We all live in a Chris Morris world

People have complained that Chris Morris's current series, **Jam**, is not as good as his two previous television landmarks, The Day Today or Brass Eye. 'Jam,' they say, 'is just not funny' – when of course, at least half of it is not meant to be. As the sub-*Viz* sixth-form Morris wannabes at The 11 O'Clock Show have discovered, the genre of news-based satirical sketches that Morris pioneered is more or less over. The outside world has made sure of that.

Real front-page stories like PRIEST BOOTS DOG IN HEAD (the *Sun*) are pure The Day Today, while BBC news reports of Zimbabwean president Robert Mugabe deriding Tony Blair's government for being 'gay' brilliantly recall Brass Eye when Morris's naval commander lambasted officers for being 'as gay as a window'. Gays are unsuitable for the military, he went on, because 'homosexuals can't swim, they get up late. They muck about.'

So, as his rivals catch up, Morris has moved on. When Tapehead reviewed the radio version of this series, Blue Jam, back in 1997, he told the great man to get well soon, but he obviously hasn't. Given the medically obsessive nature of the material in Jam and Blue Jam, the more doctors Morris sees, the worse he seems to get. Perhaps because Morris is reheating a format that is by now fairly old, Jam is softer, less stunning than the really heavy jam of Blue Jam. But in terms of what passes for 'subversive' television, even his detractors would concede some of it is still fairly amazing. CCTV footage of Richard Madeley 'being apprehended backstage while fucking a coffee machine' or of Robert Kilroy-Silk, naked, running amok in a shopping centre, urinating over a shop-window wall of TV screens bearing his own image, spring to mind.

The scene in which several German porn stars went down with 'The Gush', for example, make the notorious 'Michael Grade is a c**t' scene from Brass Eye look comparatively mainstream. Familiar Morris obsessions – apart from terrible acts against children – proliferate, notably suicide. In one long scene, Morris himself describes seeing a man throw himself on to the pavement from a first-floor balcony, and then repeat the act 40 times over, until death. The explanation that he had chosen this way of committing suicide (rather than jumping once from the 40th floor) – 'in case he changed his mind' – must have made perfect sense to Morris.

This week's episode features the innovation of throwing a six-year-old girl into the mix ('Be fucking quiet,' she screams, 'I'm only six'), as well as a woman who incites violent tragedies as a way of making friends with people. (She lies to one woman: 'Your son has just been killed in a canoe accident', then asks her if she wants to go out that night as she's got two tickets to go and see Cats.) There is also a sketch in which two men in swimming trunks bend over and shoot each other up the backsides. Fun for all the family in other words.

Meanwhile, writing about **Da Ali G Show**, certain critics are still making the mistake of thinking Ali G really is communicating in the street slang or patois of the black youth' they say he is unjustly parodying, when, of course, the whole point about Ali G's lingo is that no one ever used to speak like him in the first place, as his frustrated exchanges with his DJ, The Force, make clear. It's just his (rather sweet) white boy/wannabe idea of how to be black/hip: a junglite/Berkshire version of Westwood.

Once again, people seem to be complaining that 'it's not as good as the last series', but that, to me, is quibbling. It's impossible not to fall for him, or for his creators' sheer love of the character. He still carries the air of the unexpected. Plus he's funny. (Which is nice.) So, for his part, Tapehead continues to say big yourself up G, and would like to take this chance to show Ali some love.

Morris, of course, is not so easy – though someone somewhere should show him some love too. (If ever there was a man who needs it, it is Chris.) A lot of critics talk about Jam, Brass Eye or Blue Jam representing 'the strange, nightmarish world' Morris inhabits and praise his work as being a portrayal of his sick, twisted, unique vision. But thinking for a minute about the themes he is exploring makes it clear why this is erroneous: depression, death, doctors, fear, violence, shame, betrayal, perversity, revenge, hatred, horror. This is not 'Chris Morris's world' by any means. It is your world.

April 8–14 2000

Dumb blondes

TV's youth presenters are so anodyne at the moment, it's no wonder that 80s horrors like Keith Chegwin can make a comeback. Watching Jamie Theakston on **A Question Of Pop**, you realise with shock that, somewhere along the line, you have developed a previously unthinkable affection for ex-Pop Quiz presenter and Radio 1 DJ, Mike Read. (It will be Simon Bates or Peter Powell next.) Theakston is the kind of Thoroughly Likeable, Professional Young Person who is impossible to like. All his guests (from Barbara Dickson to the bass-player in Chumbawumba) seem to like him – the sort of dubious credential that, along with his perfect wall of white teeth and assured autocue ability, underlines the way he is the embodiment of a modern-day Smashey and Nicey we thought Harry Enfield had polished off. Introducing an old lag like Noddy Holder with 'he's got an MBE for services to pop', you can tell

Theakston really isn't joking.

The quiz itself has simply duplicated the tried-and-trusted format of A Question Of Sport – even down to the theme tune. At least half of the questions refer to some sort of venal boy band or grating girl group, with panels packed with knackered old has-beens like Holder. Mobb Deep and Li'l Kim, it's safe to say, will not be appearing.

Perhaps Theakston's single attribute is that he is not Jamie Oliver. Watching **The Naked Chef** is like being trapped in a room with an irritating version of the teenager from The Fast Show. ('Brilliant! Luvverly!!') His life, as we are forced to see it in amongst the cookery, is one long Cool Britannia summer holiday: grubby sideburns, faded denim jacket, nifty, trendy Vespa. 'Peaches! Pukka peaches man!' he cheers as hordes of Friendly Ethnic Workers pat him on the back in admiration as he patronises them. It's hard to describe how irritating and insulting the whole phenomenon of Jamie Oliver is – the way he's a 'man of the people' just because he makes references to 'sarnies' and can't put a letter 't' into 'potato'. (You irri*a*ing li**le fuckwi*.) 'It's gotta be tasty, it's gotta be simple, it's gotta be fun' is his whole ethos, but as far as Tapehead could see Jamie is only one of these. 'Anyway! Capers right?' he gushes, abjectly failing to think of anything to say abaht 'em.

The Oxbridge bods at the BBC might find this terribly charming, but the basic problem of having a twentysomething novice like Oliver as a presenter (placing energy over experience) is that he has nothing to say. 'And what you do...' he splutters manically, preparing wild mushrooms, 'is brush them – with a brush.' Of course, he's gabbling so fast, he could be saying anything. (Unlike Delia, you couldn't seriously make one of his recipes because he whizzes past all the details in favour of showing how wacky he is by bouncing a basketball round his house.) Worst of all, he is not even naked.

Modest as always, **Jo Whiley** is back for a new series of her series Jo Whiley – or as it's known in certain television circles, 'Jo Whiley: A Study In Delusion'. No matter how many credentials she has to the contrary, we must never forget that Jo Whiley is just Really Thick – witness the way she does things like ask Pete Wylie if he ever had the tabloids going through his dustbins the way Justine Frischmann did. (Guess what!? 'Er, no, not really.') 'Does it piss you off the way people keep asking you about taking drugs?' she asked Justine, with the transparent cunning of a glass of water. The frequency with which Jo chummies up to her guests by slagging off the press and 'the tabloids' in particular, you could – like Jo herself – be forgiven for forgetting that she is, when it comes right down to it, not only a DJ but a Radio 1 DJ at that. Amazing.

Her simpering and fawning to her superstar friends like, er, Pete Wylie and the girl from Moloko make her claims to 'the best talk show on the telly' a rare example of wit. Equally, the way she opened the series by reviving the old chestnut of asking her guests what they did the night of the millennium was masterful: pure vacuous pap. Like a Terrahawk without the strings, no wonder she's taken to closing the programme by grinning scarily at the camera and telling us to 'sleep well and don't have nightmares'. If only we could.

April 15–20 2000

Facing the music

When it comes to scheduling programmes about music, the geniuses running our TV stations have failed to realise only one thing: music is for listening to, not for watching. And hopefully for listening to on something better than a tinny old telly.

And so our misery continues – from Paul Weller barking at us on the excruciating Later With Jools to A Question Of Pap. Under normal circumstances, Paul McCartney's Working Classical, featuring tripe like The Lovely Linda, would represent the nadir, but that would discount Jo Whiley's modestly titled masterpiece, **Jo Whiley**. As the series has progressed, Terrahawk Features herself has continued to demonstrate her intellectual debating prowess, engaging in deep conversations with artistic heavyweights like H from Steps and a crowd of DJs (amazingly) even more thick than she is. (Why is it, do you think, that she has taken to introducing the likes of Trevor Nelson, David Holmes and, er, Brandon Block as 'superstar DJs'?)

Yes, the big stars come out for Jo (this week, DJ Gary Davies, the tambourine player from St Etienne and the singer from The Icicle Works) and when they do, music's answer to Paxman hits them with the big questions. 'So, Billie,' she confronted the 12-year-old teen sensation with the alarmingly big mouth earlier in the series, 'where do you stand on Eminem?' (Billie said she liked the red ones best.) 'Have you got plans to try and make it in America?' (Doh!) But that's Jo Whiley for you: a great face for radio. And a great mind for Radio 1.

It was only a matter of time before someone made a supposedly serious documentary about 'the phenomenon that is Status Quo', with the decision to call that programme **Excess All Areas** (geddit!!) not far behind it. The Quo, as we are forced to call them, are one of those bands of knackered old duffers still genuinely labouring under the idea that what they do classifies as rock 'n' roll. Denim jeans, a van full of amps, dandruff... they've got all the qualifications. The truth is, of course, what Status Quo do is the only musical genre even lower than being a DJ. Sunday lunchtime pub rock of the most average quality.

Rossi and Parfitt are the sort of sweaty, fat, charmless old builders who give taking Class As a bad name: for all their boasts of groupies and limos, they have all the glamour of guitarists who roll up their jacket sleeves and wear white sweatbands on their wrists. Their old drummer once filled in the 'Hates' section of a magazine questionnaire with 'recording, rehearsing and touring' and who can blame him?

The big names are all here: John Peel, Noddy Holder, Danny 'I Used to be Funny' Baker, Rick Parfitt's mum. The Quo interviews (earnestly overanalysing their hair, their wild years and even – don't laugh – their songwriting) are, as Bob Geldof puts it, like Spinal Tap – except without the humour. 'Once John left the band,' considers the bass-player (who has already used the word 'soul' in connection with their music), 'it was the beginning of the end of the whole sound.' Rossi recalls the time they put too much speed in his tea (phew, rock 'n' roll) and the drummer admits he once got up in a restaurant and left – by walking across the tables. (He apologises.) The band analyse the 'mental tension' of being on the road and appeal to journalists to stop saying they can only play three chords. (To be fair, it only sounds like two.) 'I thought everyone would like you when you were famous,' recalls Francis Rossi about why they got together in the first place – which only goes to show you how wrong some people can be.

Status Quo, Paul McCartney, Jo Whiley, Steps... None of Tapehead's loathing compares to that reserved for Elvis. Shown as part of Channel 5's Elvis Day, **Elvis In Hollywood** only confirms for Tapehead what he knew all along: that Elvis couldn't act almost as well as he couldn't sing or dance. (Didn't he ever get tired of that happy-clappy, leg-shaking wobbling thing he used to confuse with dancing?) It's time someone put the record straight. Elvis was the hillbillies' homoerotic answer to Billy Bunter, a more orange version of Simon Le Bon if he were to do Vic Reeves's cabaret singer, with all the talent of one of those fried peanut-butter sandwiches he used to live off.

Looking at it that way, Colonel Parker actually did one hell of a good job.

April 29–May 5 2000

Power, corruption and lies

Sometimes in life the temptation to be contrary can be overwhelming. But not even Tapehead is obtuse enough to try and persuade you that **The Christine Hamilton Show** is in any way OK. For a start, the idea that some BBC commissioning editor is handing over any amount of money to the Hamiltons is an insult to our integrity. Then, watching the opening titles, the sense of excruciating embarrassment is such you'd be advised to have a sick bag with you. The social shame and humiliation that the Hamiltons brought upon themselves as a result of their endeavours at the Ritz is nothing compared to what they do to themselves here.

The concept of dignity is obviously a mystery to them, as they will now do anything for whatever loose change people will throw at them, like the sort of socially debased wretches you used to find in Dostoevsky or Dickens. With supposedly gutsy but fake bonhomie, Christine sings 'I Will Survive' for the theme tune while Neil proves what a pathetic specimen he really is, posing as the monstrous bitch's chauffeur, jovially polishing her highness's car and probably licking her boots while he's at it. They sit being driven around London, lounging on the show's red sofa sipping champagne outside Harrods – a truly futile attempt to make their abject greed and corruption into something comic.

The recent (and almost successful) spin that's been put on their disgrace (her book on battleaxes, their appearance on Have I Got News For You, their continuing sense of injustice, etc.) is thus undone in seconds. You realise what shameless, self-serving creatures the Hamiltons must have been, both still completely incapable of accepting that people can see them for what they are. Still, at least they are in good company. The guests lined up on the show make for a parade of some of society's most shabby and nauseating characters, none of them worthy of the air time: Bernard Manning, Jonathan Aitken, James Hewitt and the lowest of the low, Tony Slattery.

At the other end of the production scale – but with a central female with a similar propensity for behaving badly – Channel 4's **Anna Karenina** seems so determined to disdain the type of chocolate-box commercial costume drama that the BBC go in for that, at first, it makes for deliberately dull and heavy-going viewing – so unentertaining it's as if they are trying to re-create the impression it is just like being in Russia. The prerequisite street urchins, steam trains and women in bonnets and horse-drawn carriages are all there, but unlike, say, Madame Bovary, they are bathed in a foreboding, blue light or set among beautiful, moody landscapes.

In the end, even for one of the artier period pieces, the pressures of modern commercial television prevail. There is a blow-job early on, which I'm not sure was in the Tolstoy, and a cigarette scene worthy of Ali G. 'They're Egyptian,' Vronsky tells Anna, passing one over. 'Pure opium.' (For real.) Plenty of gratuitously racy sex scenes follow, but they are cut up frenetically à la Bad Timing. In fact, the camerawork in general is what people usually refer to as 'very NYPD Blue'. This is certainly an interesting twist on how to film a costume drama, but it doesn't work – principally because the photography is too modern for the material. Does it mean the camera work in NYPD Blue is now 'very Anna Karenina'? No, it doesn't.

Finally, **Nice Girl**, a commendably challenging and actually startlingly original piece of drama from the days of A Play For Today, by documentary-maker Dominic Savage, telling a story of teenage pregnancy and betrayal between sisters that is so harshly realistic, it makes Ken Loach look like Bruce Willis. Set in the council estates of Port Talbot/HappyTown, this is one to give the Welsh Tourist Board nightmares. Everything about it takes its cue from the Nina Simone songs on the soundtrack: 'ain't got no home/ain't got no shoes/ain't got no money/ain't got no class... ain't got no mother/ain't got no culture/ain't got no friends/ain't got no love.'

Mind you, it beats watching the Hamiltons. Using improv workshops and unknowns, the quality of the acting and the subtle twists and turns of the drama put most mainstream television to shame and turn Nice Girls into a bleakly compelling soap – or rather the sort of TV you'd like to think a soap should be.

May 6–12 2000

Gay as a window

Whenever someone like Lou Reed comes to town, it isn't long before an in-depth newspaper profile will appear bearing that hoary old headline: Will The Real Lou Reed Please Stand Up? The prospect of this week's **Later With Jools Holland**, on the other hand, featuring the grumpy old tart, prompts Tapehead to demand: Will The Real Lou Reed Please Sit Down And Shut Up? Profile-writers often describe him as 'laconic' but there's nothing quite so pleasingly laconic as someone who's silent.

Not for the first time, **Reputations** also seeks to 'get beneath the surface' of another American princess: Liberace. Over the image of a hearse being given a police escort across the Nevada desert, a doom-ridden narrator hints darkly at the sinister secret the programme is about to consider, 'the one that ultimately destroyed Liberace's public image... and exposed the carefully constructed lie that sustained his career'.

Liberace – the programme reveals – was gay. First it was Florence Nightingale, then it was George Michael, now it's Liberace. Next thing you know they'll be sniffing around the Pet Shop Boys. Over haunting footage of early Liberace performing in Milwaukee, Liberace's publicist offers an insight into the great man's enigma. 'He's in control. He's a ladies' man. He walks with a brisk step. The perfect man.' Offstage, it turns out, was a completely different kettle of, erm, fish. 'Quiet. Very shy. Walks with a shuffle and was gay.' Desmond Morris: eat your heart out.

Early on in his career, in his pioneering 1950s TV show, he was rather wonderful – telling Muhammad Ali to move over because he was standing in front of his candelabra; insisting on the most fabulous piano-shaped swimming pool you have ever seen; moulding his image to look like a young Bob Monkhouse starring as the man that Gary Oldman calls 'Drahkool'. Eventually, though, his outfits – such as his stars-and-stripes shorts, knee-length socks and poncho – mirrored his decline and revealed him as a Taste-Free Zone. (Like Liberace, his talent agent in Vegas had a toupee – apparently made of shredded wheat.) Towards the end of Liberace's life, his plastic surgeon (a dope fiend worthy of James Ellroy) rearranged Liberace's lover's features to look like Liberace's own. Downing shots of vodka and snorting pharmaceutical cocaine, the plastic surgeon also ruined Liberace's looks forever. And all that time... as gay as a window.

The best thing about **Relentless** is that it offers final, indisputable, proof that the BBC's output is now so ram-jammed with brilliance that this stunning, hypnotic, kinetic live performance from the 1991 Montreux Comedy Festival can only find air time stuck away on BBC Choice. When it comes to stand-up comedy at its finest, there is Chris Rock and Richard Prior, Sam Kinnison and Bill Hicks.

Hicks notices how people who disapprove of anything sexually provocative are usually the same fundamental Christians who believe we should be fruitful and multiply. 'Maybe a centrefold in the Bible? Miss Deuteronomy!' A notoriously heavy smoker ('two lighters a day'), when he sparks up it's like watching someone light the blue touch paper. 'My cigarettes have "May Cause Fetal Injury Or Premature Birth" written on the pack. Just don't get the ones that say "Lung Cancer". Shop around. "Gimme a carton of Low Birthweight."'

He sums the Gulf war up in a sentence: 'Iraq had 15,000 casualties. The USA had 79. Does that mean if we'd sent 80 guys we still would've won. Just *one* guy in the tickertape parade.' He lambasts the quality of the Scud missile ('like launching a station wagon') and invents The Stealth Banana to feed people in Ethiopia. Sweating, angry, bitter, Hicks is so antisocial, sometimes he even mutters a scathing little comment at the end of his own joke. 'I'm a "little dark poet", that's who I am,' he niggles. Pity the strangers coming up to him, offering that monotonous mantra, 'it takes more energy to frown than it does to smile'. 'Yeah?!? Well it takes more energy to come up and tell me that than it does to *leave me the fuck alone.*'

Tapehead salutes him.

May 20–26 2000

Always (shit) & Everyone (of them is shit)

The problems with programmes purporting to be 'ironic', 'iconic' or clever postmodern 'parody' is that they are never as clever as they think they are. BBC Choice commissioning editors, for example, might think **The Christine Hamilton Show** has some sort of 'kitsch', 'camp' appeal, but the reality of her interview with Bernard Manning last week is that it was basically just entertainment for racists – for people who get some sort of kick out of hearing the words 'fucking' and 'niggers' said together on television without any kind of penalty. The Stephen Lawrence suspects, for instance, probably taped it.

Just as Eurotrash is probably more popular with masturbating inadequates than knowing students of camp/ironic wit, the TV adaptation of **Lock Stock...** will be essential viewing for moronic yobs across the country. Like Eurotrash, it is strictly Lowest Common Denominator material. Channel 4 may see it as a postmodern/iconic/larger-than-life look at 'gangster culture' but personally it's hard to see anything clever about a series that does anything to revive the word 'spade' into the language. ('Eddie The Diamond – he's the spade who runs the clubs down Walford.') Women are 'skirt', Italians are 'greaseballs', lesbians are 'a bit of fucking fuzz on fuzz'. (Wor! You're hard, lads.) Problems are resolved by 'giving someone a slap'.

What this adds to the culture remains a mystery. Unlike, say, *Loaded*, Lock Stock... has also been done with an almost dogged lack of humour or spark. It lacks that magazine's laddish authenticity too – representing a view of the young, male working classes that smacks of a load of university graduates trying too hard to boost their machismo. (Very homoerotic too.) Lock Stock is *FHM* with more pocket-money – for perpetual teenagers still labouring under the notion that Armani suits, Kenzo shoes and champagne are flash. As enjoyable experiences go, it's like watching schoolkids who think swearing or gobbing is cool/hard. (Amusing for about two minutes.)

The photography is dated, the acting is crap (aftershave advert quality) and the dialogue is gibberish. All the imagination went into the credits. As for the 'action', like the (massively overrated) movie, the makers may think they're referencing The Long Good Friday, The Italian Job and Performance, but the content is so juvenile, the Lock Stock stories are more like the sort of silly capers The Double Deckers used to get up to charging around on a bus in the school holiday in the 70s. Tarantino, it ain't. Minder, it ain't. Hazell, it ain't. It ain't even The Comic Strip or Grange Hill. In short, Lock Stock ain't The Dogs. It's just... bollocks.

Meanwhile, in the land of the TV medical drama, you'd be hard pressed to come up with a title as awful as **Always & Everyone**. Yes, it's clever (A & E – geddit?) but, on a more relevant level, it's also rubbish. *Chez* Tapehead, where virtually any medical drama series is a good medical series, Always & Everyone is known as Always Shit & Every One Of Them Is Shit.

The characters are boring (the doctors and the patients.) The photography is artificial and staid. The storylines are slow and uneventful. (A couple of weeks ago, they had TV medical drama's most boring major accident when the team wandered around a plane crash for an hour.) Not only are you not interested in any of the characters, there isn't even any sex going on among the staff – which, in a programme about the medical profession, is clearly ridiculous.

It's as if the makers were so determined to be clever and do something different from Casualty, ER or Holby City, they deliberately avoided any of the things those series do really well and just concentrated on all the dull bits. So there are no coy build-ups that allow you to play Guess The Impending Injury and you hardly ever see anyone's leg being amputated up a mountain with close-ups that make you wince. Even the theme tune is stoically uncatchy. No wonder Martin Shaw looks so uncomfortable.

Even with several episodes to go, there is no point in getting Always & Everyone into 'resuss'. No point in administering morphine or 16 milligrammes of adrenaline – unless you're part of the audience. Not even a set of those fantastic heart-thumpers they whip out at every opportunity in other medical dramas could save it. Time to say, OK people, we've done all we can. And then switch the machine off.

June 3–9 2000

Teenage kicks

Channel 4 have produced what they call 'ground-breaking new research into today's teenagers' sexual attitudes and experiences'. The 'shocking revelations' in **Sex From 8 To 18** include the following statistics: a quarter of kids under 16 are already having sex; 15 per cent started having sex at 14; 4 per cent at 13. And so on.

These are shocking revelations indeed. Tapehead thought it would be much more. What is wrong with the youth of today? Have they no sense of indecency? These figures suggest to Tapehead that today's teenagers are

229

undergoing a major crisis: not having sex as an act of rebellion perhaps, or as an act of nihilism. (Because they can't be bothered?) In Tapehead's day, 4 per cent of 13-year-olds in his class were *not* having sex, and that was on a good day. (Double geography usually.) Actually, most of the kids interviewed on the programme contradict the findings: they all seem to go like little junior steam trains. One girl complains about how useless sex education lessons are on the grounds that the only position they teach you is the missionary position. (Good point.)

Schoolboys today are, apparently, promiscuous, dirty-minded sex maniacs. They will not hesitate to dump a girl who won't put out. 'Shouldn't you respect their feelings?' the interviewer asks one, primly. 'Yeah,' he concedes, grudgingly. 'But not for long.' (Once again, fair enough.) Anyone reading this who feels they've missed out, it's too late. You will probably never catch up – especially not with Mary, 15, who 'can't remember' how old she was when she lost her virginity but presumably knows that she has done. (She is pregnant.) She thinks she was 12 but seems strangely certain that it was 'three o'clock in the morning – when we'd finished watching telly.' 'I am definitely looking forward to having sex, yeah,' explains what must be the only virgin left on the show. 'Quite predominantly.' (Which explains why he hasn't lost it already.) 'From what I've heard about other people, it would change me. I might come out different out the other side.' (Blimey.)

For the most part, though, Channel 4's research reveals, they do it because they are bored, because they are drunk or because they want to. 'Do you think it's OK for teenagers to enjoy sex?' asks the interviewer, worried. 'Ye-ah!' beams one girl. 'I mean, why else would you do it?! The whole point of sex is that you enjoy it.' A point more succinctly made than most of Channel 4's survey.

Witness, though, suggests some people aren't so lucky, following as it does the fate of the male members of the Freedom At Last Church in Wichita, Kansas, which seeks to 'convert' them from being gay and thereby save them from damnation. These men are described as 'former homosexuals' which rather suggests the programme-makers have missed the point of their own programme. Disciples are locked up, follow a set of house rules and can be dismissed for showing 'a lack of submission towards the leadership', 'not paying their fee' or 'leading other members (and their members) astray'. They spend their days doing Bible Studies and prayer. 'Lord, let me make the right decisions when I'm tempted to masturbate in the night,' which a lot of male readers might recognise, though possibly not for the same reasons. 'Neither fornicators, nor adulterers, nor homosexuals, nor thieves, nor the covetous shall inherit the kingdom of God,' a preacher booms, using some seriously poetic licence.

After the refreshing openness of the British teenagers, the combination of the nauseating, pious pomposity of the Christian counsellors and the unbearable, indulgent tedium of their patients' problems become so wearisome you could forget the subject is sex. Thank God then for Greg, who gets us out of the church when he goes home to visit his sick mother and, after 10 months in the regime, tests his resolve. 'I let one man hold my hand,' he confesses to his counsellor, suitably chagrined, upon his return. But there's something about the way he excitedly goes on to describe the man – 'He was articulate, funny, clever and very handsome' – that means the addendum at the end of the programme is not really that surprising. Since filming has finished, we learn Greg has 'dropped out of the programme. He was last heard of in New Orleans.'

As they say, the Lord works in mysterious ways.

June 24–30 2000

New balls

As predicted by Tapehead two weeks ago, despite poor Kevin Keegan's terminal delusional psychosis, England will not be appearing on this Sunday's **Match Of The Day Live**.

Portugal and France are probably the sexiest finalists, with Rui Costa as the tournament's best-looking exponent of what football should be all about: long hair, shirt untucked and 'a favourite left foot' to boot. Marvellous. No wonder Paulo Sousa and Rui Costa both perform in a Portuguese tribute band to The Verve. Inzaghi for the Italians looks like one of Duran Duran but his understanding of offside is almost as good as John Taylor's.

God knows what game England thought they were playing but it certainly wasn't football – at least not football as played by the likes of Spain, Holland, Portugal and the rest. Even Turkey and Slovenia seemed to understand that control, movement and passing were bare necessities, not something that David Beckham can do and the others gawp at. Only Germany – led by Gary Numan-lookalike Lothar Matthaus – were worse than England. England would have fitted in better (and probably had more of a chance) if they'd turned up and padded up to bat wearing cricket whites.

Perhaps next time, the likes of Michael Owen and Kevin Keegan could be forced to negotiate their advertising/sponsorship deals *after* they've qualified – thus giving *them* an incentive to win and sparing *us* from some of the most dreadful ads on television. The BBC have also had a 'mare of a tournament. The desks that Gary Lineker and the panel sit behind look like the sort of tat you get from the computer section of Ikea. David Pleat, John 'Ron Manager' Gregory and the incomprehensible Johann Cruyff have been a disaster. Trevor Brooking and Stuart Pearce offer about as much insight as Arthur Fowler and Billy Mitchell.

ITV's panel of El Tel, 'Bonkers' Bobby Robson and even Glenn Hoddle have wiped the floor, even if you do have to put up with Des Lynam, the most overrated person on television after Carol Vorderman. ITV also have Big Ron Atkinson, whose invention of non-existent football terms like 'early doors', 'a quick little eyebrows' and 'reducers' is a constant marvel. 'That's what I like to see,' Ron is fond of saying. 'Attackers asking defenders questions.' ('Oi, Desailly, what's the capital of Zimbabwe?')

Nonetheless, come Sunday, we should all be watching the Beeb for the Final. They've got Lineker, Hansen, 'Mad' Martin O'Neill who looks more like someone scary in Irish politics with every game. Hansen's love affair with Zinedine Zidane is just lovely to watch. Above all, though, they've got Motson. Motty has had a great fortnight. 'And there's a flame-thrower on the pitch!' was one highpoint, even though it was actually a flare. 'Oh! Beautiful football!' he cried during the France–Spain game, summing up the entire tournament.

From Euro 2000, like the BBC, we move straight into the tennis – a sport so boring that, like golf, it's probably very therapeutic if you're in the right sanatorium. BBC2's nightly round-up, **Today At Wimbledon**, is bordering on essential viewing, however, featuring as it does the mighty John McEnroe shooting from the lip. McEnroe talking is an almost Proustian blast of New York – the exact point where Woody Allen meets Abel Ferrara. 'I like Leyton (Hewitt) quite a bit,' he will also say, sounding like the sort of society New Yorker you get in F. Scott Fitzgerald. Then, when John Inverdale grins 'Thanks' at the end of the programme, Mac replies,

'You got it' with the sort of terse directness only New Yorkers can muster. Intelligence, sarcasm, rage: as Hansen would say, 'He's got the lot.'

Channel 4, meanwhile, are also smothering us with sport. **Today At The Test**, racing from Newmarket, and that annual drug-fest, the Tour de France. At one point during the last West Indies match, the commentators were oozing with admiration at the way that Michael Atherton had 'gone 40 minutes without scoring'. 'Another perfect forward defensive stroke there,' Mark Nicholas purred during several slow-motion, close-up, repeats. An exemplary illustration of the way that cricket has, unlike the sporting movie stars of Euro 2000, utterly failed to grasp the fact that sport is for its audience, rather than the fortunate few egotists who play it.

July 1–7 2000

Geezer

This week's viewing is like some sort of bullet-headed head to head between hard men; a decathlon of testosterone and old-fashioned brute charm, courtesy of Vinnie Jones, Frank Burnside and Grant Mitchell-lookalike Ross Kemp.

As the title of the latest plug for his career – **Vinnie Goes To Hollywood** – suggests, Jones is doing well for himself, pretty impressive for a man who frowns violently with concentration when he speaks. It's a pretty funny notion – Vinnie Jones co-starring alongside Brad Pitt and Nicolas Cage – but there is the severe danger that not only is Vinnie starting to miss the joke, but is even taking himself seriously. 'I would like to be a major player,' he says. 'I would like to say, "I want 20 million for that movie". I would like to be a Brad Pitt.'

The prospects for his improbable film career are looking pretty rosy – as long as the line of roles requiring virtually Neanderthal silence don't dry up. 'I fink that's harder,' he insists gamely. 'Harder than having lines.' Course it is, Vincent. He bluntly declares himself to be 'the only English actor around who can do these roles. Sean Connery cannot do the fings I can do now', and genuinely seems to believe it. He's got the friends, the house – up in the Hills next to Springsteen, Beatty and Nicholson. It's just the pesky matter of the ACTING that gets in the way. He was up for Numbers – a true story alongside Travolta – but didn't get the role on the pedantic grounds that Vinnie couldn't do an American accent.

Vinnie is a walking (but not talking) gimmick and, as his latest director Dominic Sena confirms, could turn himself into the New Arnie, which these days is something no one else wants. 'We weren't looking for him to be a thespian,' Sena reveals supportively. 'If he got into a fight with three guys, he looks like he would win.' Possibly only Vinnie could win testimonials from everyone from Jerry Bruckheimer and Robert Duvall to Joe 'Straight Outta Watford' Kinnear and Lord Guy Ritchie who, like a lot of toffs, hasn't worked out that talking and trying to drink coffee at the same time can't be done. Worryingly, Vinnie is already lamenting being typecast ('playing Big Chris in a different suit') – the first step to becoming an out-and-out luvvie. Like John Thaw before him, Ross Kemp has the same problem – stoically trying as hard as he can, without frowning, not to sound like Grant.

The only thing wrong with Kemp's latest star vehicle, **In Defence**, is, predictably, the star (and the star's car – a hopelessly nonsensical Renault). When he says, 'I lost sight of what matters', the strain of pronouncing every 't' nearly turns him puce. He runs through the gamut of Grant's facial expressions: a bulldog looking puzzled, a bulldog looking as if he's been stung, Nookie Bear being a chump. He keeps saying/shouting things like 'I can blow this case wide open' and making Grant-like declarations like 'I'm. On. Your. Side.' Kemp can also do a solitary raised eyebrow that would give Roger Moore a run for his money.

Finally, our old friend Frank Burnside is having similar problems readjusting to life on his own in the imaginatively titled **Burnside**. Five years ago (when they should have started this series) Burnside used to get all the juicy storylines in The Bill. He was a lovable rogue, a rough diamond. These days, though, stories about toms, ponces and shooters are ten-a-penny in Sun Hill, the crime capital of Europe.

Burnside has still got the Big Ron big coat, the Big Ron suntan and the banter, talking in strange staccato haiku. ('Two days earlier/I came across Buchan in the pub/We had a ruck/Couldn't resist it.') The problem is, it's all a little bit too knowing, too obviously Sweeney-esque and too humorous, whereas five years ago, Burnside was just Hard. 'You don't like me very much, do you?' asks a female detective. 'No.' 'Why not?' 'I'm a sexist bigot. I don't have to give a reason.' Not only unconvincing but unnecessary. (We know he is.)

It doesn't help that Frank's frontline has been moved to Margate. So

Frank has to keep a straight face when a gang of Jamaican gun-runners come down from the smoke to hit the local rock shop. ('Oh shit! It's the Yardies!') Burnside's even got his own website: www.burnside.co.uk. What is the world coming to?

July 8–14 2000

So I face the final fucken curtain

In a dream, Tapehead sees himself disappearing, shutting down like HAL the computer from 2001. The summer schedules are getting him down. Visibly wearying of so many programmes featuring Carol Vorderman, his doctors give him only three weeks to live before he climbs into the TV set screaming. Only regular doses of **The Sopranos** are keeping him going. It was only when the rerun started that Tapehead realised how depressed he had become since the guys from Noo Joysey had gawn and what feelings of loss he was experiencin'. He was like Tony Soprano and his ducks.

By the end of last week's episode, Tony was beating one of his goombahs over the head with a telephone receiver, in much the same way that Tapehead has fantasised about pistol-whipping Carol Vorderman with the TV remote. This week's violence involves the bell at a hotel reception desk, which, in Carol's case, could also work. Thankfully, a year on, The Sopranos has not dated one iota. The direction, the dialogue and the soundtrack are all a TV dream.

The language too is still exemplary: 'sorry I'm fucken late'; 'they'll do it fucken tomorrow'; 'I'm fucken Rockford over here' and so on. Tony is still beautiful – a noble, haunted bear, trapped in a corner of his own making. 'Everything I touch turns to shit. I'm fucken King Midas in reverse here. I'm not a husband to my wife. I'm not a father to my kids. I'm nothing,' he laments, like a suburban Marlon Brando. Watching him driving out to the freeway every time he has to make a phone call makes your heart bleed. Only Carmela ('What?! Do I look like a fucken Thorn Bird over here?') and Christopher can upstage him. Christopher's greeting to Martin Scorsese – 'Hey Marty! "Kundun"! I liked it!' – takes some beating as the

235

best line of the series, right up there with his assessment that next time Uncle Junior wants to make a hit 'he won't send Boyz II Men'.

Even now, The Sopranos will still stop you from feeling depressed. It's a salutary experience, considering what the British equivalent of The Sopranos would be. Badger, for instance. Or Border Café? If you were going for a title with the word 'The' in the title, you'd have to go for 'The Bill' – Sun Hill being pretty much based on New Jersey.

Time was when Frank Burnside was as irresistibly charming and tough as Tony Soprano. But so far, in his own series, **Burnside** still seems a bit lost. The thriller aspect in the current storyline ('Exposed') is reasonably sophisticated – Cracker meets the Colin Stagg case – but it has a basic problem in that it doesn't actually need Burnside popping up doing his Ron Atkinson act at all. The team refer to Burnside as a 'dinosaur' and these days that's what he seems. 'If he wuz gonna kill 'er, he'd surely 'ave done it by now,' he explodes sensitively when the token female detective on his team takes a suggestion to go undercover with the local serial killer too far. Later, when he's sitting in his car, listening voyeuristically to the completely convincing scenario of the officer letting the suspect shave her pubic hair, you can even see his suntan go slightly pale.

Glasgow Kiss on the other hand is a right load of old MacRubbish – like Hearts And Bones without the heart, or bones. It makes Badger look like The Deer Hunter. The problem with any male Scottish voice-over is that it always sounds like Renton. A female Scottish voice-over and it's Anna from This MacLife. In Glasgow Kiss, the painstakingly earnest Iain Glenn does a fine impression of Paddy Pantsdown, while the feisty Anna character is a Sheena Easton lookalike played by Fiona MacFullerton. The inevitability of the two characters (who live in Glasgow and, er, Clapham) enjoying a wildly improbable chance meeting is painful to behold. It is, inevitably, only a matter of time before they have a MacShag.

As for the tenuous metaphors involving football and the football reporter's love life ('friends and relatives, that's your defence and midfield. Work and home – that's your striking partnership'), they are so laboured that the assessment that Glasgow Kiss is just asking for the transfer list/the red card is equally inevitable.

July 22–28 2000

Press the eject

In a final dream, Tapehead is watching himself host his own awards show. After wrestling with his demons for seven years, three hundred columns and a quarter of a million words, the chance to resolve all the traumatic issues that have kept him awake at night has come: who is Tapehead's most hated person on television? Who is Tapehead's all-time favourite character in soap? Who is Tapehead's TV Personality of the decade? The awards show is like a cross between Tapehead's Hall of Fame and the BAFTAs (the TAFTAs?). Frank Sinatra opens the show, singing 'And now the end is near/And so I face the final Tapehead'. Eric Cantona sings 'Tapehead ne regrette rien'.

Competition for the first award is intense.

Most Irritating Creep On Television 2000: Male: Nick Hancock; Female: Sada from Big Brother.

Favourite TV Moment In 2000 So Far: Sada being voted out on Big Brother; Runner-up: Chris Evans reminding TFI Friday viewers that they were missing The Simpsons 10th Anniversary special on the other side. (Nice going, Chris).

Best Impression Of A Rat In Human Form: Nick Hancock; Runner-up: Ian Beale.

Genuinely Unpopular 'Popular' TV Personality: Nick Hancock; Runners-up: Denise Van Outen, Chris Evans, Frank Skinner, Ruby Wax.

Most Talentless Autocue Reader Posing As A Comedian/Lad: Cambridge graduate Nick Hancock; Runners-up: Jonathan Ross, Jamie Oliver, David Baddiel, Lord Guy Ritchie.

Worst Interviewer: Nick Hancock on You Only Live Once; Runners-up: Martin Bashir, Christine Hamilton, Frank Skinner.

Best Sex Symbol: Male: David Wicks (EastEnders/Holby City) Runners-up: Swiss Tony, Anton 'Walk With Me' Meyer (Holby City); Female: Carol Jackson (EastEnders/Out Of Hours) Runners-up: Caroline Aherne, Fiona Griffin (Coronation Street/Holby City).

Most Sexless Sex Symbol Award/Stupid Tart: Denise Van Outen; Runners-up: Donal MacIntyre, Lindsey Corkhill.

Funniest Thing On Television: Chris Morris; Runners-up: Swiss Tony, Alan Partridge (A-ha!).

Unfunniest Thing On Television: Chris Evans/Danny Baker; Runners-up: Baddiel & Skinner, Neil Morrissey, Rhona, Jim Davidson.

Favourite TOTP2 Clip: Billy Mackenzie singing 'Party Fears Two'; Runner-up: Mobb Deep – 'Quiet Storm'.

Best Animal In A Documentary: The rattlesnake in The Incredible Journeys; Runners-up: Thorny Devils (Supernatural).

Best Cartoon: Taz – the Taz-ster, the Taz-eroonie; Runners-up: The Simpsons, King Of The Hill, Foghorn Leghorn.

Most Overrated Cartoon: South Park.

Best TV Detective: Jim Taggart (RIP), even though he did only ever solve the case when virtually everyone else bar the suspect was dead; Runners-up: the fuck-ups in The Vice, Jim Carver (The Bill), Columbo.

Scariest TV Detective: Maisie Raine; Runner-up: Frank Black (Millennium).

Favourite TV Police Officer: David Caruso (NYPD Blue); Runners-up: Giardello, Munch, Kellerman, etc. on Homicide: Life On The Street, Reg Hollis (The Bill), Dean (The Cops).

Favourite Nurse/Nymphomaniac: Tina in Casualty; Runner-up: Claire Maitland (Cardiac Arrest).

Least Favourite: Duffin (Casualty); Runner-up: Moll Flanders (ER).

Loveliest Hair On Television: Gary Mavers (Peak Practice); Runners-up: Richard Madeley, Noel Edmonds.

Best Haircut In A Soap: Les Battersby.

Worst Haircut In A Soap: Ian Beale/Ian Beale's kids, Annie Palmer, Melanie Healey at the Soap Awards.

Maddest Accent On Television: Niamh Musgrove: 'Joe-weeeeeh' (Brookside); Runners up: That Bitch Lorraine (EastEnders), Rose Gray and Ruth Rodgers murdering Italian on The Italian Kitchen.

Maddest Programme: Richard And Judy; Runner-up: Badger.

Most Overrated Programme (general): Anything with David Jason; Runners-up: ER, Absolutely Fabulous, Friends, Red Dwarf.

Most Underrated Programme (general): Oz; Runners-up: The Tony Ferrino Phenomenon, Cardiac Arrest, Dial Midnight, Gazzetta Football Italia.

Subject Matters To Be Prohibited By Law: Programmes about airports; Runners-up: programmes about sex, drugs, football, gangsters, cookery, gardening, DIY, lonely detectives.

Best Presenter: James Richardson.

Most Overrated Presenter: Des Lynam.

Best Double Act: Hayley/Harold; Runner-up: Andy Sipowicz and his hairdresser.

Most Deluded Egomaniac: The unassassinated Donal MacIntyre; Runners-up: Clive James, Chris Evans, John Peel, Michael Palin, Ruby Wax.

Arse: Richard E. Grant.

Twerp: Oliver James.

Dickhead: Neil Morrissey.

Lifetime Achievement Award For Inspiring Gratuitous Insults: Lindsey Corkhill; Runners-up: Gail Tilsley, Mandy Jordache.

Too Thick To Be Allowed On Television Award: Jo Whiley; Runners-up: Lindsey Corkhill, Edward Windsor, Deirdre Langton-Barlow-Rashid, Mike Dixon, Sada from Big Brother, Frankie Fraser.

Go Away, Leave Us Alone Award: Davina McCall (even popping up for no reason to ruin Big Brother); Runner-up: Graham Norton (in Brookside).

Mystery Phenomenon Award/No Noticeable Talent Award: Carol Vorderman; Runners-up: Jamie Theakston, Kirsty Young, Barry Venison, Garth Crooks.

Too Offensive To Be Allowed On Television Award: Ron Dixon; Runners-up: Neil & Christine Hamilton, Jim Davidson, Jimmy Savile, Jeremy Spake, Craig Charles.

Maddest Soap: Revelations/Brookside.

Best Children In Soap: The Wonderful Tyrone, Sonia, Emily Shadwick, Janine (Julie Burchill), Sarah-Lou, Candice, Jamie Mitchell.

Worst Children In Soap: Steven Beale, Our Kylie, Rosie Webster.

Favourite Female Soap Character: Beth Jordache (RIP); Runner up: Sexy Cindy (RIP also).

Favourite Male Soap Character: Trevor Jordache (RIP); Runners-up: Barry Grant (RIP), Tommy McArdle (RIP), Des Barnes (RIP).

Worst Family In Soap: The Fowlers, The Musgroves, Ollie and Bel Simpson, The Shadwicks.

Scariest Character In Soap: Danniella Westbrook; Runners up: Gita, Christian and Simon the Cult leader (Brookside), Pauline Fowler.

Most Hated Male Character: Our Little Jimmy/anything in Brookside to do with smack heroin; Runners-up: Racist Ron Dixon, Jashun Shadwick, Robbie Jackson's Grandad, Mark Fowler.

Most Hated Female Character: Pauline Fowler; Runners-up: That

Bitch Lorraine, Mandy Jordache, Lindsey Corkhill, Gail Tilsley, Patricia Farnham.

Favourite All-Time Tapehead TV Moment: Christopher Walken reading *Three Little Pigs* on Saturday Zoo: 'Goodbye Piggy. Buongiorno salami'; Runners-up: Brass Eye's 'as gay as a window' sketch; Kevin Keegan saying he would love it if Newcastle beat Man United now.

Tapehead Respect Is Due Award: Tom Fontana (Oz, Homicide); Runners-up: David Chase, Tony Merchant, Tony Soprano, Chris Morris.

Tapehead's Best TV Personality Of The Decade: Alan Partridge (A-ha!).

Worst TV Personality Of The Decade: Chris Evans (har har).

Best Programme: Brass Eye; Runners-up: Oz, Knowing Me, Knowing You (A-ha!), Match Of The Day, Holding On, The Sopranos.

Worst Programme: Baddiel & Skinner Unplanned; Runners-up: Nantcheroo/Dr Willougby/anything with Joanna Lumley.

Tapehead's Most Hated Person On Television Award: Male: Richard E. Grant; Female (allegedly): Jo Whiley.

In the dream, Tapehead is watching the show (slagging it off), watching it end. The show closes with Tapehead singing 'we had joy, we had fun, we had seasons in the sun' with the winners. All of Tapehead's demons and dilemmas are resolved. He reaches for the remote and switches everything into darkness. Then Tapehead rests in peace.

August 5–11 2000

Acknowledgements

The person most responsible for Tapehead is former editor of the Guide, Ben Olins. (In other words, blame him.) Ben studied every detail of Tapehead and gave me the sort of leeway that has probably made it impossible for other editors to work with me ever since. He even let me carry on writing Tapehead when I was holed away in the Hotel 17 in New York, and you can't get fairer than that.

The first person to ask me to write about television was Bonnie Vaughan when she asked me to take over Paul Morley's Telecide column in Blitz. So, several thousand videotapes later, I would like to thank her. While I'm at it, not only were Morley and Dave McCullough the writers who made me want to become a journalist, they were the ones who encouraged me more than most.

Thank you to Trisha Watt, Harry Royal and Eamon Grant who taught me right.

Helen Oldfield was the first person to commission me to write for the Guardian, reviewing Brookside, where my first sentence was, 'What's happened to Brookside?' Sinbad was, apparently, living in a shed living off cream crackers at the time. Or at least I said he was.

I would like to thank all the kool kats at the Guide who helped to produce Tapehead, particularly Kathy Sweeney, Teri Grenert, Mr Jones (Ross Jones), Tim Lusher and Amelia Morgan, who for years had to type up the columns from faxes.

Thanks especially to all the Tapeheaderz and Sudz for all their e-mails and hate mail, particularly Mari.

Serious cheers to Mathew Clayton of Guardian Books and to Toby Mundy, Alice Hunt, Chris Shamwana and Helen Ewing of Atlantic Books – above all for their desire to get the detail right and for making this book possible.

A big kiss to Julie B, aka Janine. Thanks to boy wonder Kez Glozier for putting Tapehead into pictures and to Merlin. Thank you to Richie Hopson at Lapmonkey for the sunglasses shot, to Francis Jago at MPA Fingal and Gorm and everyone at Bullet for cover input.

Above all, thanks to Reg for the quote. Have a chorus of the Swaziland national anthem on me.

Speaking of which, thank you to legal eagles and advisers, Sarah Davis and Ruth Gladwin, Michael Tulloch and especially Sandra Casali PR (or Peeeee Rrrrrrr as Donal MacIntyre would say), the creator of Jim Shelley On The Telly.

Thanks to Deborah Orr for Zeitgeist and High Anxiety.

For all their consideration and cooperation, I'd like to say thanks to Ben, Garry, Ernie, John Malkovich, Abel Ferrara, Richard 'Man With A Mission' Wallace, Morrissey/Marr, Paul, Paolo, Vicky M, Jefferson, Noel Gallagher, Joanne Mallabar, Shirley Manson, the Spice Girls, Iggy Pop, Steve Coogan, Lisa P, Maxeeeene, Jo, Lulu (not that one), Johnnie and Sam and Uncle Junior, Jimmy White and Ronnie O'Sullivan, Nicola Jeale, Nicole, Nicola, Ruth and Heather at Sainted, Chris Petit, David Cronenberg, Grace Jones and Alan Whicker.

Thanks to Jo-Ann Furniss who, in the nicest possible way, inspired the title, along with New Order.

Thank you to Sky for the satellite dish. Thank you to Alan Sugar for the Amstrad double video. Thanks to Brass at Centonove, W2 and Billy Candis at the Hotel 17, NYC.

Finally, I should say thank you to my mum and dad for letting me stay up late during the seventies and watch Match Of The Day, Hazell and the first two-thirds of The Sweeney, and for taping Twin Peaks and Hill Street while I was away on tour.

Consequently, this book is dedicated to Frank Furillo and Joyce Davenport and to Joseph and Susannah, whose laughter makes me marvel and is the main reason I did Tapehead for so long.